Transplanting the Agora

Hellenic settlement in Australia

Yiannis E. Dimitreas

ALLEN & UNWIN

First published in 1998 by
Allen & Unwin
9 Atchison Street
St Leonards NSW 2065
Australia
Phone: (61 2) 9901 4088
Fax: (61 2) 9906 2218
E-mail: frontdesk@allen-unwin.com.au
Web: www.allen-unwin.com.au

National Library of Australia
Cataloguing-in-Publication entry:

Dimitreas, Yiannis E.
    Transplanting the agora: Hellenic settlement in Australia.

    Bibliography.
    Includes index.
    ISBN 1 86448 430 6.

    1. Greeks—Australia—History. I. Title.

305.889094

Set in 10.5/12pt Plantin Light by DOCUPRO, Sydney

Printed and bound by SRM Productions Services, Sdn Bhd., Malaysia

10 9 8 7 6 5 4 3 2 1

TRANSPLANTING THE AGORA

To my beloved mother Stavroula Spyrea-Dimitrea,. daughter of Aikaterini Spyrea, whose faith in my endeavours has never dimmed.

Τα ξένα θέλουν φρόνημα,
θέλουν ταπεινοσύνη
θέλουν λαγού περπατησιά
κι αετού γρηγοροσύνη

Αναθεμά σέ Αμερική,
αναθεμά σέ πόλη
που σ'στεί τον άνθρωπο,
και μ'στειλες το βόιδι!

Αικατερίνι Σπυρένα

To go abroad requires discipline,
requires humility,
requires the hare's speed
and the eagle's wings.

Curses on America
curses on cities,
I send you my man
and you send me a bullock!

Aikaterini Spyrea

Contents

Preface

The central theme of this book is the impact of immigration from Greece (*Hellas*) to Australia, particularly in terms of the social mobility and political affiliation of the immigrants. I include an analysis of migration and social mobility in my discussion of the theoretical framework, defining and placing both within socio-economic and socio-historical contexts. Such an inter-disciplinary approach cuts across the fields of political economy, sociology, politics, law and demography. I draw from both Weberian and Marxist traditions in order to offer the most comprehensive testing possible of the empirical analysis of the immigrant experience. Chapter 2 seeks to determine the causes of present Greek-Australian social mobility and related traits, in terms of pre-migration, migration–settlement and post-migration socio-economic experience. In Chapter 2, I give a brief account of my research methods: these include an empirical inquiry based on various questionnaires; detailed personal interviews; and other primary sources for the trends and variables in social mobility, such as data from the Australian Bureau of Statistics. In order to comprehend the values and cultural features which contributed to the decision to migrate, in Chapter 3 I examine the symbols of Hellenic national identity that have derived from a mythical past, including the symbols and legends that continue to shape everyday human interaction. I also look at the outstanding features of the typologies of migration, from the pioneer settlers of the mid- to late nineteenth century, through to the inter-war years. I have included biographical accounts of the 'scouts' who pioneered Hellenic settlement in Australia, as well as of those who came after the initiation of mass migration from Greece. I also examine the socio-economic development of the Hellenic nation state, as both a cause and effect of mass out-migration from Greece to America and Australia over the past hundred years, and how the major factors of economic underdevelopment and rising unemployment forced Greeks to abandon their rural and farming communities, choosing first urbanisation then mass out-migration. *Transplanting the Agora* analyses Australia's history, its socio-historical development and how its changing immigration policies affected public attitudes both before and after World War Two, as well as focusing on the attitudes of the Australian public towards the settlement of non-British migrants in their country. Until multiculturalism was established many southern European migrants experienced the closure to them of social structures and the general unreadiness of Australian society to accept these migrants led to its failure to capitalise on their skills and initiatives, until the implementation of multiculturalism in the 1970s.

The main purpose of this book is to present the key social, cultural and political aspects of the evolution of Hellenic life in Australia by exploring the social and historical context of both cultural continuity and change in the course of Hellenic migration and settlement in Australia. These key elements of the book reveal the core of the individual and group 'cultural capital' which not only forms the basis of cultural continuity, but also recreates the social and material structures indispensable for community life. The book argues that this stock of cultural capital, derived from its historical and mythical past, has been crucial in the development of the 'Hellenic-Australian' identity. The distinctive claim of this book is that cultural continuity is at the centre of individual and communal adaptation and the attainment of social mobility in societies of settlement.

As a child of Greek migrants I have shared, and continue to share, the experiences, history and myths that define the Hellenic identity in diaspora. I have taught a variety of courses, including Hellenic language and culture, English, sociology and multicultural studies in secondary schools and at tertiary institutions in Australia for 16 years. *Transplanting the Agora* represents the culmination of this experience and involvement with the issues confronting migrants in countries of migration.

I examine the history of Hellenic immigration to Australia since European settlement, with special emphasis on the social mobility of Greeks in Australia during the postwar years. Personal interviews have revealed the racism, discrimination and exclusion experienced by Greeks in their efforts to achieve occupational, residential, educational and other forms of mobility in their adopted country. Faced with this reality Hellenes responded by organising themselves in a struggle for rights, by joining, for example, what became known as the Ethnic Rights Movement and by participating in the political movements which became the main driving forces behind the establishment of Australian multiculturalism.

RESEARCHER'S NOTE

The writing of the present book is based on an interdisciplinary investigation into the social mobility of Greeks in Australia that, in 1995, was submitted as a PhD thesis at Victoria University of Technology. Due to constraints of space and literary convention, the methodology chapter of the original thesis has been omitted and, in its place, a much shorter version has been incorporated in Chapter 2. Researchers and other scholars interested in the full account of the research strategies used in the writing of this book should refer to the thesis, 'Social mobility of Greeks in Australia', which can be found at the Victoria University Library.

Acknowledgements

I wish to thank all those friends, who because of their numbers must remain anonymous, who either directly or indirectly gave me their assistance and valuable comments on this book as it progressed. This book has arisen out of my PhD thesis at Victoria University of Technology, Australia. I am indebted to my thesis supervisors, Professor Ron Adams and Professor Robert Pascoe for their consistent encouragement, patience, understanding and invaluable advice. In this context, I would especially mention my debt to Ron for helping me to appreciate more fully the power of the word and singer Stelios Kazantzidis, the troubador of Greek social folk for his songs connected with the power of the word, migration and success. My special thanks go to the late Leon Peres, Reader at the University of Melbourne, who was my first supervisor. I wish to express my gratitude to Dr Judy Brett for teaching me about the power of single concepts and metaphors in her course 'Language and Ideology', which she ran in the Politics department, University of Melbourne, 1981. I am indebted to John Marinopoulos for his expert statistical advice. Furthermore, I want to thank the members of the Hellenic community for their extraordinary hospitality, cooperation and courtesy during my research. The Greek leaders of the community were unsparing of their time and knowledge to aid me in my attempt to provide a socio-historical and sociological account of Hellenic settlement and social mobility in Australia. I am deeply grateful to them. I wish to express special thanks to Meng Lim for her constant support during the writing of *Transplanting the Agora*; to Les Terry for sharing with me some of his views and interest in areas relating to the study; and to the following people and organisations for providing me with access to material in their possession: Effy Alexakis; Associate Professor Gillian Bottomley; Evangelos Dedes; Leonard Janiszewski; Panayiotis Kalantzis; Sofia Kalantzis; Yiannis Kalantzis; George Kallianis; Dimitris Kalomoiris; Theo Koulochris; Stelios Kourbetis; Eric Lloga; Johna Low; Alan Matheson; Joan Messaris; George Mihelakakis; Chris Mourikis; Tom Oikonomou; George Papadopoulos; Professor Charles Price; Stathis Raftopoulos; Theo Sidiropoulos MLA; Katerina Skoutas; Dr Anastasios Tamis; Harry Trahanas; Dr Michael Tsounis; Dr Dorothea Warr; and George Zangalis; the Greek Orthodox Community of Melbourne and Victoria; the Greek Orthodox Community of Sydney and New South Wales; Achileas Paparsenos from the Greek General Consul of Melbourne; the Holy Archdiocese of the Greek Orthodox Church of Australia; and the Greek language newspapers *Neos Kosmos* (Melbourne), *O Kosmos*, and the *Hellenic Herald* (Sydney).

Abbreviations

ABS	Australian Bureau of Statistics
AIMA	Australian Institute of Multicultural Affairs
ALP	Australian Labor Party
AMA	Australian Medical Association
BCN	Bilingual Consultant Network
BIR	Bureau of Immigration Research (subsequently BIMPR)
CPA	Communist Party of Australia
DIEA	Department of Immigration and Ethnic Affairs
ERM	Ethnic Rights Movement
GOC	Greek Orthodox Community
GOCM&V	Greek Orthodox Community of Melbourne and Victoria
ICEM	Inter-Government Committee for Migration
ILO	International Labour Organisation
IRO	International Refugee Organisation
L/LM	Lower/Lower Middle
NCP	National Country Party
NESB (or NES)	Non-English-Speaking Background
NOOSR	National Office of Overseas Skills Recognition (previously COPQ)
NSSG	National Statistical Services of Greece
OMA	Office of Multicultural Affairs
PASOK	Panhellenic Socialist Movement
SBS	Special Broadcasting Service
UNGA	United Nations General Assembly
VEAC	Victoria Ethnic Affairs Commission

Illustrations

1

Introduction

Contemporary migration from Greece has been to various destinations in the industrially advanced nations of the world, including Australia. Following migrant settlement, host societies have paid little attention to studies of migration and social mobility from the migrants' perspective. In the studies currently existing it is maintained that the attainment of social mobility by migrants is only a matter of time and that it will be achieved, though perhaps not until the second or even third generation. The initial disadvantages and difficulties that migrants experience following migration and settlement can therefore be expected to disappear, also, over time. This view appears to be supported by the census data of the Australian Bureau of Statistics that clearly show social mobility as an aggregate statistic over an extended period of years. This proposition appears to be quite straightforward. It does not, however, explain the complexity of the steps, issues and factors in this seemingly linear and inevitable process; nor does it reveal the multifaceted and involved nature of adjustments that have to be made by individuals, families and whole communities both in the migrant and the host society.

This book, by contrast, explores the issues involved in the process of migration and settlement by examining the experiences of the Hellenic community and the way its members have struggled over the years to gain acceptance and greater social mobility in Australian society. Many other studies have been carried out by people who have described ethnic population groups from an outsider's perspective, but this study is carried out from an immigrant's view. In general terms all ethnic communities that comprise Australian society do adjust to the social, cultural, economic and political circumstances in the host society, but the nature of this process of adjustment is neither simple and smooth nor predictable.

My basic research objective was, therefore, to investigate the social mobility of Greeks in Australia. I begin with the second half of the nineteenth century and follow through the subsequent developments of the Hellenic[1] presence to the more recent post-World War Two years, paying particular attention to Greeks' social mobility patterns in the context of Australia's different stages of cultural and economic development. The term 'social mobility'—as used here—refers to any movement in the occupational, economic, educational and residential hierarchy of the Australian social stratification system.

Migration, like social mobility is, in essence, a social process leading towards social change (Byrne 1977: 248–9). Following settlement in their new country, the migrant family requires more material—and orientation—assistance than families already established in Australia. As Byrne states, the family is the 'social microcosm in which the dynamics of personal and group adjustment to environmental stress largely take place following migration' (Byrne 1977: 248).

Most contemporary migrations have involved mass population shifts to places such as the United States, Australia, Canada, Western Europe and other industrially advanced regions, as migrants search for work and better opportunities for themselves and their families (Castles & Miller 1993). For most migrants, the socio-economic deprivations in their country of origin are generally significant causes of out-migration (Castles & Miller 1993). Migration, therefore, whether internal or external, remains an attempt at economic and social advancement. When the migrant[2] becomes an immigrant (that is, settles permanently in his or her new society), theoretically he or she is then free to search for better socio-economic opportunities, thus indicating that the socio-economic forces that initiated the migration are still in action.

In order to understand better the difficulties implicit in the migratory experience, both migration and settlement need to be understood in the context of 'social mobility'. Like migration, social mobility is used to designate the phenomenon of movement within human societies. What makes the *movement* of people important is their belief that by moving (or attempting to move) within or between given societies, they will be able to take advantage of potential opportunities and, ultimately, will improve their social and economic status within that society.

When western sociologists speak about social mobility, they usually mean mobility within the social stratification system of a given society, that is, a society with *structured inequality*, where the population of some strata have more power, rewards and opportunities for advancement than others. Structured inequality occurs through property ownership, and/or access to the acquisition of control and power, which can be granted either through legitimate or tolerated action.

Often, the occurrence of upward or downward movement of social status depends upon the socio-economic structures of host societies and the extent to which such societies are characterised by structures and processes which are closed or open. For example, in caste or feudal societies, social positions are fixed and cannot be changed. Social positions and status are therefore ascribed or inherited and transmitted across generations. These structures are unlike those of modern or postmodern societies[3] such as the United States and Australia, where social positions are gained through individual achievement rather than accidents of birth. Modern and postmodern industrial societies offer equal opportunities to all members of society in the competition for unequal positions, with the allocation of the available positions being made meritocratically (Giddens 1993: 212–49). In these situations, a major interest of sociologists is how the individuals concerned mobilise themselves, and what obstacles they face—occupationally, educationally and economically—in seeking to fulfil their aspirations and to achieve positions of higher status.

When social mobility is discussed, it is important to note that, due to differing theoretical frameworks and theoretical presuppositions, there are differences in the interpretation of data on mobility. The main differences occur between Marxist (and other radical sociological critiques), and non-Marxist, for example, Weberian, positions.

This book draws on both the Weberian and the Marxist traditions in order to offer a more comprehensive testing of the empirical analysis of the immigrant experience. Using such a theoretical framework and, at the same time, applying the relevant historical and sociological research methodologies, the measurement of differential rates in the social mobility of Greeks in Australia is possible. A Marxist analysis enables the researcher to ascertain whether there have been significant differences between Greeks in terms of achieved higher social class and to determine if this relates, as Marxist theory claims it should, to corresponding changes in political voting patterns. In contrast, the Weberian theory provides the framework for the measurement of a wider range of social class categories.

Furthermore, the social mobility of Greeks in Australia can be placed in a longitudinal perspective, thereby exploring the *incremental* process, whereby the socio-economic and political incorporation of members of the Hellenic community into Australian society is effected in structural and policy terms. I discuss this process against the background of contemporary socio-economic and political changes in Australian society, in which the Greeks' pursuit of social mobility exposed them to a new set of issues and specific socio-economic conditions. The impact of these conditions on their life and culture has had significant implications for Greeks in terms of maintaining continuity of status while, at the same time, making concerted efforts to achieve a higher degree of participation in the socio-economic life of Australia.

In contrast to the general view held by sociologists of mobility, the questions which are central to this research relate to issues of access, equity and social justice, not only for members of the host society, but also for migrants and other disadvantaged groups. There are also important questions relating to the actual or imagined ability of some sections of society, such as ethnic population groups, to take advantage of the opportunities made available to them by receiving societies.

Traditionally, and for many years after World War Two, it was intended that migrants would settle in Australia permanently and that 'assimilation' or 'integration' would modify or eliminate the cultural differences between incoming migrants and members of the host society. Unlike many other western countries, Australia intentionally recruited migrants for permanent settlement rather than as guest workers (Castles 1988). For this reason neither the government nor the community considered it appropriate that immigrants maintain their cultural traditions in their new home. Rather, immigrants were expected to assimilate largely unaided; to 'deny and forget their origins', while 'wholeheartedly embracing' the Australian way of life (Secretariat to the Committee to Advise on Australia's Immigration Policies 1987: 14).

Ethnic population groups arriving in Australia *en masse*, especially through the chain migration processes which characterised the Hellenes and the Italians in the 1950s and 1960s, found themselves consistently encapsulated—residentially, occupationally and economically—in the so-called 'ethnic enclaves', often until subsequent generations broke away from these 'social mobility traps'. Many first-generation immigrants were forced into the secondary labour market (Storer 1975), especially in the manufacturing industry. This was due to a number of social factors operating against them, including lack of appropriate language skills, non-recognition of skills and qualifications gained overseas, and the host society's lack of readiness to accommodate its newly-settled migrants.

Pascoe (1992) holds that migrants often moved to particular geographic locations because these settings either offered opportunities for developing services, or enabled them to do their shopping in traditional markets or shops and live within walking distance from their work—an important factor, since most could not afford a motor car following initial settlement. Such locations allowed them—through social interaction—to identify with a social and geographic space and to redefine their worldview of place and belonging in their new social context, thereby establishing a much-needed sense of continuity.

Hellenic migrant settlement has been a significant part of Australia's post-1945 non-English-speaking background (NESB)[4] immigration program. The historical longevity of the Hellenic presence in Australia, combined with its significant expansion in terms of mass migration and settlement over the past 50 years, enables the researcher to conceptualise a number of important research questions, pertaining to the social, economic and political mobility not only of the Hellenic community[5] but also of other migrant groups in this country.

As a theoretical study, this book seeks to determine the factors and related issues involved in the social mobility of Greeks in Australia by exploring pre-migration, migration-settlement and post-migration socio-economic experiences. As an empirical inquiry, it relies on questionnaire surveys, detailed personal interviews and other primary sources to establish trends and to identify variables relevant to social mobility. In contrast to the Weberian approach, however, this book uses a set of strategies which attempt to construct a more wide-ranging and inclusive investigation and analysis of the experience of migration as well as of the social mobility of immigrants within Australian society.

My research is based on the general hypothesis that the level of upward mobility of Hellenes in Australia is a continuation of the migration process that began with people moving from impoverished rural areas to overpopulated urban centres firstly within Greece and subsequently joining the worldwide Hellenic diaspora.[6] This process involves a multiple stage migration: from rural and urban centres in Greece to industrial urban centres of Australia; and from inner-urban industrial settings in Australia to newly-developed suburbs and housing estates.

Migration was the end result of a drastic decline in a Hellenic economy drained by years of war and administered by an inadequate system of government unprepared for autonomous rule. The system failed to: (1) provide work for the growing rural population; (2) cater for the growing socio-economic and welfare needs of the country's population; and (3) keep up with a modernising and changing world. These failures led to out-migration, a complex multifaceted chain-like process, in which relatives, friends and, ultimately, entire villages, followed pioneer migrants to the new industrialising regions such as America, Western Europe and Australia.

Research on the social mobility of ethnic groups in Australia has generally used conventional quantitative methods, which tend to focus on a single point in time and assume that the existing social and economic mechanisms of both host and migrant societies are stable and given. There has been extensive discussion as to whether social mobility is greater in some ethnic groups than in others, and whether the respective rates have been rising or falling.

A socio-historical approach allows these variables to be taken into account by comparing their different effects under different internal and external conditions, although there are various limitations which face the contemporary investigator, usually arising from scarcity of data and the lack of relevant social history studies. Existing evidence of the Hellenic migratory experience reveals an overlapping of related patterns across a series of historical Hellenic settlements in Australia during both the pre- and the post-World War Two periods. In each of these periods, and in each settlement stage, we can see countervailing tendencies, reactions or attitudes to the prevailing social, political, economic and mobility trends. Even so, each historical stage presents certain unique qualities regarding the patterns of Hellenic–Australian migration as well as settlement and mobility indices. Examination of these patterns allows comparative analysis over a longer period of time.

What has been increasingly evident during the latter half of the twentieth century is that the level of involvement of various ethnic groups in Australia's social, economic and political structures is dependent upon a framework of social incorporation. Much of the migrant success in Australia, as in any host society, is associated with the type of 'social incorporation' model in place and its capacity to accommodate migrant workers and their families. The presence, or absence, of a formal social incorporation model militates either for or against the further development of a partnership with socio-economic opportunities for ethnic population groups in Australian society.

Government commitment to an Australian multiculturalism has at times been cautious, superficial or even suspicious about the preservation of ethnically diverse cultural heritages. It is often argued that government commitment to multiculturalism has been utilised as 'political rhetoric'—a placebo for ethnic communities, particularly their leaders, who have occasionally 'been alerted to the superficial character of multiculturalism'. For almost 20 years, this model has remained an 'ambiguous and ephemeral phenomenon in Australian politics' (Castles et al. 1988: 78).

In this book, therefore, I examine the theoretical and cultural aspects associated with Hellenes' efforts to achieve social mobility. In order to explain the motivation of Hellene migrants in Australia and elsewhere, I will provide accounts of the main socio-economic trends in Greece and aspects of the modern Hellenic national character in regard to their social and cultural orientations.

In general, *Transplanting the Agora* examines Australia's economic development which, like that of most other western nations, has always been its first priority and, historically, has shaped the formation of its immigration policies accordingly. There have been discriminatory policies and public attitudes which had an impact on the experiences of immigrant groups in terms of achieving acceptance and upward social mobility in Australia. State bureaucracies had to overcome the twin hurdles of discriminatory policies and the nation's state of 'unreadiness', in order to recognise migrants' skills and qualifications and to provide them with fair access to the job market.

The book provides a critical account of the socio-economic forces which operated behind the increasing participation of Hellenes in small business and as labourers in the nation's manufacturing industries throughout the post-World War Two era. The nation's current socio-economic order and job market availability make it possible to raise serious questions as to whether full engagement within the general society, to the point of allowing social movement within the confines of the dominant group has been achieved. This evaluation is placed in the context of a discussion about the acquisition by ethnic population groups of economic security, the construction of ethnic organisations as a means for collective ethnic community action—which itself requires an adequate familiarity with the wider social system in general.

Furthermore, it can be argued that social mobility has a major bearing on the political behaviour of the Hellenic community within the Australian political system and that the legislative innovations of the post-1970s period have, for the first time in national history, led to the emergence of 'bipartisan acceptance'. The importance of the legislative component lies in its ability to enable further improvements in the cultural and structural incorporation of ethnic population groups within Australia.

Of the few existing studies on Greek-Australians, most have dealt with the years up to 1970, when most of the ethnic communities' concerns were directed inwardly—towards individual, ethnic group life, ethnic organisational practices and ethnic social and cultural institutions. Petrolias' (1959) study of the ethnic Greek and ethnic Italian leadership in Melbourne found that Hellenic community leaders were predominantly involved within their own organisational institutions. Petrolias also found that the most important qualification for Greek leadership was a commitment to the preservation of ethnic values. Competence in dealing with the outside world, although appreciated, was not considered essential (Petrolias 1959). Tsounis found that even the most politically active and outward-looking sector of the Greek community, the progressive Left, tended to give priority to internal community politics and conflict (Tsounis, interview with the author, 1989). In fact, Tsounis saw little evidence of social mobility by Greeks into or across the wider Australian society, other than through ethnic Greek institutions. Reich's (1981) study of Greeks and Jews in Australia indicates that there were different historical and subjective factors which operated behind the socio-economic status, the ethnic organisations and the level of participation of each of these groups in Australian society.

An analysis of the 1981 Census found that Greeks and other Mediterranean immigrants were still over-represented in the lowest echelons of society (Collins 1988: 79). This apparent inequality placed migrants in a disadvantaged position in comparison with members of the host society, who monopolised positions of power, thus controlling the 'culture of the established society'. The socio-economic and occupational 'gap' existing between immigrants and members of the host society cannot be comprehended without a detailed understanding of the migrant experience in social mobility.

This book establishes a theoretical framework based on different perspectives of the migration phenomenon and the social mobility of immigrants. Specifically, Chapter 2 establishes a multi-disciplinary theoretical and methodological framework that can accommodate the complex range of factors which lead people to migrate from familiar to unfamiliar social

9

and geographic spaces. In contrast to most studies, it is argued that migration, migrant settlement and social mobility cannot be understood or defined in terms of a single theory or by the theoretical perspective of any one discipline.

Chapter 2 also relates Hellenic-Australian experiences to historical and cultural themes stretching back to antiquity, thus exposing the nature of the underlying motivation and goal orientation associated with the upward social mobility of Greek-Australians.

This aspect is further developed in Chapter 3, which focuses on the Hellenic cultural features and values which contributed to the decision to migrate away from familiar social and geographic spaces to remote countries of the world, such as Australia. The chapter also provides an analysis of key symbols and values derived from the mythic past. It argues that the myths and stories told in the *agora* became part of the 'social memory', informing the ideas and actions of those social actors which, in turn, helps to explain both the migration and post-migration history and social mobility of Greeks in Australia.

In the context of these cultural themes, Chapter 4 provides an analysis of the sporadic arrival in Australia of Greek pioneers during the nineteenth century. Through an examination of these pioneer Greek settlers, it provides an account in terms of which the typology of sporadic migration can be understood. In considering their biographies, Chapter 3 stresses that many of these individuals, who arrived as isolated seamen, eventually established themselves in Australia and, in the absence of eligible Greek women, married local women and Anglicised their names, thus becoming the forerunners of chain migration from Greece.

However, the typology of mass migration cannot be explained solely on the grounds of the achievements of the Greek pioneers to Australia. A whole range of complex factors operated behind the post-World War Two out-migration (one of the largest 'volunteer' migrations on record). To reveal the complexity of this type of migration, Chapter 5 locates the migration debate in a broader historical conceptual framework, connecting out-migration to the socio-economic and political changes which occurred after the foundation of the modern nation state in 1828. The chapter indicates how Hellenic economic underdevelopment and underemployment were major factors in the abandonment of rural and farming communities in favour of urbanisation, internal migration and mass out-migration.

Turning from what are seen as the 'push' factors of migration to the 'pull' forces that attracted Greeks to Australia, Chapter 6 provides an analysis of the arrival of Greeks in Australia in the context of Australia's immigration history. Treatment of this history includes an analysis of Australia's immigration policy together with relevant details of Australia's socio-historical development. Specifically, Australia's pro-British immigration policies and Australian public attitudes towards Hellenic migration both before and after World War Two, are examined. The question of the origins of immigrants (which was central to the nation's immigration policy) is scrutinised, as well as the types of socio-economic mobility Greeks were afforded in Australia during the period preceding the abolition of the 'White Australia Policy' in 1972.

Chapter 7 examines the social history of the Hellenic presence during the pre- and inter-war years, until the dawn of Multiculturalism during the post-World War Two period. The chapter looks at how Hellenic organisational life, which was the result of the mode of immigration in the Australian social context, initially led to the concentration of particular ethnic groups within a limited range of occupational practices and, at the same time, followed a particular pattern of settlement within the host society both during the inter-war and post-World War Two years, before these patterns began to change.

Chapter 8 examines the extent to which the social mobility of Greek-Australians has begun to reverse previous trends, following the increasing interaction and participation of the Hellenic community and its leaders within the wider Australian society. Hellenic community leaders no longer limit themselves to the activities of their own ethnic organisations alone, but participate instead within the organisations of both worlds—those which represent their own ethnic cultural and political interests as well as the organisations of the host society.

This social mobility, upward and downward, is then measured in the first section of Chapter 9 using indices for individual progress against the collective advancement pre-

11

sented in correlated class ranking terms in Chapter 8. A single factor analysis is presented which relates to the social mobility of Greeks in Australia—namely the occupational, financial and residential status of participants—collected from a sample, consisting of 353 participants, ranked and correlated to provide a perspective of the developing differentiation in class status rankings of present-day Greeks in Australia. The class patterns that emerge are of intra-generational and some inter-generational mobility, although the latter is not yet fully visible. In the second section of Chapter 9, the socio-economic characteristics of the participants are derived from a structured questionnaire survey and correlated with political preferences, which are shown to be changing for the second time since Greeks came to Australia.

After considering a number of diacritical indicators relating to the forces of migration, the post-migration and social mobility experiences of Greeks in Australia, Chapter 10 discusses the implications of this study for a better understanding of the migration experience. This discussion deals with issues of development theory relevant to ethnic diversity, the development of multicultural policies in Australia and the challenges posed by mass population movements in the 1990s.

Types of migration

Modern migratory forms, currents and trends are not stable in either direction or population volume, unlike those of pre-industrial periods. Migration, together with various forms of occupational social mobility, has now become a necessary feature of post-industrial societies in the context of the widened scope of an international community (Richmond 1988: 1; Withers 1990; Stahl et al. 1993). It is within this global context that there has been increasing labour mobility inside and between nation states, through improvement in communications and cheap transportation. In the modern and postmodern periods, unlike earlier historical periods, it may be 'anachronistic' to assume that people will always seek to remain permanently in any particular country to which they have migrated (Stahl et al. 1993). In very broad terms, this chapter establishes a theoretical framework to accommodate the complex range of factors which lead people to migrate from a familiar social and geographic space to an alien space. In contrast to most writings on migration, it is argued that migration cannot be understood or defined in terms of a single theory, such as neoclassic or Marxist, or in terms of a single discipline. This chapter suggests that such approaches provide only a partial explanation of the process of migration in general, and of social mobility in particular—a multi-theoretical and multi-disciplinary approach is necessary in order to grasp the complexity of the subject of migration and social mobility of migrants.

'Migration' as a general term is used to refer to the geographic movement of an individual or group (Kuper & Kuper 1985: 524; Cigler & Cigler 1985: 6). The motivation to migrate emanates from an ordered set of values that are of utmost priority to given individuals or groups of migrants and that are not adequately met in the home country. For example, people migrate in search of better economic opportunities, as a result of political or religious persecution or to escape various forms of exploitation, alienation or cultural deprivation experienced in their country of origin. At the same time, migration, together with various forms of occupational mobility, constitutes the basis for the explanation of the reasons behind people's movements along the different systems of social stratification within, as well as between, nation states in modern and postmodern societies.

The experience of migration involves not only people's geographic movement, but also questions of status as migrants within host societies. A migrant, whatever his or her status—for example, a refugee, a legal or an illegal migrant—becomes an immigrant when a decision is made to remain in the new country and/or otherwise qualify for permanent settlement status. Generally speaking, only when a migrant has been granted permanent settlement status may the goals which prompted the decision to migrate be fully pursued and realised.

When immigration involves permanent settlement in contemporary societies, it is usually legitimised through the operation of Immigration Acts implemented by the governments concerned. In modern times, other than de facto permanent immigration, only Australia, New Zealand, Canada, the United States and Israel are said to still accept permanent immigrants per se (Richmond 1988: 1). This acceptance, however, involves questions of protocol for each nation state, in accordance with the way immigrant citizenship rights are defined and conferred upon entry (Kritz 1987).

Social investigators now recognise that migration is a multifaceted social phenomenon, comprising many different types or forms (Richmond 1988; Salt 1989; Castles & Miller 1993). Whatever the form or type of migration, and its underlying causes, two geographic areas (those of the out-migration (migration abroad) and in-migration (internal migration)) and three societies (the society of origin, the host society and the immigrant group itself) are usually affected (Velikonja 1989: 710). These areas or societies are interchangeably linked to the phenomenon of migration, that itself is effectively a form of social mobility, involving processes of social transition which lead to social change. For example, when migrants move between or within nation states they may do so in order to improve their socio-economic opportunities. However, their full potential to do so is enhanced in democratic societies, where social structures are more open and where freedom of expression is encouraged. In such a society the migrant, acting either as an individual or as part of a collective social unit (for example, an extended family group), may be regarded as a social force which, by exerting its influence, ultimately contributes to social change within the host society. As Byrne has commented, 'the migrant family is the *microcosm* in which the dynamics of personal and group change, of acculturation and identity, and of adjustment to environmental stress, to a large extent, take place' (Byrne 1977: 248 (emphasis in original)). Viewed from this perspective, few of the characteristics of migration, either external or internal, can be explained outside the context of social mobility. There is a whole series of settlement issues linked to migrants' accommodation and success within host societies that may have to be faced during migration–settlement.

Migration exerts a demographic effect because it involves movement of people between geographic and social locations. Together with mortality and fertility rates, migration constitutes one of the three factors which affect the structure, composition and distribution of a population (Petersen & Thomas 1968: 289; Wooden et al. 1990: 62). Because of the interrelation of migration, fertility and mortality, their different rates, together with the size of migration, may have a permanent effect on the demographic composition of a population. This effect has been felt not only in societies which have suffered mass out-migrations but also within industrially advanced societies such as the United States, Canada, Australia and Israel where immigration programs have had a significant impact on the demographic composition and expansion of their population. For example, according to the 1986 Australian Bureau of

Statistics (ABS) Census, one-fifth of the Australian population was born overseas (Richmond 1988: 10). Moreover, as commented on in a Bureau of Immigration Research (BIR) report:

> if [the immigrants] have distinctive fertility and mortality patterns which differ from the Australian-born, the immigration program can have an influence on patterns of fertility and mortality as well (BIR 1990: 63).

Over the last 20 years, there has been scholarly as well as governmental recognition of the social impact of migratory movements and the sheer diversity of types and currents of migration. Prior to the post-industrial period, most authors conceptualised migration as a one-way process or single-pattern movement over a single historical era. In this sense, international migration was regarded very much as a homogenous process, that is, a process directed towards single destinations with no significant re-migration. Consequently, research on migration remained limited within single scholarly disciplines. Whether they were geographers, economists or historians, most authors treated migration mainly as a relocation of people within given geographic parameters (Conway 1973: 3–11; Cross 1973: 5–45). In addition, until well into the twentieth century, most authors reflected on people's migration experience and its social mobility dimension as a supplementary issue, rather than as a subject in its own right.

This approach to the subject was maintained despite the systematic inquiries into migration *per se* which started to appear in specialised literature just over 100 years ago with Ravenstein's 'The Laws of Migration' (1885: 167–235; 1889: 241–305). While Ravenstein was limited in his treatment of migration by his neoclassic economic approach, he did at least treat migration as a subject in itself. His writings coincided with the expansion of industrialisation and the development of the capitalist economic system within the affairs of the nation state that increasingly sought to pursue its interests far beyond its national boundaries. The nation state controlled political and military affairs and exercised the rule of law over society at large. As such, the administrative apparatus of the nation state legitimised the interests of the bourgeoisie or capitalist class which, according to Marx, owned and controlled the means of production (Marx 1983). This control occurred through the legal protection of the profit-making advantages the nation state provided to capitalist activities and interests. Ravenstein, like Marx before him, noted that the changes occurring in economic circumstances due to industrialisation were accompanied by population shifts from rural areas to newly-built industrial centres. The initial migratory movements first became evident within Britain itself, then in the other nation states of Europe (Jansen 1970: 3–9) and subsequently spread elsewhere with external migrations to the United States, Canada and Australia. These migrations were often accompanied by internal population movements in each of the host countries.

Despite Ravenstein's studies and the contributions made by authors from different scholarly disciplines, the subject of migration remained narrowly perceived and largely unexplored. Government immigration policy remained based on either the micro-economic or macro-economic imperatives of migration, as in the case of the United States and Australia respectively (Dawkins et al. 1992: 110; Foster & Withers 1992: 90). Such economic imperatives have remained constantly reflected in the selection criteria applied by host societies to potential immigrants, with the selection of different national groups exhibiting an order of priority based on race and ethnic origins, as well as the potential migrants' knowledge of skills or trades and/or educational level. These priorities have reflected the assimilationist views and/or melting-pot philosophies adopted by their governments. These issues relate to economics and development and also reflect the thinking of the times, both in connection to the level of tolerance of organised labour and of the host societies in general. Thus, governments organised the selection of immigrants in a way that minimised social upheaval or disruption, in order to show that immigrants could serve the economic interests of host societies.

Countries with high immigrant intakes, such as the United States, Canada and Australia, not only chose migrants who, through lack of marketable skills or a knowledge of the English language, were limited to certain categories of work, but also anticipated that these immigrants would adapt and assimilate more readily within the cultural framework of Anglo-conformity. Within this framework there was a widespread but narrow view

17

which asserted that migrants ought to forget their past way of life, their culture and their language and adapt to those of their hosts. This argument remained prevalent until the 1960s (Gordon 1964: Price 1963; The Secretariat to the Committee to Advise on Australia's Immigration Policies 1987: 14–17). One of the effects of these assimilationist attitudes was the failure of different governments to address adequately what was actually meant by the words 'migrant' and 'migration'. There was lack of consensus, by both researchers and the international community, as to how the words 'migrant' and 'migration' were going to be understood and defined in the context of host societies (Gregory 1928; Petersen & Thomas 1968: 289; Bowen 1977).

For their part, analysts of the phenomenon of migration were influenced by the requirements of their own governments' policies and had little interest in human rights issues, such as the migrants' right to maintain their languages and cultures, or to repatriate. As a result, for many years questions of possible re-migration were excluded from immigration policies. Scientific inquiry into the subject of migration remained limited as it dealt with migration only in terms of single-factor analysis. Immigration authorities assumed that people migrate for single reasons, and that they migrate only once in their lifetime (Withers 1990: 10–22), an assumption that was soon disproved by real-life experience.

However, socio-economic changes in the advanced industrial world brought about changes in people's understanding of migration. As time passed, scholars and governments throughout the industrially advanced world began to realise that people migrate for all kinds of reasons—it became obvious that migration should not be treated as a one-way relocation of migrants from the country of origin to the country of destination or, that following settlement, migrants ought to abandon their language and culture and adopt those of the new country. This approach, whereby migrants who acculturated fast were praised for their achievement and others who failed to do so were condemned by members of the host societies, was now regarded as simplistic. It is now known that currents of migration have changed many times, both in volume and direction, since the turn of the nineteenth century. It is also known that, by the 1950s, difficulties in migrant adaptation and integration in the United States, Canada and Australia led many people to return to their countries of origin. Governments could no longer ignore scholarly reviews of earlier theoretical works and policies associated with migration, the status of immigrants themselves and their increasing demands, and therefore began formally to recognise evidence of existing problems in relation to migrant presence, including lack of tolerance and racial and cultural prejudice in the host societies, especially towards certain ethnic population groups. In the United States, Canada and Australia, this awareness gave rise to legislation addressing prejudice and discrimination towards racially and ethno-culturally diverse groups living in host societies (Richmond 1988). The historical experience which generated legislation in each country was different, both in terms of the migrants (size and settlement histories, race, and ethnic group origins) and also in regard to the status of the indigenous populations (for example, the American and Canadian Indians or the Australian Aborigines). Through the implementation of legislation, however, the governments of Canada and Australia enshrined the rights of newcomers to maintain, if they so wished, their ethnic identity and cultural practices and to make submissions to their host governments seeking funds for cultural programs to be carried out by their respective ethnic organisations. Immigrant adaptation and integration within host societies were reconsidered in the light of new developments conceived and defined within the framework of cultural pluralism (Gordon 1964; Schermenhorn 1970; Bowen 1977).

Within this context of cultural pluralism, theoretical contributions often came from a critical perspective that challenged conventional or traditional perspectives on migration. Researchers and governments increasingly recognised the subject of migration as a multi-faceted and multi-dimensional social phenomenon, requiring complex research methods for analysis and definition. In contrast to earlier theories, contemporary research is increasingly studying the multi-factor causes of migration, addressing it longitudinally rather than merely as a one-way relocation of individuals within and between geographic areas. This approach, which permits the use of multivariate models of analysis, more accurately addresses the diverse factors associated with migration, and provides the capacity to consider a range of social factors which are connected to pre-migration, migration and settlement experiences (Goldlust & Richmond 1974: 193).

Individuals or groups of migrants are now increasingly being classified according to the specific category to which they belong, or in accordance with the kind of forces that either motivated or forced them to migrate. The most commonly employed typologies may be outlined as follows:

Table 2.1   Major types of migration

Archaic and contemporary migration	Mass and independent migration	Voluntary and involuntary migration
Refugee migration	Colonisation migration	Associational (or chain) migration
Internal and external migration	Professional and skilled migration	Transient migration
Conservative and innovative migration		Permanent migration

Most types of migration presented in Table 2.1, in spite of having distinct qualities and meaning, are often interrelated in that they overlap with each other and form part of the debate that help to understand the complexity of the causes and effects of the migration phenomenon. *Archaic migration* refers to migration that occurred in response to some kind of ecological push and was generally due to basic environmental changes, such as the exhaustion of food or water supplies. *Contemporary migration*, however, occurs because of the availability of natural resources in the place of destination (Petersen & Thomas 1968). The features which apply to archaic and contemporary migration can also apply to *mass and independent migration*. What distinguishes mass and independent migration, however, is the role or the impact of socio-economic forces, as well as the size of population shift. Mass migration, as the term implies, involves very large population shifts, while independent migration involves the migration of isolated individuals, that is, sporadic migration or the migration of pioneers who migrate outside of chain or associational migration (Petersen & Thomas 1968; Schermerhorn 1970).

Mass and independent migration, along with *voluntary and involuntary migration*, are central to any study of most Greek migration to Australia as they often tend to overlap, not only with each other, but also with voluntary and involuntary migration. What distinguishes voluntary from involuntary migration is the extent to which migration is the result of free choice by the individual or group (mass) concerned (Castles et al. 1988: 81). If individuals are forced to migrate because of restrictions imposed on them or discrimination against their social, political, religious and related practices connected with their basic human rights, such people are classified as refugees and can be granted refugee status by host societies. Refugee migration is generally forced upon peoples by dictatorships, civil wars or colonisation. *Colonisation* also is a major type of migration and can occur because of overpopulation in the sending society, or because of political, commercial or even military considerations (Schermerhorn 1970). For its part, *associational migration* is usually the product of other types of migration as, for example, independent (or pioneer), mass, and/or colonisation. What distinguishes associational migration from other types of migration is the existence of strong associational or communal ties, feelings and concerns (Rex & Mason 1986).

All types of migration have as a point of reference the nation state since all migrations occur within and between nation states. As a consequence, all types of migration are indiscriminately categorised as either *internal or external migration* (Rex & Mason 1986: 90). Since migration occurs nationally as well as internationally, this also sets the framework of most analyses of social mobility. The movement of people from point A to point B within and between nation states, is best realised and defined in a social mobility context, regardless of whether or not people cross an international border. Migrants, like everyone else, strive to become upwardly socially mobile either within or beyond the national borders of their own country of origin. They aspire to migration hoping that increased opportunities for social mobility will enable them to achieve their goals beyond their country's national borders. Consequently, migrants offer their occupational services in host societies, hoping that on arrival they will be provided with

21

opportunities which will produce benefits for themselves and for their families.

Adams asserts (1968: 29–48) that the out-migration of scientists and other skilled personnel deprives developing societies of much of the 'know how' normally needed for their industrial 'take-off' stage. The labour mobility of scientists has been conceived in terms of their contribution to the national interests of host societies, for example, in the arenas of technological and economic development. In modern and postmodern times, some professional and skilled personnel may be classified as transient migrants as opposed to those professionals who are granted immigrant entry status. What distinguishes the transient type of professional migrant from the immigrant professional, therefore, is the residential and citizenship status granted by receiving countries. The transient migrant category also includes members of the diplomatic corps, teachers, engineers, scientists and guest workers, who cross national borders to work or to represent their country of origin and, in so doing, retain their sending country's citizenship (Richmond 1988: 2). Generally speaking, all migration can be defined in terms of permanent or temporary status, depending on the immigration authorities of the host societies.

Whether or not residential status is granted to migrants depends on a number of different but interrelated factors, including the extent to which migrants fit *conservative* or *innovative* categories. Some countries, especially multicultural societies like Australia and Canada, attract both types of migrants. Conservative migrants, as the word implies, may wish to conserve or retain their original lifestyle, but if the migrant is classified as innovative, the contrasting situation may occur, that is, the migrant adopts and adapts to the customs and language of the host society.

Implicit in any discussion about the types of migration is the assumption that certain types—such as refugee movements, professional migration and a few colonising migrations—tend to be conceptualised as variants of models applied to labour migration. These variants generate some of the complications evident in current theorising on migration since, in general, theories do not follow a uniform pattern nor do they attempt to encompass the totality of the different processes and/or aspects of the subject. Instead, theories tend to concentrate on the specific aspects of the migration experience. Some of these aspects are, for example, the origins and effects of labour flows; the socio-economic forces which determine movements of migration and the formation of their categorisations, (including migrant direction flows); the determinants of stability of migrant movements; the uses of immigrant labour; and migrants' adaptation within host societies. These factors are the key issues of current theoretical interest in the subject (Portes 1985: 57).

Taken together, the various categories of migration contribute to a fuller appreciation of what we term 'Hellenic migration to Australia'; but individually, however, they lack the theoretical power to adequately explain Hellenic migration to Australia. Furthermore, although specialisation in defining key aspects of migration has increased, because of theoretical differences between disciplines research still fails to encompass certain particular characteristics of migration evident in modern and postmodern times. Thus economists, drawing from the neoclassic and Marxist schools, refer to the economic impact of migration, while sociologists and demographers who draw from social themes associated with the regional or national composition of given populations, provide accounts which relate to the causes and effects involved in the cycle of migration and re-migration. Between these two approaches, however, characteristics which do not fit neatly into either approach remain undetected and undiscussed.

Despite the diversity of approaches, the real value of contributions made by single disciplinary research is not denied. In fact, the different approaches to migration—irrespective of idelogical background or directing theory—have, in one way or another, contributed toward or stimulated consideration of a wide range of factors and indices, and helped to answer more complex questions on the subject. Moreover, over the last 30 years, theoretical trends on migration tend to emphasise reciprocity and inter-dependence in terms of understanding migration and the extent to which it is beneficial to migrants as well as to the sending and receiving societies (Thistlethwaite 1960; Boyd 1989: 630–61).

A number of attempts, from inter-disciplinary schools, have been made to study and explain the typologies of migration. Some of the better-known attempts are set out in historical

Table 2.2   Theories of approaches to migration

Neoclassic economic theory of migration	Marxist critique of migration	Socio-historical approaches of migration
Sociological theory of migration	Demographic theory of migration	Multivariate approach of migration
Socio-psychological theory of migration	Psychological and cultural deprivation theories of migration	Multivariate approach of migration
Globalisation and migration (or labour mobility)		

context in order to illustrate the contributions made by different scholars and/or different disciplinary schools of thought ranging from economic to psychological or theoretical approaches. This information enhances the theoretical framework of this study on Hellenic migration and the social mobility of Greeks in Australia. The readings representing the different theoretical approaches on migration are illustrated by Table 2.2.

Ravenstein (1885) examined how lack of labour in a given geographic region could be supplemented by migrants relocating from another region where labour is plentiful. He also noted that people migrate because they follow the direction of migratory currents, or because the geographic distance covered makes it possible for people to re-migrate if they wish to do so. He argued that tendencies to migrate vary between rural and urban regions, and between the sexes. Ravenstein also regarded highly-populated regions as a main cause of migration towards regions where resources of wealth remained unexplored and could provide migrants with satisfactory employment benefits. Furthermore, he stressed that migration can be caused by a nation's oppressive laws, heavy taxation, poor climatic conditions and depressive social settings. The predominant cause of migration, however, is what he called 'people's natural wish' to improve their economic status (Ravenstein 1889).

Although Ravenstein's work is a study of geographic movement of people, with its emphasis on the importance of economic opportunities, his work is also an example of the neoclassic economics of migration as a 'pull theory'. Neoclassic economists are concerned with the benefits—as opposed to the costs—resulting from migration and this is central to their view of free market economy theory. They adopt this view in response to concerns raised over the last 20 years in countries such as Australia and Germany, as to whether or not migration is a true contributing factor to the economic development of host societies, rather than simply detrimental to sending societies. In these discussions, economists have been less concerned about any possible advantages or disadvantages exhibited in the cost-related aspects of the migratory experience, and more with the extent to which contributions made by migrant labour have slowed down or increased the speed of the developmental advancement processes of host societies.

The neoclassic economic theory emphasises the importance of individual motivation in pursuit of personal gains (Kindleberger & Herrick 1977: 180). The spirit of the neo-classic model, as studied by scholars since the end of the nineteenth century, is to be found in its perception of economic stimulation and response mechanisms displayed by individuals and decision-makers. Policy-making draws from the neoclassic economic theory in order to encourage individualistic competition and promote monopolistic activities in the context of capitalism and the nation state. For its part, the state—as a corporate body and the arbitrator of the capitalist economic system—is limited to 'essential services' in order to ensure the maximisation of profit to individual parties involved in the profit-making competition.

Developments of the neoclassic theory, based on Adam Smith's (1776) treatise on political economy, underpin the economic causes of migration and the economic policies of the modern nation state. He analysed the relationship between freedom of trade and order of economic processes. He attacked the British mercantile system for its limitations on free trade, and argued that free trade based on individualism led to order and progress. This view stemmed from his economic theory on the supply and demand of labour, goods and factor substitution, which aimed at maximisation of profit. Smith stressed that all barriers to labour mobility should be lifted and justified this position by claiming that the development of trading through the international distribution of labour was of crucial importance for the general well-being of all (Smith 1954: 54–137).

Smith's work was supported and extended by David Ricardo, a leading British economist, who helped to establish the classical economic theory. Ricardo (in Sodersten 1988) considered labour the most important source of wealth, and accumulation of capital the key to rapid economic growth. He emphasised that the conditions that enable a nation's economy to reach its greatest potential were realised through income distribution and the use of the principle of comparative advantage in international trade. His views were further refined by Heckscher-Ohlin, who argued that factor price equalisation was influenced by trade in compensating factors of production (in Sodersten 1988: 41–6, 67–75). The transference of capital investment and labour from one nation state to another meant (potentially) that there would be an increase in world production. Combining the transfer of capital investment with labour, as well as with the transfer of technology, could lead to speedier developmental processes and to productivity increases that, in return, would be to the benefit of all (Ohlin 1952: 354).

In applying neoclassic economics, Thomas (1954) focused on the impact on economic development in Britain of migration to the United States. He did this by examining the relationship between emigration and real income in Britain and economic fluctuations in the United States (prior to World War Two). He focused on economic gains arising from railway construction and its cost output, against four substantial migrations to the United States. As these migrations coincided with periods of relatively rapid economic growth in the North Atlantic economy (in contrast to the lower developing status of sending countries), Thomas, like other neoclassic economists, supported the theory of pull towards the host country, rather than push from the sending country.

In further stressing the neoclassic economic model, Kindleberger and Herrick claimed that migrant labour is drawn to regions where working conditions and remuneration are most attractive and where benefits and returns generally could be maximised (Kindleberger & Herrick 1977: 180). People migrated to host societies which usually possessed abundant natural resources, capital, advanced technology and higher wages for both skilled and unskilled labour. Similarly, for the individual capitalist, migrant labour was an investment in human capital. The return on investment in migration could be measured as the difference in net earnings, which were the result of the difference minus the costs between sending and receiving countries. In terms of neoclassic economic theory, migrants can be defined as 'free riders' who usually take advantage of 'external benefits', which have been created by the administrative elite, and the socio-economic process by which that elite transfers wealth to itself from the rest of the society (Kindleberger & Herrick 1977).

Charles Kindleberger[1] claimed that countries like Britain, and some of the Scandinavian states, which did not experience an increase in the availability of labour, experienced a slower pace of development.[2] He believed that the availability of plentiful labour might *promote* developmental processes but it could not *provoke* them. This has been evident in situations where the levels of development reached by post-World War Two Europe were determined by technological change and progress, but also by better organisational methods of production and distribution. Kindleberger (1967: 4) described the income increase of 6–8 per cent per capita in the 1950–60 period as 'super development'; he also maintained that this achievement was due, in part, to migrant mobility of labour from agriculture to industry and related administrative services, but even more to the occupational practices of guest workers in West Germany, France and Switzerland.

In the context of economic gains resulting from migration, other commentators such as Boyd (1989) emphasise the importance of remittances for the economic development of sending societies. Remittances (or the sending of money by immigrant workers to their family household) are said to 'provide the litmus test of benefits from labour migration'. As indicated by Boyd, remittances are noteworthy for four reasons: firstly, remittances show the existence of social networks across geographic space; secondly, they have economic effects in the sending country; thirdly, remittances maintain the use of migration as household strategy; and fourthly, migrants send important messages about comparative opportunities and standards of living, thereby stimulating future migration flows (Boyd 1989: 651).

In viewing migration from a slightly different angle, Myrdal (1957: 54) argued that the law of supply and demand of international trade leads to polarisation of development. He further hypothesised that countries or geographic regions with expanding economic activities tend to be attractive to migrants and that migration is a selective process—at least as far as the age of migrants is concerned. The latter is an essential factor in the assertion that younger migrants can contribute more towards the development, or the speed of the developmental processes, of host societies. Migration to host societies can have detrimental effects upon the population structure of sending societies when the migrants are younger, since they are regarded as the driving force behind the development of sending societies. Myrdal justified this theory by arguing that during the mass migration period toward the industrial centres, for example, the United States, the poverty of rural regions of Europe occurred largely because of the poor age-to-population ratio that had resulted from migration.

During the 1960s, when economically less powerful European states were facing problems of increasing unemployment or a surplus of labourers, the nations which were facing labour shortages took advantage of this oversupply, in order to maximise social and economic benefits from migration. Job seekers saw their movement elsewhere—in response to the labour demand—as a means of economic survival. Eventually, however, due to advances in technology and increasing unemployment within these receiving states, a number of indices were adopted as criteria to reduce migrant entry.

Undoubtedly, certain types of people, who fall outside the socio-economic selection criteria of immigration policies of host societies, tend to remain less mobile even within the boundaries of their own nation state. Some of these people who are restricted from gaining migrant status and have to remain in their home countries often face limitations in the level of their socio-economic advancement. This situation usually occurs where out-migration did not solve the sending societies' development problems and, consequently, the surplus of labour could not be absorbed by their manufacturing sector.

Central to the neoclassic theory of supply and demand is its connection to the criteria adopted by host societies for immigrant workers. There are various socio-economic indices which influence the supply and demand of workers, and/or influence them to migrate (OECD 1976: 55–66). Some of the indices which influence labour supply are: the degree of industrialisation (on primary, secondary and tertiary levels) of the receiving society; the natural population movement; the duration of compulsory schooling; the occupational status; and post-occupational training. Labour supply is also affected by the ratio of males to females occupied in industry; the return to employment of economically active migrants; and their integration in the occupational practices. In contrast, factors which influence labour demand in host countries include: the educational and occupational training of migrants and the level of integration of first- and second-generation migrants. Labour demand is influenced further by the number of working hours performed in each occupational category and the kind of welfare services that are available for the unemployed, as well as being conditioned by problems associated with migrant pensions, vocational issues, absences from employment, social conflict and political selection (OECD 1976: 55–6).

There have been important objections, however, to the rationale adopted by the neoclassic model. Not all authorities agree with the neoclassic or external economic model of development and the justification it provides about the causes of labour mobility and the use of migrant labour. It has been criticised for maintaining that the same forces that cause migration to occur also determine the social mobility within a country or region and the direction of rural–urban migration. Much of the criticism directed against the neoclassic model has come from the Marxist radical critique, which regards certain typologies of migration—such as mass, voluntary and involuntary—as failing to provide sufficient explanation for the better understanding and analysis of labour mobility between countries under capitalism.

In delineating its criticism, Marxist radical critique portrays neoclassic economic theory as an artificial, notably ahistorical, state of affairs and sees it as a mechanistic mode of analysis of historical development, rather than a study based on stages of development. Marx (1983; Kamenka 1986: 201–8) regarded socio-economic evolution as a process based on the dialectic materialism of historical development. This process was one where thesis and antithesis clash and combine into a synthesis.

For Marx, capitalism as a mode of operation was doomed by internal contradictions which harboured the seeds of its own destruction. Periodic economic crises wreck the capitalist system and these crises grow in size and duration. A continuous class struggle occurs between owners of capital and production forces and the workers.

Radical critique associates migration of human labour with Marx's notion of the industrial 'reserve army'[3] or with the use of the proletariat class under capitalism (Marx 1983: 589). Marx indicated that every special historic mode of production has its own special laws of population movement. He argued that, under capitalism, the working population 'along with the accumulation of capital produced by it, the means by which it made itself relatively superfluous, is turned into relative surplus population; and it does this to an always increasing extent' (Ibid.: 591).

The 'reserve army' is a product of the associated increase in labour productivity and an ever-increasing level of capital accumulation. It is Marx's notion that a surplus of labourers, which he regarded as an artificial state of affairs under capitalism, was a condition purposely worked out by the capitalist system in order to achieve greater profits through the exploitation of the working class. Exploitation is carried out through capital accumulation and labour control, as well as through the ownership of the means of production by the capitalist class (Marx 1983: 632–3). The sterilisation in capital formation of increasing amounts of output is associated with rising unemployment, or with the creation of a bigger 'reserve army'. This army, consisting of unemployed workers, one may add, contributes to internal and external migration as its members travel from place to place in search of employment.

For Marxists, migration will not relatively improve the workers' situation in host societies. This situation occurs partly because as capitalism advances internationally into the developing countries of the world, it uses all available labour to extract higher profits. In doing so, the domestic class struggle is extended worldwide. In the Marxist view, the capitalist class makes no contribution to the process of production—the source of all value is the workers. They are the ones who contribute to the process of production (Marx 1983). Lenin's definition of imperialism as the highest stage of capitalism saw this exploitation of workers as a logical expansion of local capitalism to world dimensions. This expansion resulted from the nineteenth-century colonial system (Lenin 1978).

Lenin's views on migration are founded on the law of unequal economic and political development among different nation states—created by imperialism—that is, the monopoly stage of capitalism. For him, imperialism, or finance capital, has created the new epoch of monopolies, bank cartels, domination of the world market, and the exploitation of labour in other countries in order to amass vast profits. Because of the inequality between nation states, workers from the less advanced countries of the world migrated to the industrially advanced nation states of Europe, as well as to the United States and elsewhere in search of material rewards. This inequality was a main cause of the division of the working class within different nation states.

Unequal development exists within and between countries, and is reflected in the remunerations and special privileges granted to local, as opposed to immigrant, workers. Engels referred to the special privileges which were given to British workers in contrast to immigrant workers (Engels 1962: 119). These privileges were given to them by virtue of their training, which meant that they could not be replaced by members of the industrial 'reserve army'. By conceding privileges to specific organised sectors of labour, 'above all to craftsmen', the labour aristocracy were in a position to utilise class consciousness to secure an opportunist non-revolutionary leadership for these sectors. This manipulation is the method of divide and rule, expressed in special advantages (which take the form of higher status symbols), rather than higher material rewards. This situation misleads workers, causing some to identify with the capitalist instead of with the rest of the working class (Lenin 1977: 244–6).

One of the special features of the monopoly stage of capitalism, according to Lenin, was the decline in emigration from imperialist countries and the increase in immigration into these countries from underdeveloped countries. Engels, and Lenin after him, also point out that imperialism had the tendency to create privileged sections among the workers and to 'fetch' them from the broad masses of the proletariat. In doing this, imperialism bribed the upper strata of the proletariat—thereby fostering, shaping and strengthening opportunism and permitting lower wages to be paid (Lenin 1977).

Samir Amin, like Lenin before him, saw migration as a phenomenon connected to the capitalist system of unequal development between geographic regions. This unequal development could exist within single nation states as well as between countries or geographic regions and is characterised by development between the developed centres and underdeveloped peripheral areas (Amin 1977).

Amin argued that the era of imperialism still continues and should be subdivided into two phases. The first phase stretched from 1880 to World War One (perhaps to the 1930s), and opened with a structural crisis at the centre, which was overcome by the appearance of monopolies and capital exports to peripheral countries. The second phase of the imperialist system was marked at the centre by large-scale state intervention, new forms of surplus absorption and changes in the forms of dependency between nation states. During the first phase of imperialism, the period of relative stagnation of real wages was at the end, and a period of relatively high wage increases began (Amin 1977: 232). Also, the first phase was characterised by very high growth rates of both the product at the centre and world trade. In contrast, during the second phase of imperialism there was a tendency by foreign capital, particularly towards the latter part of the period, to assume direct domination. This domination took place through the technological domination of developing countries and the adoption of their consumption patterns. During this time, the main source of growth shifted from export to import industries. This shift distorted the development of the peripheral mode of production and created a problem of absorption, which was solved firstly by export of capital to the countries of the capitalist centre and, secondly, by an increase in the proportion of the surplus value spent on imported luxury goods. The importing of technology, and the production policies connected to small local import 'substitutions' coming from monopolies, permitted this form of consumption of surplus (Ibid.: 233–4).

Much of the blame for this kind of development has been associated with the role of the bourgeoisie of the underdeveloped countries. Amin argued that the bourgeoisie of these countries did not enter the phase of competition necessary to create the favourable conditions which could lead to a more advanced capitalist mode of production. Instead, the local bourgeoisie became dependent on the bourgeoisie of the developed centres of the United States, western Europe and Japan. These countries were where the capitalist mode of production and capital accumulation were concentrated and mainly developed. From there, they were extended to the underdeveloped countries of the periphery where pre-capitalist conditions prevailed. Furthermore, Amin argued, the refusal to industrialise was accompanied by a division of the local bourgeoisie—into a comprador section whose future was linked with foreign domination and a national section which came into conflict with imperialism (Amin 1977: 232).

The inability to industrialise of the developing economies led to underemployment or labour surplus. The relationship between dependent (that is, industrially underdeveloped) countries on the one hand, and independent (that is, developed or industrialised) countries on the other, created a system of unequal capitalist regional or international development which promoted migration to the developed centres (Amin 1977: 66–7). Under such conditions, however, it could be argued that migration did not constitute a natural relocation of individuals based on people's free choice.

According to Castles and Kosack (1980), contemporary currents to western Europe present two new features when compared with earlier patterns of worker immigration. The traditional Marxist conception of the industrial reserve army of men and women thrown out of work by 'rationalisation and cyclical crises is hardly applicable today. Thus, immigration is of key importance for the capitalist system' (Castles & Kosack 1980: 119–21). The authors argue that, from 1945, migration to the developed countries led to large numbers of immigrant workers taking more stable positions in the productive process (since the domestic reserve army was inadequate), so that their labour could not be dispensed with in periods of recession. This repopulation led to their second point, that the role of the modern industrial reserve army conceivably might be fulfilled by other groups, for example, immigrant workers in industrially developed European countries (especially West Germany), who had migrated there from underdeveloped areas of southern Europe or from Third World economies, forming the 'latent-surplus' population or reserve army (Ibid.: 119).

Furthermore, Castles and Kosack argue that under modern capitalism workers were divided to ensure their maximum exploitation. This division occurred between immigrant and indigenous workers. They were 'split along national and racial lines'. By allowing this division to exist, the capitalist class of these countries offered its indigenous workers better conditions and status than its immigrant groups, encouraging 'large sections of the working class to identify with the consciousness of labour aristocracy' (Castles & Kosack 1980: 121).

In summary, it appears that migration is essential to the capitalist system for a number of reasons. It is essential because capitalism facilitates the exploitation of the working class worldwide. Migration is also used to provide the reserve army of labourers—as traditionally conceived by Marxists—thus enabling the bourgeoisie to proceed with the segmentation of the working class within host societies. At the same time, the classic and neoclassic economic theories identify migration as a component of modern economic development, which is related to unemployment and the obvious needs of developing nations for capital investment and foreign exchange. The foreign exchange resulting from mass labour migration, return migration and remittances[4] is assumed to produce real income for the remaining population of sending societies.

Although remittances are noteworthy for the reasons discussed earlier, they do not, however, redress the economic imbalances between developed and underdeveloped economies. Migration outflows continue due to the economic structure and/or economic dependency of the developing nations. As previously noted, the economic or external model of migration draws from capitalism and the nation state. Both neoclassic economic theory and Marxist critique tend to emphasise the importance of economics in defining migration. As such, the economic model completely ignores the social and psychodynamic model theories of migration. It is now accepted that migration is influenced not only by the powerful pull factor of host societies, but also by local developments and temporary influences.

In contrast to other theoretical approaches, socio-historical perspectives of migration are not limited to single-factor analysis. Instead, they stress that the influence often exerted on people to leave their home country could have a wide range of origins. Fairchild, for example, established that the most significant causal forces behind the individual's decision to migrate were the familiar ones of economic, political, social and religious pushes. Human motives to migrate can be distinguished between those which have 'subjective', as opposed to 'objective', causes, but all migration incentives 'can hardly arise, without some exterior cause' (Fairchild 1925: 3–20).

Similarly, Jones claimed that there was a further dimension of a subjective nature—namely, the hopes and fears of millions of individual migrants—which was no less important in understanding migration. In viewing the social history of European migration to the United States in the nineteenth and twentieth centuries, Jones stressed that not only were the push and pull of economic forces present but there were also other subjective aspects. For example, some migrants were caught up in prevailing involuntary migration resulting from political or economic strife and were classified incorrectly as voluntary immigrants, or listed as refugees (Jones 1960: 94).

Unlike the socio-historical views, the demographers' and sociologists' scholarly perspectives usually employ the push–pull approach in their analysis of the migration phenomenon. Such authors distinguish between the associated factors involved in the process of migration and re-migration, which could be both economic and non-economic. When studying migration, demographers tend to speculate on whether or not factors which 'push' populations from their countries, such as poverty, overpopulation and social upheaval, were more or less important than forces which 'pull' migrants to the place of settlement. These forces may be high wages, unoccupied areas, refugee migrations, the lure of distant lands, or the wish to be with friends happily settled elsewhere.

Sociologists, too, emphasise that there is a combined 'push versus pull' principle in migration. The two forces involved work selectively on different migrants. The *push factor* includes unemployment and economic hardship, food shortages, racial or religious discrimination, political oppression, deteriorated environments and overcrowding. The *pull factor* refers to job availability, cheap land, political and religious freedom and increased educational opportunities. The forces relating to the 'push versus pull' principle were 'mitigated by inhibitory effects of sentiment, habit and fear of the unknown' (Broom, Selzwick & Broom 1981: 280).

Sociologists often base their observations on information obtained from migratory experience on a longitudinal approach. According to Goldlust and Richmond (1974: 193), such an approach is useful because it 'permits the linkage of records of individuals'. This kind of research was obviously based on empirical methods and could include indices of migrant experience from country of origin to country of settlement. Such an approach, however, is time consuming, and few of the studies have collected data beyond the third year of migrant residence within host societies.

The 'push versus pull' approach to migration fails to deal with the more subtle aspects of an individual's cultural and subjective, or psychological, make-up. It does not, therefore, constitute a fully adequate model to understand migratory movements, or the development of people's attitude towards out-migration. While the 'push versus pull' considerations are central to an *external* model of migration theory, they do not form the focus of the equally important *internal* model. This approach is human-centred, in that it is concerned with people's feelings and emotions. It considers migrants as individuals who are exposed to cultures or civilisations, not as mere organisms that strive egotistically to attain economic and occupational aspirations, or to take advantage of perceptible differences across national or regional boundaries.

In applying a human-centred approach, one could argue, as Zubrzycki did, that the act of migration might be accompanied by great mental pressure once the migrants arrive in their host societies. His research demonstrated that social workers find that this mental pressure affects different ethnic groups differently (Zubrzycki 1973: 1–10) and he argued that pre-existing states of alienation have also been responsible for re-migration. Following these suggestions, Zubrzycki went beyond the mere 'push and pull' of economic forces in his attempt to explain the causes of out-migration, for example, immigration might be chosen as a remedy for psychiatric problems resulting from financial, social and interpersonal difficulties. He concluded that departures (re-migration) from Australia were generally due to more complex reasons (Ibid.).

The mental pressure on an individual to re-migrate or return home does not always result from the migration experience abroad—it is often embodied within the network of the migrant's culture of origin. Traces of 'migration mentality' can constitute part of a culture's norms or its inhabitants' attitudes towards migration. This mentality can simply be an outcome of people's interaction with the geographic characteristics of their country or could further involve people's past and present settlement histories or myths, the value system of their society and whether or not human experiences such as seafaring, travelling and/or migrating have been important features of their history and traditions. Such an approach to migration seeks to trace the extent to which the cultural traits of given nations reflect popular thinking which, in turn, enhances migratory movement across the world. For example, some peoples, such as the Greeks (Andrewes 1984), the Filipinos and other islanders, have, over time, settled on many small islands that are scattered across the seas. As a consequence, they tend to regard seafaring as a common feature of their culture, indeed, as an attractive and even inevitable part of their lives. Cultural traits may also be clearly apparent when observing the behaviour of a people or listening to their traditional tales of migration and travel. The power inherent within a culture that propels individuals to migrate or shapes their habits of travel can be part of the everyday life of a given people, regardless of whether or not the factors that sparked the migration in the first place still apply. Within this cultural framework, therefore, the need to meet challenges outside people's national borders may be seen as a norm.

This cultural framework leads to 'stunting' and 'liberating' theories (or approaches) which stress the social and psychological elements found in migration outflows (Martin & Meade 1979: 6–7). The study of migration from a stunting and liberating perspective is a subset of the psycho-social framework and is generally disregarded by other theoretical approaches, but it is an important aspect of migration at the experiential level—one that has an impact on the economic and related development level—at least in terms of innovative choices about life's chances. Stunting and liberating theories place increasing emphasis on the subjective experience of migration in spite of the overlapping of conventional factors such as economics.

The *liberating* approach to migration 'is concerned with the fresh vision brought to bear by migrants on a group level as strangers' (Martin & Meade 1979: 6–7) while, on an individual level, it directs attention to the release of individuals from the national or ethnic parameters of a culture. The liberating approach frees participants' creative and critical faculties from preconceptions so they can gain insights into more than one culture. The migrants' role in society is supposed to be that of 'innovators and catalysts for social change and even as prodders of slumbering conscience' (Ibid.). A liberating *mentality*, as the word implies, encourages people to experience cross-cultural communication through their participation in different societal and cultural settings. In conceptualising the liberating theory Cahill states that it 'highlights the inter-cultural communicative aspect of inter-marriages which leads to the rupturing of monolithic groups based on ethnicity, religion or culture. It facilitates broader inter-cultural interaction between various groups or societies which is the basis of intergroup co-operation' (Cahill 1990: 3).

The stunting and liberating approaches imply that the migration phenomenon is of a multifaceted nature and, as such, requires in-depth analysis in order to be adequately understood. It is asserted that, since the migration experience is an interactive process related to multifaceted factors and indices, each of which exerts particular influence on the decision to migrate, the various aspects of migration interact with each other. Therefore, except for purposes of specific analysis, migration cannot be treated discretely. In a study of migrants in Canada, Goldlust and Richmond (1974) found that post-migration experiences of adaptation, for example, could no longer be based on simplistic suggestions, nor could difficulties associated with immigrant adaptation be explained in terms of monocausal relationships between particular eco-nomic, biological, or even psychological, variables. There has been a growing dissatisfaction with monocausal explanations of the migration experience—and an increasing recognition of the complexity of both the dependent variables such as the migrant's main motive to migrate—and correlated factors.

If the stunting approach is adopted as a tool of analysis of migration, attention must be drawn to the possibility of immigrant self-hatred, and the concern of certain ethnic groups that they will be used as the scape-goats for the socio-economic or political failures of the established community. These outcomes could eventuate in ethno-racial definitions against migration on a group level—thus focusing attention on the defensive nature of migrants and their organisational practices. When the social status of a migrant group is attacked, the individual migrant is believed to suffer insecurities, loss of a sense of identity and organisational disorder.

An essential aspect of the stunting approach to migration is its capacity to overlap with existing theories of cultural deprivation. This capacity is attributed to the cultural and intellectual poverty of people who are placed in the lower social rankings of a given society. Cultural deprivation is often attributed to working-class children whose families have limited earning capacity or education, and/or to immigrant children who belong to the lower socio-economic stratum of the host society. It has been proved that cultural deprivation can prevent children from lower-class backgrounds from achieving satisfactory educational results or meeting parental expectations (Seitz 1977: 21–2; Halsey 1972: 8). The child's 'normal' mental and psychological development can be inhibited, lowering the child's 'maturational ceiling' (Martin & Meade 1979: 6–7).

As well as the stunting and liberating approaches to explaining the complexity of migration, Goldlust and Richmond proposed an equally important model, which dealt with a wide range of issues connected with social mobility factors and indices of immigrant life. Their study employed advanced research methods and strategies to examine specific issues of immigration which, when addressed by previous studies, had foundered on problems of linearity and overgeneralisation (Goldlust & Richmond 1974: 193–225). Their study examined the impact of the migration experience upon the cognitive mechanism and psychological condition of individual migrants in connection to their adaptation within the host society. Their model was somewhat compatible to the 'push and pull' approach, but its advantage lay in the fact that it was based on a longitudinal, or simple survey study and applied regression analysis in order to explore the more subtle aspects of migrant experience. Their model assumed that the immigrant population is heterogeneous and is influenced by a range of variables. The adoption of multivariate factors and smallest variable analysis allowed the independence or interdependence of several different issues to be considered together more effectively.

In contrast to subtle, multivariate analysis, most theories concentrate on the 'objective' concrete factors—features often reflected in popular reports, which are influential in shaping the migrants' own explanations behind their decision to migrate. Factors that are usually reported by the mass media, for example economics and politics, form what has been defined here as the *external* model of migration. One of the outcomes of this model is that migrants find it difficult to go beyond the rational explanations which led to their decision to migrate. They are unable to enunciate any factors other than the conventional ones—economics, increased job opportunities or a house of their own.

Unlike the external model that remains at a 'superficial rational' level, Luthke and Cropley (1990) pointed to the importance of confronting the deeper or *internal* psychological issues involved in migration. They viewed migration as a dissolution of attachments to objects, both at the place of origin (the push area), and the place of destination and settlement (the pull area). They pointed to the interrelationship between concrete (objective), and non-concrete factors, but argued that in the final analysis decisions are governed by non-concrete or non-rational factors. They also argued that the external or rational model theories containing the 'push' perspective of migration were characterised by limitations in scope, especially when potential migrants were struggling to reach rational decisions in relation to voluntary migration. As Luthke and Cropley indicated, the external model:

> while undoubtedly of some value, is obviously limited in scope, especially as a source of insights and associated strategies and tactics for practical counselling of potential or actual migrants wrestling in their minds with the uncertainties of the decision-making process in the homeland, or with the stresses and strains of adaptation in the receiving society (Luthke & Cropley 1990: 152).

To prove the strength of their internal model, Luthke and Cropley investigated the non-rational considerations involved as well as the rational or concrete factors. They did this through empirical and theoretical research, questionnaires and personal interviews. Participants were asked to respond to questions which related to the interrelationship between concrete (objective) factors and non-rational (psychological) aspects found in people's motives to migrate. To do this, the following categories were considered:

(1) Concrete Motives (e.g. house of one's own or job availability in Australia, need for a drier climate for health reasons). (2) Social Motives (reasons which make the wish to emigrate seem more rational and convincing to other people). (3) Cognitive Motives (reasons which make the wish to migrate seem rational to would-be migrants themselves). (4) Psycho-dynamic (motives to migrate which include a desire for change and exposure to challenges, an urge to 'avoid conflict-laden family relations', and earlier traumatic separation experiences) (Luthke & Cropley 1990: 156).

The authors found that motives to migrate included in category (1), although they were 'plausible and commonsensical', were given low priority by the participants. In contrast, the dominant categories were (2) and (3), but when these were further analysed it was found that these categories too were associated with the fourth category. This finding meant that the 'real motives for emigrating lie with the fourth domain (psycho-dynamic motives)', which constituted part of their internal model approach. The theoretical approach of the internal model can be related to the false consciousness that often results from an individual's disenchantment or alienation in the subject–object relationship, or from people's mental and psychological state when trying to understand the meaning of social values (often due to the rapid transformation of values). Depending on the strength of its impact, alienation can deprive individuals or whole ethnic groups of their ability to act rationally when making decisions about migration.

According to Fried (1970), alienation often stems from people's dissatisfaction with their society of origin—therefore only a small proportion may be said to migrate voluntarily.

Fried maintained that it is not always the poorest who migrate, but also a substantial number of migrants who are already partially alienated, or dissatisfied, with their country of origin because it does not meet their physical and spiritual expectations. Similarly, data relating to migrants' social origins, skills and education suggests that it is not so much the most adventurous who migrate, but rather those who suffer continuous deprivation—such as religious, social and political discrimination—whether due to racial or ethnic oppression, poverty, famine or lack of opportunities (Fried 1970: 29).

In presenting the different theories of migration, it has been argued that single theories only enable us to grasp some of the complexities of the subject. Again, part of the problem in single-theory models is that their theoretical contributions to understanding immigration in its various forms and/or classification categories come from various single disciplinary schools of thought which do not follow a uniform pattern leading to a holistic model of migration. At the same time, migration currents have increased and migrant categories have become more complex, thus making it more difficult to analyse and explain by single theories or perspectives.

The theoretical complexities of migration have expanded during the post-World War Two period with the numbers, origins, scope and influences of migrants also expanding, so that they have become a more permanent phenomenon of the contemporary global community. This trend towards globalisation appears to be increasing as civilisation proceeds towards the post-industrial or postmodern social system. The emergence of post-industrial societies—and the increasing penetration by capitalism of every corner of the planet—has led many more nation states to be involved as either sending or receiving societies of migrants and, in some cases, both. Persons of diverse cultural and educational backgrounds travel across many more borders and oceans than in previous eras. Migrants move internationally, in an increasing variety of forms and occupational categories, seeking better employment and rewards. Women are also seeking social mobility status across nation states, overcoming previously imposed gender differences and, like men, are being recruited more than ever before either as individuals or groups (World Council of Churches 1991; Stahl et al. 1993). Labour mobility presents a significant movement of workers and professional personnel, within regions from less developed states to newly developed industrial or technological sectors. Accordingly, the movement of workers now takes place not only from a developing to a developed country but also vice versa, depending on the technological needs or projects under way in the countries concerned. People migrate to take up employment opportunities that are available in industrially developing Third World countries. In such cases migrant workers, or professional personnel and their families, who cross the borders of nation states are regarded as non-nationals or people in transit while residing in their place of employment. Unlike the industrial period, temporary, contract and illegal migrants have become the dominant feature of population movement of modern and postmodern times over the last 20 years. As a result, global labour mobility often reduces migrants to the status of unprotected individuals, without citizenship rights within their host societies. They remain unprotected as long as their rights are not addressed by the national legislation of receiving states, or by their own state of origin while on an overseas employment contract (Stahl et al. 1993).

Over the last 20 years, international organisations and conventions have been expressing their concern about the protection of migrants but migrant status as a social category is determined differently by 'settler societies' like Australia and New Zealand. Definitions of migrants' status may be subject to both societal attitudes and outdated legislation implemented by governments which, in the past, discriminated against certain rights for migrants. Host societies may, for example, define people of Anglo-Celtic origin as British citizens and all non-Britons as 'migrants'. Traditionally, this has been one of the difficulties associated with the rights of migrants in certain host societies—including Australia and New Zealand (Victorian Ethnic Affairs Commission, National and Regional Conference 1988). The possibility of inadequate protection of the migrant by nation states has gained international impetus and is now associated with questions of the citizenship rights of migrants and migrant workers' rights within host societies. The phenomenon of migration is now more complex than ever before because, unlike in earlier historical periods, it does not only entail economic considerations or a single-theory approach but also humanitarian, political and social considerations. The apparent complexities of migration, and the reluctance of host societies to tackle migrant needs, have not only raised questions about the capability of the nation state in its traditional role as arbitrator, but also generated an increasing number of Non-Government Organisations (NGOs) and International Organisations which *are* ready to deal with the problems. Some of these organisations are: the International Labour Organisation (ILO); the World Council of Churches; and the United Nations General Assembly (UNGA). The UNGA resolution 34/172 of December 1979 established an open-ended Working Group to consider the desirability of a new instrument on human rights to be applied to migrant workers.

The recruitment of migrant workers and the remittances they send to their families while working abroad have created the latest form of global financial interdependency between sending and receiving societies. There are also many more questions raised by both scholarly theories and governments regarding the status of migrants in the context of an international community. As Shirley Hume has commented:

> Many [Nation] States of employment now recognise that migrant workers and their families are a permanent rather than temporary part of their society (ie, the ongoing 'guest worker' systems in many countries), requiring new strategies and policies for peaceful national integration. [Nation] States that have historically viewed themselves as relatively homogeneous, often find their own citizens opposing the permanent presence of migrant workers whose race and culture is considered distinctly different and are therefore seen as a threat to the national character. Tensions between nationals and migrant worker communities are further exacerbated when the economy stagnates. As non-nationals in states of transit and employment, migrant workers and members of their families remain relatively defenceless, open to exploitation and often legally unprotected by national laws or civil rights codes. Hence, the need for international protection and universal standards (Hume 1991: 3).

It follows, therefore, that theories of migration—and theoretical approaches to migration in general—have failed to provide a critical insight into the lack of civil rights granted to migrant workers and their families while living in host societies across the world. This failure indicates not only the limitations inherited in the definition of migration by receiving societies, but also the distinctive theoretical differences on migration that are attributable to different intellectual traditions and disciplinary backgrounds. These theoretical differences have maintained some kind of discriminatory profile towards each other, disregarding the fact that there are apparent similarities and overlapping indicators concerning, for example, the economic development within and between nation states. Migration theory limitations are most apparent because they fail to address questions related to migrants' rights as members of an ever-increasing international community.

Finally, despite the theoretical developments on migration which have arisen out of inter-disciplinary research, the definition of migration remains basically the same. Migrant recruitment is still viewed in terms of economic inducement and it is in this context that migrant workers have been defined as the midpoint of a process that has ranged from involuntary labour extraction to the spontaneous initiation of migration flow on the basis of labour demand in societies of migrant intake (Collins 1988; Freeman & Jupp 1992).

The first stage of the completion of the migration cycle is the actual contact between different ethnic groups following migrant settlement. From the starting-point of initial contact, the various migrants begin their struggle for socio-economic advancement within the host society. This occurs irrespective of whether people migrated because: (1) they suffered from the impoverishment—whether by overpopulation or natural disaster—of their home country's agricultural system; (2) they were victims of political or religious persecution, war or revolution; or (3) they wished or needed to join relatives and friends. Research has shown that whether the act of migration is voluntary or involuntary, most people migrate in search of new opportunities or better financial rewards.

In theory, migrants have not been seen as conquerors but as newcomers to be exploited—either temporarily as guest workers, or permanently as settlers—subject to specific government regulations and policies at the time of migration. In *economic* theory, at least as far as the immigrants are concerned, host societies are meant to provide much-needed labour

45

because of a rapidly expanding economy and, as such, migrants are given entry permits.

Following settlement and contact with members of the host society, there follows competition. The first phase is for real estate, and jobs with greater benefits and returns. With the minor exception of some professionals and skilled artisans (whose qualifications are recognised), most migrants start their struggle for upward social mobility as unskilled industrial or agricultural workers. The outcome of competition is conflict— for accommodation, more prestigious jobs and better remuneration. Then follows the establishment of relatively stable patterns of concerted action (with conflict in the competitive context) until some kind of *modus vivendi* is arranged. The working arrangements by which members of different ethnic groups are able to approach one another with fixed expectations constitute traits of, or are images of, ethnic stratification based on the host societies' social class structure.

MARXIST AND WEBERIAN VIEWS OF SOCIAL STRATIFICATION

To enable a better understanding of ethnic population groups in relation to social mobility, this book draws on the Marxist as well as the Weberian perspective since, in migration theory, there is no single theoretical explanation available which can provide a sufficient analysis of the social mobility of individual migrants or ethnic population groups following settlement within host societies. This combined approach provides a better and broader mix of theoretical elements to apply to the study of social mobility within ethnically diverse societies.

Marxism points to discrepancies between the ideology of equal opportunity and reality in terms of opportunities for true mobility. This theory rests on the tenet that the highest social stratum controls the means of production in developed capitalist societies and that the working class has been faced with a reduction in occupational independence and self-employment. Under capitalism, class stratification is divided between 'haves' and 'have nots'—two historically significant classes, the bourgeoisie and the proletariat.

Like Marx, Weber was aware of discrepancies between

objective and subjective location within the stratification system, though he argued that there was mobility of varying kinds and that people moved for different reasons from one stratum to the next. Unlike Marx, he did not reduce the question of stratification to class consciousness or a class dichotomy and he distinguished status from economic class. He attempted to show that society was not monolithic or polarised in terms of power relations (that is, power was located in the antagonistic struggle of the two major classes), as if society was not influenced by the role played by other social groups or social factors. *Status*, or the subjective perception of class, is the honour bestowed on a person by their peers, while *power* is related to the ability of a person to lead others by compulsion or persuasion. Although Weber suggested that ownership of property is the basis on which a class forms, he added that the amount of property and skills a person had determined that individual's chances of owning goods, being successful and content with life (Weber 1968). Someone who is *nouveau riche* may not necessarily have equal status with someone who inherited their wealth or position. Status groups usually attempt to maintain their status privileges by excluding others from entry into their group. This can happen through a process of social closure, for example, endogamy, although Weber does not imply that these groups always succeed in achieving this closure.

For Weber, the existence of classes—consisting of economic or property groups, status groups and members of organisations such as political parties—reflected how power was structured in society and, like Marx, he stressed that even in capitalist societies there were two bases on which classes formed: ownership of property and commercial success. Although he regarded these criteria as belonging to a more traditional and pre-capitalist group of classes, whose status was determined more by what was owned than by the owners' occupations, at the same time he believed that the commercial classes were associated with the emergence of capitalism. Class position—in those terms—was equivalent to the market situation in which people found themselves, and those situations determined people's available 'life chances' in society. Weber pointed out that limited life chances reflected a lack of property which could be used in the market place as a kind of bargaining power, either as a means to generate income or to acquire certain kinds of 'rewards', such as expensive consumer goods (Weber 1968). It is these 'rewards' which give privileged classes prestige in the eyes of others, although they do not need to be determined solely by property ownership or lack of it. Individuals might lack property but they may be able to offer services or 'marketable skills' for which there is a demand and which may, in return, determine their access to various kinds of rewards (Ibid.). Weber identifies these individuals as the 'commercial classes'. This analysis generates a scheme of six class positions and it is this scheme of multiple class positions that makes Weber's theory particularly useful when studying the social status or mobility of ethnic population groups in the context of the social stratification system and processes of contemporary Australia. Examples of class positions include the dominant entrepreneurial and property-owning groups, the intelligentsia, those who possess specialised marketable skills (but who own no property), the petty bourgeoisie and the manual working class. His approach enabled this research to apply additional indices in order to study the more subtle aspects of the way power is allocated in society and thus proceed with a more thorough analysis of immigrant social mobility.

In Marxist terms, however, single indicators cannot account for real mobility nor do they explain the population masses of migrants who find themselves in single occupational categories. Although being employed in a white-collar occupation is considered as non-proletarian, occupation alone is not sufficient to raise one to a higher class, that is, to the bourgeoisie. The latter owns and controls the means of production and, by virtue of that ownership, is able to exploit the labour of the proletariat which only owns the labour which it must sell to the bourgeoisie in order to earn its living. For these reasons both classes are interdependent. At the same time, they have fundamentally opposed interests (whether class members are aware of this or not). The dominant class has its vested interests in maintaining the status quo, while the proletariat's interests lie in destroying the existing system and replacing it with an alternative. Thus, for Marx, class structure under capitalism is both dichotomous and antagonistic. There are also some intermediate classes which share some of the characteristics of each of the two main historical classes mentioned. Classes for Marx, then, cannot be either income or occupational groups. Income is not a fundamental generating factor, unless the capacity to generate income depends on the amount of property ownership and the control of the means of production.

Weber argued that there is a link between power, economics and social class over different dimensions which are not limited by the dichotomy of two major class groups argued by Marx, and that possible 'bases for the formation of status groups include also the features of age, occupation, race, religion and ethnicity' (Najman & Western 1988: 61). Weber's evaluation of class analysis can be based on one or more of a number of characteristics, for example, occupational prestige or sanctioned monopoly of occupational skills and political access; hereditary membership of a particular family; ethnicity or race; education; and religion. Whereas status differences could lead to variations in lifestyle, people in similar positions would tend to acquire the same sort of material possessions, follow similar leisure pursuits, have similar norms of family life and family size and have similar tastes in food and music—similarities in lifestyle that would lead to the formation of status groups. A status group is a group of persons making a claim for special privileges or treatment by virtue of holding a socially recognised position (Weber 1968: 302–5, 926–40).

In conclusion, drawing from both the Marxist and Weberian traditions enables a better understanding of the social mobility of immigrants within host societies. This mobility often begins with competition for jobs, which results in the distribution of ethnic groups into different kinds of employment. The social mobility of ethnic groups is also characterised by shared experiences which become evident over time, as reflected in their various settlement features. The more advanced phase of social mobility draws on the outcome of immigrants' struggles to achieve their goals, including status in terms of social stratification, political participation, assimilation, segregation, integration and, generally, the level of their social incorporation within receiving countries. It is, therefore, the complexity of immigrant experience which necessitates the use of a combined theoretical approach to understand social mobility within receiving societies. Such a combined theoretical approach requires equally complex methodological strategies in order to research Hellenic group experiences in Australia.

METHODOLOGY

One of the major limitations encountered in conducting this study was the dearth of previous studies directly related to the present issues. The existence of such studies would have provided me with a starting point, as well as allowing for the comparison of findings. Hellenic language data and literature such as interviews, radio and TV programs, books, government reports and organisations' minutes had to be translated into English. This required specialist professional expertise and a considerable period of time in which to collate the resulting data. There is always the possibility of slight literary misinterpretations, and all documents, including newspaper articles and media reports in general, should not be accepted as literal and accurate records of events, but as the author's (or the editor's) opinion.

I applied both qualitative and quantitative methods in this study, as complementary to each other rather than mutually exclusive (Paton 1990; Bryman 1992). The qualitative aspect to the research (utilising a field study approach) provided me with raw material derived from subjective information, which I use in different ways: firstly, to guide the formulation of problems which preceded the collection of survey data; secondly, to assist in the discussion and analyses of various chapters, while at the same time providing a balanced and systematic research strategy for discovering themes; and, thirdly, to associate the themes generated by the categories and discerning patterns suggested by the responses of participants (Paton 1990: 390).

I used a three-stage approach during the research process. Stage 1 employed qualitative methodology—through formal interviewing—to establish a quantitative approach to the collection of data in order to develop a theoretical framework for a social mobility questionnaire. Twenty-seven individuals were contacted, with 17 agreeing to participate in a formal interview. The formal approach was guided by an interview schedule comprising carefully selected and systematised sets of open-ended questions (see Appendix 1). The participants were

Australian residents: elderly immigrants (30 per cent); younger immigrants who arrived in Australia during the pre- and post-World War Two periods (45 per cent); and second-generation Hellenic-Australians (25 per cent). One criterion for selection was that participants could articulate clearly their various experiences of migration. Stage 2 (utilising information from stage 1), involved the use of a survey questionnaire made up of fixed structured questions (see Appendix 1). The choice of this strategy was subjected to the following considerations: the need to employ statistical analysis; the time frame; monetary costs; and the geographical problems associated with administering a questionnaire to 1000 Greek residents of Australia. In stage 3, informal interviews were conducted with individuals of Hellenic extraction to provide supplementary information related to participants' own experiences in Australia. Nineteen out of the 30 people I contacted agreed to participate in informal interviews. Complex 'photo procedures', or the identification of specific themes or sub-themes from a theme for further elaboration and subsequent development were applied. These procedures provided me with further information from the participants, by detecting and analysing underlying themes they suggested. Keeping the interviews informal helps the participants and the interviewer to be relaxed, and encourages them to interact with each other. The interviews were based on a broad set of questions derived from a questionnaire (see Appendix 2), which allowed participants to dictate the structure of the interview by acting as either conferers or conferees in the interpretation and analysis of the material under discussion. This strategy was designed to maximise participant input and minimise interference by the interviewer.

Qualitative and quantitative research methods are both used to explain, systematically, the nature of social interaction. Generally, quantitative methods are supported by the positivist paradigm and lead the researcher to regard the world as made up of observable and measurable facts (Glesne & Peshkin 1992). Conversely, qualitative methods are supported by the interpretivist paradigm and portray a world which in reality is socially constructed, complex and ever-changing (Glesne & Peshkin 1992). Although some social researchers (Lincoln & Guba 1985; Schwandt 1989) perceive qualitative and quantitative approaches to research investigation as incompatible, others believe they are not mutually exclusive (Paton 1990; Reichardt & Cook 1979). Different authors believe that the skilled researcher can successfully combine both approaches, so that they support and complement each other (Eisner 1981; Firestone 1987; Howe 1988). This complementary approach enabled me to explore, discover, uncover and understand the multiple social, economic and political factors that have a bearing on participants and the reality of their socially constructed world (Paton 1990). In the quantitative part of the present study, survey methods are most appropriate, as they allow researchers to collect data from populations otherwise too large to interact with directly. By engaging in this method a number of strategic tasks become necessary: questionnaires have to be delivered; responses coded; and data analysed statistically (Denzin 1978).

In conclusion, by employing a range of research techniques, including qualitative and quantitative methodology, this study on the social mobility of Greeks in Australia has been able, firstly, to avoid, as much as possible, research bias and research limitations; secondly, to minimise considerations arising from the limitations of one type of research method; and, thirdly, to compensate for the lack of related studies on Greek-Australians. This study also allowed the use of secondary research data and, therefore, by adopting a range of methods, it has been able to draw on sociological and socio-historical evidence to investigate the various hypotheses longitudinally—addressing pre-migration, migration–settlement and post-migration socio-economic experiences of the social mobility of Greeks in Australia. The socio-historical approach enabled me to examine Hellenic migration as an assertive factor behind social mobility trends following the processes of settlement and resettlement of Greeks in Australia; understand the forces which operated for or against the Hellenic presence in Australia in each historical period and settlement stage; and compare the social, economic and political fluctuations of the host society in each historical period. Yet, as has been argued, to adequately conceive the forces behind Hellenic migration and the social mobility of Greeks in Australia, we need to understand the more subtle psycho-social aspects of Hellenic culture which underpin the Hellenic national character and the Hellenic connection with Australia.

Hellenic values and national character

To understand the significance of the decision to migrate for the individual pioneering Greeks who travelled to Australia, the United States, western Europe and elsewhere, it is necessary first to identify the Hellenic cultural values in which they were nurtured. This chapter examines the symbols and legends of Hellenic national identity derived from a mythical past—symbols that continue to shape everyday human interaction and legends that underpin the open debates and stories told through time in the *agora*. These stories are embedded in Greece's historical heritage and philosophy and in the Greeks' passion for freedom and democracy, their pioneering pursuits and their strong individualism, which contrasts with their close-knit social structures.

Greece, or (Ελλάς *(H)Ellás*) as Greeks prefer to call their country, is a contemporary nation state whose national identity and character has been moulded by at least 3,000 years of history and culture. Two of the most important features of the development of the Greeks as a people are the country's geographic location and long-established traditions and culture. The country is located in the south-eastern region of the European continent and the southern part of the Balkan Peninsula. It constitutes the point of convergence for diverse national cultures and is at the crossroads of three continents: Asia to the east; Africa to the south; and Europe to the north. The geophysical environment (about 3,000 islands spread across the Aegean and Ionian Seas) has itself created a unique natural structure where localised customs have developed over the centuries. This diversity of geographical and cultural features has left its mark on the Hellenic character.

The strength of this cultural diversity as expressed by locals is one of the most obvious elements of Hellenic national life. Just as in ancient times Hellenes identified themselves by their city-states, modern Greeks, although unified under one state, also distinguish themselves according to the names of their respective regions, for example, Macedonia, Epeiros, Thessaly, Dodecannesos, Eptanessos, Pelloponnesos, Sterea (H)Ellás Thrace, and so on. Thus, whilst emphasising their Hellenic origin, Hellenes speak with pride about their particular place of birth and their local, often unique, customs. The geography of the country, in particular the geographic diversity in terms of mountainous slopes, islands and seas, is identified as one of the most influential factors in shaping its inhabitants' attitudes.

Greece's location in the midst of three continents has meant that, historically, Hellenes have witnessed many conflicts over territorial, cultural and racial issues. As a result, Hellenic society has been a proverbial battlefield of social and political unrest from within, though the cause of this internal unrest has often had its roots in external pressures. This historical background has been maintained in Hellenic life and has led to the development of an awareness in Hellenes of the importance of their geographic location, their political and cultural history and the potential of invasion by 'barbarians' (that is, non-Greeks), with the result that modern Hellenic culture and the identity of the Hellenic national character have been subject to an interplay between the ideological influence exerted by the local geographic location and the features of localised customs. From recent history, one major example of external factors which helped to shape the national character is the 1821 struggle for independence from the rule of the Ottoman Empire, the time when Greece became a modern nation state. Although some parts of the country gained freedom shortly after this revolution against the Turks, the struggle for independence continued well into the twentieth century, with further parts of the country joining the new nation state while other parts remained under Turkish rule.

For these reasons, it is difficult to describe the Hellenic national character in precise terms. None the less, the history of the Greek people is underlaid by certain uniform cultural characteristics and values that are common to all Greeks, irrespective of local cultural variables. The Greeks have managed to keep their traditions and customs relatively intact—within the broader uniform cultural framework of Hellenism—despite the invasions of the Romans, the Arabs, the Crusaders and the Turks. This cultural stability is reflected in the Hellenic national identity today, even though the Ottoman occupation hindered communication among Hellenes living in different territories of their country to a greater degree than previously experienced under other invaders. This restricted communication did not stop the Hellenes from practising their customs and traditions, however, particularly in the more remote areas away from the occupying Turks, who were mainly garrisoned in the larger towns and cities.

According to the historian Vakalopoulos (1983), outstanding features of the national character remain intact to this day. The Hellenic individualism and love of freedom have been shaped by a number of factors that tend to exercise their influence on the nurturing and socialising of people. He stresses that:

> The passion for freedom and strong individualism, gave birth to feelings towards the need for equality ever since Homer's epoch. There were no major social differences. The people spoke always in the singular and the king never stood higher than the people. Thus, although the country was subjugated first to the Romans and later to the Turks, the Hellenes had the capability to live free in the nearby or distant mountains and the [geographically] spread out islands (Vakalopoulos 1983: 109–10).

The physical environment itself isolated sections of the population. This isolation may have hindered the development of communication between people from different regions but it fostered the continuation of cultural variety. In ancient times, the country's division into a multitude of natural regional territories contributed to the establishment of small independent city-states or *poleis*, where the inhabitants were encouraged to pursue individual and political rights. An obvious consequence of this division was the enhancement of localised forms of individualism. As Vakalopoulos argues:

> The influence of the conquerors did not occupy the whole of the life and the soul of the Hellenes. Consequently, the ancient characteristics expressing the individualised and mainly group-like life style survived, although in forms of fluid diagrams (Vakalopoulos 1983: 108).

In addition to the factors of individualism, other features have contributed to what appears to be a common body of Hellenic culture. These features are social, historical and philosophical experiences that are common to all Greeks irrespective of regional location—for example, all Greeks share a common language, common institutions, a common religion, a distinctive set of family values and strong feelings for the family, especially the extended family unit (Bottomley 1979; Storer 1985a).

In writing about the Greek national character, one of modern Greece's best-known playwrights and scholars of social history and culture, the late George Theotokas, reflected on the question and offered the following description:

> Odysseus is suffering from this position that modern history has placed him in, and does not want to accept it as definite. Resting on the prow of his ship, under the star-lit night of the Mediterranean, he is dreaming of the Renaissance that escaped him and another Renaissance, his own, that he promised to himself and which he wants with all the strength of his soul. A Renaissance of Hellenism, a new flooding of intelligence, strong and long lasting, that would develop again all the charismata of the Hellenic people and thus decorate (this people) with glory. Such is the golden vision that the 'Hellenic demonic' plays on occasions in the eyes of Odysseus in order to keep him in restless καημό = *kaemo*, [that is, in restless yearning] (Theotokas 1961: 68).

Moreover, Odysseus' yearning is undoubtedly linked to Hellenic history and cultural identity and it is this that keeps him in restless καημό. As a consequence, when Hellenes today think of their identity, they tend to extract cultural material from debates and written works. They also project present-day experience backwards on to ancient philosophy and culture and, through self-reflection, select outstanding features from both their present and ancient histories. This attempt to locate meaningful and exemplary explanations of contemporary life in ancient cultural and literary traditions means that the modern Hellenic national character is constantly informed by and related to the works of Socrates, Plato, Aristotle, Thucydides and others. For example, modern Hellenes identify with Aristophanes' classical play about the man who, unable to stand women any longer, leaves his village to go to the mountains where, he believes, the peaceful environment and exclusive company of the trees and animals will stimulate his mind. However, eventually Aristophanes' protagonist realises that he cannot live by himself and that even the company of women cannot be as bad as loneliness and isolation. He returns to town to share his life with his people, including of course, women. Similarly, Hellene readers of Nietzsche's *Thus Spake Zarathustra*, find they have many things in common with the author's hero. Like his Hellenic counterpart, Zarathustra, in the prime of life, leaves his village and the serenity of its lake and journeys to the mountains to search for spiritual stimulation. Zarathustra returns to his village after ten years because he realises that, unlike other human beings, neither the Sun, the Moon, nor the trees can share in the power of his 'wisdom'.

In contrast to the themes of seclusion and retirement from life, it is equally true that the theme of Hellenes as a gregarious people requires attention. Aristotle, one of the best-known Greeks to propose this theme from a philosophical perspective, argued that the elemental unit of *anthropos*, the human being, is that he or she is what Aristotle termed a *political zoon*, that is, a social and political animal. Aristotle held that humans only develop their full spiritual and psychological potential in the context of the *polis*, that is, within the city-state (Stocker & Langtry 1986: 26–38). This philosophy is one of Aristotle's great pronouncements about the nature of human life and human organisation. In stating it, Aristotle drew upon the scholarship of Socrates and Plato as well as his own experience of the *polis* of ancient Athens. Similar views were held by the Oracles of Delphi, Dodoni and Dion.

The individual, therefore, can when necessary survive in isolation and solitude, but does not thrive on mysticism alone. The Hellenic spirit demands the *agora*, the marketplace, the square, the *kafeneion*, the harbour, the piazza, places where there are people; and this gregarious element is a feature of modern Hellenic life as well as the ancient village or *polis*. In these social settings new ideas and discoveries can be tested through dialogue, by the fire of debate. The spirit of the *agora*, with a free and open exchange of ideas, is conducive to independent thought and resourceful action, both of which are of vital significance to the Hellenic conception of participatory democracy. Clearly, therefore, the environment of the *agora* and the experiences gained from personal involvement in public debate are very enriching in terms of the intellectual stimulation of daily life. The *agora* is the catalyst that allows individuals to initiate cultural development, political discussions and personal or group interaction. It is within this social milieu that what the Hellenes call Φιλότιμο = *philotimo*[1] is best tested, ensuring that, at all times, Hellenes remain a sociable people as much as strong-minded individualists who share a common set of values (Vlachos 1968; Kouvertaris 1971; Vakalopoulos 1983).

'Values' are usually defined as abstract constructs, often contained in meaningful or effective sociolinguistic terms, which reflect underlying assumptions about the nature and functions of language and culture—the nature of human beings' relationships to the concrete world. Human values are subjectively defined and yet they have concrete effects and psychological implications in the way they contribute to the meaningful shaping of everyday human transactions (Berger, Berger & Kellner 1973; Dimitreas 1981, 1994). Throughout the long history of the Hellenic world, questions about values have been pursued with immense interest and passion by citizens engaging in exhaustive debates, both of an academic and a popular nature. The issue of the importance and ranking accorded to values in human affairs is central to these discussions. The placement of values, in order of priority, reflects the universality of choices by people in terms of which values are most or least important in Hellenic life. The following remarks are indicative of the values which have the highest priority within the Hellenic value system:

A people's soul can best be discerned in their perceptions of the supernatural, in the wisdom of the man in the street, in their collective social action and in the melody, tempo, and the lyrics of their popular songs. An old drinking song that could be heard in the local taverns of Attica as early as the fifth century BC, describes the Greek hierarchy of the needs: 'To mortal man, the first gift is Health; the next is Beauty; third is Wealth that no shame attends; the fourth is to be young amongst one's friends' (Burn 1930: 40).

Fame has been considered an important element of Hellenic life, indeed, it has been regarded as an essential aspect of the much sought after quality of honour. As an alternative to fame, some Greeks have sought honour through the accumulation of wealth (Andrewes 1984: 227), but this behaviour has been criticised, especially in regard to the effects of excessive wealth. Concern with the way wealth is both acquired and distributed has been and still remains central to Hellenic society. Historically the core of the Hellenic value system centres upon honour and fame rather than wealth per se. To cite a modern popular saying, widely held as a high ethical value, Η τιμή, τιμή δεν έχει και χαράστον που την έχει ('honour has no price and (praise)worthy is the one who has it').[2] If a person is poor and honest, this person is still honoured, and has a place in society (Monos 1976).

People with honour in Hellenic society are categorised as *philotimoi*, those with a deficit of that value as *aphilotimoi*. To be regarded as *aphilotimos (aphilotim(oi)* = plural), that is, to be stripped of honour, integrity and self-esteem, generosity, altruism and egalitarianism is (when applied seriously) one of the gravest social condemnations. Living for wealth or for the sake of accumulating more and more riches carries no honour when this practice lacks moderation; above all it fails to effect a healthy balance of mind and body, both for the individual concerned and for other members of society. This view was emphasised by ancient classical scholars and traditions found in modern Hellenic society point to its continuing relevance. Pericles sums up this view in the eulogy for the first dead of the Peloponnesian Wars, when he states:

> One's sense of honour is the only thing that does not grow old, and the last pleasure, when one is worn out with age,

is not, as the poet said, making money, but having the respect of one's fellow men (Thucydides 1985: 150).

The folly of the pursuit of money is dramatically illustrated in the tragic Hellenic myth of King Midas. An overriding desire to amass wealth for its own sake arouses suspicion in modern Hellenes, and the myth of Midas is a significant theme in everyday Greek conversation. The newly rich are urged to be cautious and the undesirable consequences of amassing excessive amounts of wealth are stressed. These attitudes are related to the view that the practice of increasing wealth jeopardises the desirable balance of moderation often referred to as παν μέτρον άριστον ('the golden mean'). Thus, when Hellenes see individuals like the shipping magnate Aristotle Onassis behaving like another Midas, they tend to suspect that this state of affairs must have serious implications for the individual's personal and family life, as well as his social status.

For Greeks, the impermanence of wealth and the means by which it is acquired are important issues for debate. They are frequently concerned about the means by which wealth is acquired, considering human preoccupation with it to be undesirable. Solon, the lawgiver of Athens, declared: 'Wealth, I desire to possess, but would not have it unrighteously'. Greeks believe that, by the very nature of human destiny, there will be an eventual retribution if wealth is acquired 'unrighteously' or by unethical means. A related concern is that acquisitiveness is to be feared because it becomes a passion— often reducing men to what in Hellenic mythology is the most despicable condition of all: slavery (Kouvertaris 1971).

The concepts of slavery and freedom form a major Hellenic preoccupation. Hellenes have always maintained a very strong sense of freedom, and it is a theme of extraordinary importance in Hellenic culture—both in ancient history and modern nationhood (Andrewes 1984: 293; Theotokas 1961). True freedom was viewed not only as a physical state but also as a spiritual and intellectual condition. A character greatly admired by modern Hellenes is the Titan Prometheus—the 'Liberator' in Hellenic mythology—who disobeyed the gods by imparting to mortal men the secret of fire. Caught by the vengeful gods, he was chained to a rock and suffered the agonies of an eagle devouring his liver, which grew again during the night, so that his punishment was never-ending. Prometheus remains a strong symbol of universal human liberation within the Hellenic tradition.

Freedom, as first propounded in Hellenic mythology, has become the rallying-point for patriots in major historical events. The leaders of the struggle for independence against the Ottoman Turks campaigned under the banner of freedom, in order to gain the support of their compatriots. Moreover, this call for freedom not only came from intellectuals, poets and literary figures, but also from ordinary (even illiterate) people. These individuals stepped forward with slogans of freedom reminiscent of classical Athens, or Sparta's Νικη ά Θήνατος ('Victory or Death'), Ελευθερία ή Θάνατος ('Freedom or Death'). This tradition is manifest in contemporary Hellenic life on National Independence Day (celebrated each year on both the 25th of March and 28th of October), when banners bearing slogans of freedom honour those who gave their lives for this great ideal which, today, is characterised by Hellenes as the 'eleventh commandment'. The eighteenth-century Hellene poet, Regas Feraios, neatly encapsulated the concept of freedom in the following way: καλλίτερα μιας ώρας ελεύθερη ζωή παρά σαράντα χρόνια σκλαβιά και φυλακή ('An hour's freedom is better than forty years of slavery and imprisonment'). Feraios was later executed by the Turks for espousing such ideals about freedom, but his verses were learned by heart by many of his compatriots, and his famous slogans calling for freedom became even better known during the nineteenth and twentieth centuries.

The importance of freedom is also emphasised by modern Hellenic poets and prose writers, such as Yiannis Ritsos, Odysseus Elytis, Kostas Varnalis and Kostis Palamas. In the works of Nikos Kazantzakis, one of the nation's better-known modern writers, freedom is clearly of paramount concern. In *Zorba the Greek,* as well as *Captain Michalis,* Kazantzakis is clearly making personal and national freedom the dominant issue. Many of these writers' works show that accumulated wealth has no value when compared to freedom.

A number of other related ideals which constitute part of the living experience of modern Hellenes have their origins in the social and cultural perceptions of their ancient ancestors. The ancient and classical Greek city-states or *poleis,* especially

61

Athens and Sparta, set down distinctive paths and trends for the future well-being of their respective societies that remain landmarks of Hellenic heritage to this day. In both Greece and Australia these ancient ideals and values often find expression in everyday discussions, academic debates and social gatherings. (They are discussed in subsequent chapters.) Athens developed its political system through a number of stages that reflect a shift from aristocracy to democracy, whilst Sparta maintained, for 1,400 years, a monarchical system of government that provided the city with political stability. Athens became the principal city of the arts and sciences and its value system centred upon the goal of making its citizens *kalos k'agathos* (beautiful and ethically good). This goal was conceived as the embodiment of excellence and was achieved through educational training that emphasised a healthy balance between mind and body. On the other hand, although Sparta pursued this same goal—of producing citizens with a harmonious balance between mind and body—what emerges as this city's outstanding feature is not the cultivation of the arts, but a high regard for military prowess and the adage Το Λαχονίζεεν Εστίν Φηιλοσοπηείν ('to speak laconically is wise').

Ancient Hellenic values that remain influential in modern Hellenic culture play an important role in shaping people's views about what is good. An example is the term ευδαιμονία: goodness, happiness, a concept of the good. This value is probably as important today as it was in the classical *polis*, where individuals of the *demos* insisted on having, as a right, the social conditions necessary for satisfaction and happiness. This right was invariably understood in terms of citizens' well-being being furthered by public contribution. As early as the eighth century BC, the epithet *aristos* was used as an honorific, chiefly to reward military exploits and successes. In Homeric Athens, a citizen's social position was based exclusively on his military career and the part he played in protecting the well-being of the city. During the classical period, however, military prowess was not as highly regarded and was replaced by other forms of honour. For example, if a citizen was considered *kalos kagathos*, it meant that he was seen as a distinguished and respected citizen and afforded highly preferential treatment by both officials of the *polis* and ordinary citizens—to the point of being granted an acquittal when brought as a defendent before a court of law. At times, the status of individuals who were considered to be *kalos kagathos* was regarded as being comparable to the status associated with any other kind of fame.

It is important to note that in Ancient Greece the various forms of honour and fame were achieved by individual effort and accomplishment through social mobility within the structures of the *polis*. They were not a birthright. By its very nature, the social system of the *polis* had to be an open one where individuals from different social backgrounds could pursue their own interests on an equal footing. Pericles made this clear when he reminded citizens that fame and honour are not inherited (Thucydides 1985). At the same time, Isocrates lauded the path of individual effort: 'It is the most experienced and the most capable who in any field of action deserve to be honoured' (Isocrates 1938: 131). An impressive example of this attitude is reflected in the story about Leonidas, the Spartan king, who, questioned about his family tree by a group of Peloponnesian kings, responded by saying 'if the rock is strong, it does not need the support of stones'. With this metaphoric statement Leonidas made the point that one does not need royal blood to be a good and worthy king. Today, Greeks refer with pride to Leonidas' statement about the significance of the family tree, often to support an argument during a popular discussion.[3]

The notion of honour is, therefore, linked in Hellenic society to all forms of liberation—material and non-material. Over time, the situation changed from one where honour was bestowed in exchange for military achievements, to another where the well-being of the city-state and artistic or academic accomplishments were given greater importance. As a result, involvement in politics became a more central source of fame than either military prowess or the amassing of wealth, a point emphasised in many works of Hellenic history and philosophy. For example, both Solon and Pericles advocated the bestowal of honours in the public political and artistic spheres of life—spheres in which they believed all citizens should be encouraged to participate. While both Solon and Pericles had brilliant military and political careers, their fame was primarily based on contributions to the establishment of a more democratic and peaceful political society—Solon was known as 'the lawmaker', Pericles as 'the statesman'.

The city-state became an obvious political focal point for honour by virtue of the importance it had in Greeks' lives: even a citizen's identity was inextricably linked to the citizen's birthplace. The 'seven wise men of antiquity'[4] were always identified by name and city of origin. This practice of giving importance to the relationship between a city–state and the individual was incorporated into the philosophy of the Olympic Games. The Hellenic conception of the city-state fostered the development of the highest forms of social organisation and attracted the most highly qualified personnel from both the provinces and overseas Hellenic colonies. The most skilful craftsmen, the most lyrical poets, the most renowned sophists and philosophers, the most persuasive lawyers and orators and the most sophisticated *hetaerai* could be found in the *polis*.

The basic prerequisite for attaining status in the *polis* was high respect for and adherence to its laws. This was no minor matter, and the Greek conception of the strong relationship between duty and obedience to the law is illustrated by the inscription on the monument erected in Thermopylae where, in 490BC, Leonidas and 300 Spartans fought to their deaths against the invading Persians: 'Oh, passerby, tell the Lacedaemonians that we lie here in obedience to their laws'. This obedience to state laws was often accompanied by a humble philosophical and dialectic frame of mind. Thucydides, for example, when recording the Spartan king Archidamus' speech, delivered in Sparta, during the debate and declaration of the Peloponnesian War, has been recorded as stating:

> We are not carried away by the pleasures of hearing ourselves praised when people are urging us towards dangers that often seem to us unnecessary; and we are no more likely to give in shamefacedly to other people's views when they try to spur us on by their accusations. Because of our well-ordered life we are both brave in war and wise in council. Brave, because self-control is based upon a sense of honour, and honour is based on courage. And we are wise because we are not too highly educated as to look down upon our laws and customs, and are too rigorously trained in self-control to be able to disobey them (Thucydides 1985: 83).

64

In broad terms, Hellenic culture has its roots in the symbols and images of the Olympian gods, whose cultural and philosophical heritage has been represented by the Apollonian and Dionysian traditions. These permeate every aspect of modern Hellenic life—language, food, dance and celebrations, as well as modern Greeks' ideologies and philosophies of life and religion. In a sense, the Apollonian and the Dionysian traditions constitute the two sides of the same coin which are depicted and described by the activities of everyday Hellenic culture.

The Apollonian tradition epitomises Helios (sun) and light. Intelligence is depicted in the form of light, often represented by Apollo and the qualities of the mind are contrasted with those of the body. The Dionysian tradition, on the other hand, epitomises the physical aspects of life, the hedonistic face of Hellenic culture and the emotional side of human nature. It can be said that the Apollonian side of a person often stands apart or aloof; on the contrary, it can be bewildering to observe the Dionysian side of life when primitive lusts and animal drives produce emotional and physical suffering and, in some cases, cause a being to be torn apart as Dionysus was himself.

The Dionysian or physical sphere of Hellenic culture has strong links with Hellenic notions of honour and fame as the ancient Hellenic value system was strongly oriented towards the body, and emphasised the physical attributes of youth and their associated pleasures. Since the Hellenes place such emphasis upon the body or physical impermanence, it is logical for them to be preoccupied by lasting and enduring pursuits which enable them to develop notions of honour, prestige and fame—criteria by which they will be judged and remembered when they die.

The modern Hellenic conceptualisation of the notion of honour constitutes a major component of a cultural ideology which can be traced back to ancient times. From being the nexus between the Dionysian emphasis upon the physical and particular forms of honour, it eventually found impressive expression in the phenomenon of the Olympic Games, a series of contests based upon fair competition between athletes from different states and social classes.

[Eventually material rewards that were granted to Olympic victors] paled into insignificance however . . . when

65

compared with the immortality with which their fame endowed them and of which the simple crown of olives was the guarantee. It is not surprising, therefore, that kings and rulers strove with all their might, alongside ordinary men, to win the crown of honour that would guarantee to them the right to perpetuate their name by erecting a statue of themselves in the Sacred Altis. An inscription accompanying the statue included the name of the victor, his father's name and the name of his city, and often also the contest proclaimed by the victor (Ekdotike Athenon 1982: 137).

This passage implies that not only were Olympic victors the most highly regarded individuals of their *polis*, irrespective of their social background, but also that the Games highlighted aspects of deeper pedagogy and enculturation representing the supreme values of Hellenism and accepted as such by every participating Greek city-state. The Olympians honoured the gods and the 'good contest' with their naked bodies.

In classical Athens, the education of the young was aimed at achieving the simultaneous development of the two elements of life: the Apollonian *mind* and the Dionysian *body*. A fundamental principle of this education was that physical exercise was part of social life and was inseparably connected with the cultivation of the mind. The Olympics were an expression of this concern which involved the citizens of every city-state. The gathering of the Hellenes at the Olympic Games was an event of great importance signifying, as it did, the universal gathering of free men who, in an atmosphere of truce, experienced the ideals of peace, freedom and equality— ideals that were conceived and made real by men reared with this simultaneous representation of 'the beautiful and the good'.

Later in Hellenic history, particularly after the seventh century AD, the growth of Christianity and the fear it inspired of the physicality of the human body attenuated the influence of sport and the sporting spirit and displaced them into the sphere of artistic expression. Body movement found significant expression first in the Italian Renaissance (Hellenic Ministry of Culture 1989: 26) and later in the art of the rest of western Europe. However, through the centuries, the Hellenic traditions and customs as practised in the more isolated mountainous regions of the mainland and on the islands continued to emphasise the importance of the human body. Despite the restrictions on freedom of speech imposed on the Hellenes by Ottoman rule, these values have survived into contemporary culture, mainly by transmission into hundreds of demotic or folkloric songs and festivals. These festivals and songs extol various bodily characteristics and personality traits, such as beauty, bravery, generosity and caring for others, personified in what Greeks today call a *leventis* or *palikari*, an individual who is *philotimos* [5] and characterised by a strong sense of personal freedom.

The increasing influences of Christianity on the one hand and the Ottoman Empire's despotic rule, on the other, impelled those who upheld the Hellenic traditions and customs associated with the human body to practise their culture in secret for four centuries. While a significant part of Hellenic culture remained insulated from foreign influences, both Christianity and the Ottoman rule adversely affected the Greek reverence for law.

The moral teachings of Christianity and the lifestyle imposed on Hellenes by the restrictions of Turkish rule, fostered an attitude of indifference towards law and discipline, especially when the Turks regularly monitored and interfered with the social practices of the people. From the Greek point of view, Christianity remained above all a mystical, apolitical and *ecumenical* philosophy of life. It glorified revelation through ecstasy and the guidance of one's 'inner light'. This emphasis upon ecstasy generated a strong affinity with the Dionysian element of Hellenic culture. Also, by making the quest for salvation supreme, Christianity encouraged the individual to disregard secular law when this law happened to conflict with personal conceptions of the divine Christian law. By transferring law to the metaphysical realm, Christianity also thereby transferred the related concepts of honour and self-esteem (*philotimo*) to the metaphysical spheres (again encouraging a wider acceptance of the Dionysian tradition). The effect of this transference was to minimise the importance of the state as the administrator of civil society, and to make political careers unimportant as sources of achievement and fame (*philotimo*). Moreover, the Ottoman's deliberate policy of marginalising the state as the administrator of civil society eradicated open debate in the *agora* (and other social gatherings) and discouraged direct political participation in community affairs. During this period, two distinctive features stand out in the history of Hellenism. Firstly, Ottoman rule over secular affairs of state resulted in the granting of additional powers to the Greek Orthodox clergy and, in particular, to the Patriarch, who became directly responsible for the civil as well as religious affairs of Orthodox Christians. Secondly, the Patriarch became the political representative of Christians. In other words, the Patriarch was responsible for the *ethnos* (nationhood, peoplehood) of the Christians.

The Ottomans' abolition of the civil state, its replacement by the clergy and, above all, the oriental despotic administration that lasted for four centuries, had adverse, and perhaps unexpected, consequences not only for the occupied Hellenes but also for the rest of the free world. Hellenes could not participate in the administration of the state or exercise constructive criticism of its rulers, unless they were willing to compromise with the Ottoman administration. Unwilling to do this, people often resisted or violated laws and regulations imposed by the Turks. This civil disobedience grew through the period of Ottoman occupation, as these rulers suppressed not only traditional freedoms prized by the Hellenes, but also undermined innovative practices in both the arts and sciences. This latter form of suppression forced many educated and talented Greeks to flee to Italy and other European countries, where they contributed to the flowering of the Renaissance, but this migratory outflow robbed Hellenes of the opportunity to have their own Renaissance, as well as undermining the Apollonian side of the Hellenic character—the main source of Hellenic manly behaviour—honour and pride. Yet this migration brought about the establishment of expatriate communities that made up the pre-industrial European Hellenic diaspora, which drew its inspiration from Greece and, like the loyal Odysseus, participated in her struggle for independence and emancipation.

To preserve the important quality of *philotimo* under this domination, and to honour those who had died for the attainment of universal human values, the Greeks were forced to make one of two choices: to modify their definition of 'humanhood' in order to allow for periodic states of bondage; or to prove that they could preserve a degree of civil autonomy and identity even under the heaviest yoke of their Ottoman rulers. They chose the latter option and, while the Hellenic Orthodox Patriarchate cooperated (under duress) with the new administration, many Hellenes who were insulated from direct Turkish rule continued to observe their traditional customs, maintaining their strong sense of freedom. Also, whenever an opportunity arose, the Hellenes defiantly and enthusiastically circumvented and ridiculed the Turkish laws, rejecting the rule of oriental despotism which was abusive of and in conflict with the Hellenic *philotimo*.

In the context of migration, because the Hellenic character carries with it a strong sense of *philotimo* to the countries of migration, the social and political nature of the country of settlement can have a marked effect on the attitudes and behaviour of the migrating Greeks. As we have seen, there is, in the Hellenic national character, strong resistance to compliance with the directives given by a master, or a superior ruler. Because the tenets of *philotimo* are unfamiliar to or misunderstood by members of host societies where Hellenes live and work, their experience, particularly in the early phases of settlement, is characterised by compulsion and degrees of suppression over their activities by rulers or people. When such compulsion or force is used, what is normally understood or seen as δουλειά (in the sense of *work*), is transformed into δουλεία (in the sense of *slavery*). This notion of δουλεία is an important one for Hellenes and is used in everyday discussion. This term is spelt the same way regardless of the meaning intended, the meaning being chosen by simply moving the accent from the last to the second last vowel, thus denoting the opposite idea (Kouvertaris 1971: 39).

In the context of working for an employer, Hellenes tend to despise what they define as αφεντικά, namely 'bossy' behaviour or what Hellenes in Australia refer to as *bossiliki* (a compound term which is Hellenised by Greek-Australian workers and is derived from the English word 'boss').[6] When an employer's behaviour becomes authoritarian, that is, when he or she imposes their *bossiliki* over an employee, it is like using their position and power to interfere in their employees' freedom to perform their work—such behaviour being regarded as abusive of the employee's sense of *philotimo*. Working for others has not always been desirable in the Hellenic tradition, unless *philotimo* has a full and central application in human interactions in the workplace and working conditions guarantee a 'fair' spiritual as well as material independence for employees. Although it can be argued that the concept enables people to be as individualistic as possible, at the same time it requires such individuals to be careful not to upset the independence and harmony of others that is granted to them through *philotimo*. It is important to note that *philotimo* (in this sense) is not a rigid concept which does not allow change. Change is inevitable and *philotimo* requires social actors to cooperate with their fellow workers or bosses and not to act individual-istically or egocentrically in cases when their individual working tasks affect the work undertaken by others. Collaboration with others is part of being altruistic and generous to other workers who are contributing towards the making of products. *Philotimo*—with its underlying meanings described above—was evident not only when Greece gained independence from Ottoman rule during and after 1821 but even when Greeks migrated to other European and intercontinental destinations such as America, Canada and Australia (Kouvertaris 1971; Bottomley 1976; Dimitreas 1981, 1989, 1994; Storer 1985). Greeks became one of the most law-abiding ethnic population groups in the new countries of settlement. This reversal in attitude towards legal and political institutions, as discussed, has been related to the implied meanings connoted by the concept of *philotimo*. In fact, it can be argued that the preservation of Greece's good name and the peaceful estab-lishment of Hellenic communities abroad has been mainly due to the Greek immigrants' sense of *philotimo*.

The same cultural indicators that are in operation when attempting to define *philotimo* also explain the Hellenes' behavi-our in their gatherings and organised festivities in Australia. The habits and behaviour patterns that characterise the Hellenic personality are largely distinguished by concrete socio-linguistic communication involving face-to-face 'organically' defined rules and expectations in social interaction. In contrast, the British-Australian cultural experience, from a Hellenic perspective, appears to be the opposite, where human inter-action occurs within an urban environment in which human communication is dominated by a reserved, impersonal, bureaucratic and abstract public culture. As a result, these cultural realities represent barriers that often alienate individuals from directly participating in a given social situation. Traditionally, after migration, Hellenes maintained an all-embracing communal framework of interaction in human relationships in Australia. Concretely practised through personal contact enhanced by strong demotic themes—such as folk songs, music, regular celebrations and an extensive traditional cuisine—a focused view of life was shared by the community as a whole.

It is understandable that in times of deep political instability, war and especially dictatorship, Hellenes felt a strong desire to leave their native land in search of what they perceived to be democratic societies, with a tradition of freedom of speech and tolerance, such as Australia. This expectation is an important factor in the decision to migrate, particularly when the *agora* is unable to function effectively at home. The search for places where 'freedom of speech' is practised is a significant pull factor, holding the promise of allowing community life to continue uninterrupted—as in the *agora*. Given that the *agora* has a specific function for 'place and placemaking' and, generally, is an informal public forum where people practise participatory democracy in the Hellenic tradition, it is not surprising, therefore, to find that it is recreated in the new environment.

Travelling or migrating to faraway places in order to escape the social, political and physical restrictions of Greece constitutes part of the mythological and historical Hellenic culture of seeking to escape non-democratic conditions in order to re-establish the *agora* in more sympathetic environments. For example, Odysseus, the crafty king of Ithaca, no doubt needed to escape the boredom occasionally felt in the social space of a single *agora* and travelled to distant and unfamiliar places in search of both pleasure and knowledge. However, in spite of the lures and pleasures of beautiful Amazons and powerful women such as Calypso and Circe, Odysseus returns home to face the challenges awaiting him in the *agora*. Others like Dionysos, the god of wine, who travelled across Asia to India for the enjoyment and celebration of life in conditions of brotherhood, kept practising a form of living which he learned in the *agora* symposia at home and which he took with him to those faraway places.

The theme of escaping from the *agora* and returning to it, as in the case of Odysseus, or recreating it in faraway places, as in the case of Dionysos, is a theme to be found throughout Hellenic mythology and history of migration. Odysseus' adventures away from Ithaca, which involved him in endless struggles over many years, on land and at sea, relate to one of Homer's main themes of discussion. This theme was of particular concern to Homer because his hero's experiences at home and abroad were a matter for ideological and cultural challenge. As Monos comments:

> the starting point of the world's most famous saga is to be found not only in the romantic frivolity of a love affair but in the anxious and wandering spirit of a paradoxical race who possess thirst for adventure and a knowledge of faraway places, juxtaposed to a powerful attachment to home, to gods, to festivities and traditions of the native land (Monos 1976: 19).

Similarly, in the pre-industrial era, Hellenic out-migration contributed to the flowering of the Italian Renaissance. This migration occurred, as we have seen, following the fall of Constantinople to the Turks (and the subsequent collapse of the Byzantine Empire) in 1453AD. Migration became a flight from tyranny, and countless descendants of Odysseus started a migratory pattern that has continued through the centuries. For the first time Hellenes experienced life in a state where independence of thought and action was severely curtailed, a state in which they could not practise their traditional mode of life and, as a consequence, many Hellenes chose self-imposed exile and migrated to the distant lands of the New World.

From the fall of Constantinople until the eighteenth century, Hellenes migrated chiefly to Europe, where they became immigrants in what they regarded as countries populated mainly by non-Greek Orthodox Christians. Despite the ancient 'echoes of paganism, which resounded through everything Hellenic, the basic Christianity of the Hellenes and their suffering at the hands of the "infidels", evoked the brotherly concern of the Roman Catholic Church', which recognised the Hellenic contributions to the philosophy of Christian religion and the development and establishment of Christianity (Monos 1976). In this way Hellenic refugees established their first communities in Europe in the fifteenth century and continued to do so until the twentieth century. These communities became centres for the preservation and dissemination of Hellenic language and culture and contributed to the life of the Renaissance through the revival of the classical arts. Refugees, being both gregarious and determined to practise and preserve their languages and traditions, contributed to the preservation of Hellenic values and provided the foundation for the European Renaissance.

Hellenes have also migrated from their homeland for a variety of other reasons. In peaceful or more tolerable periods of their history, it was the merchants, scholars and adventurers who left, motivated not only by the obvious economic and political reasons, but also by curiosity about people in other lands. 'Possessed by restless minds, full of enquiries, they have always been tantalised by what lies beyond the *agora*', the towns, the mountains and/or islands, and beyond the Ionian and Aegean seas (Monos 1976: 20).

As myth has it, those who leave the *agora* behind are expected to return home eventually, like Odysseus. Moreover, Hellenes who travel or migrate abroad for either a short or long time are expected to renew the strength of their wisdom as Odysseus did before embarking on his return trip. The idea of returning, therefore, is a key theme for those who migrate for whatever reason or whatever length of time. It is often expected that, having gained greater experience by living abroad, they will reassert their original views with increased vigour upon returning home.

As an anxious and wandering spirit the Hellene travels abroad to face the challenges of the unknown. This wanderlust often occurs during long periods of peace and tranquillity when the Hellene becomes bored and restless with life in the *agora* (Monos 1976). As settlers in their host countries, however, they do not forget the values and ideals which comprise the good life, the ideal social environment of the *polis*, and the debates of the *agora* which have been pursued with limitless energy and imagination by the Hellenic soul in its attempt to maximise mental and physical satisfaction in an ever-changing world.

Once the number of Greek migrants in any one place is sufficient to allow them to found their own institutions, their search for *agora* environments becomes a priority. Like their ancestors, these migrants use their 'modern' *agora* settings to gather collectively to debate issues of personal and social interest within their host societies. They often spend hours debating history, philosophy, or the meaning and function of culture within *agora* settings such as the *kafeneion* (cafe). The modern *agora*, or 'small parliament' as Hellenes call it, is vital to direct participatory democracy and communal responsibility. By drawing on the legends and stories which are part of the collective social memory, they inform themselves about modern-day social phenomena and discuss ways of dealing with their migration and post-migration experiences.

The term 'modern' has been used here in relation to the *agora* because, in Australia, there is no equivalent to the *agora* most often found in Greece. Usually, an appropriate model of an *agora* is set up in one of the busier and culturally diverse parts of a town or village. A typical *agora* normally includes a variety of architectural forms of buildings painted in a variety of colours and usually incorporates one or more of the following institutions—a central community head office, a church, social clubs, markets, coffee houses, the tavernas, or even a court and police station. The *agora* would also include the main square of the town or village, which is usually shaded by trees and provides a suitable place for sitting and strolling. Individual attendants of a modern *agora*, therefore, as in ancient times, expect to gather and meet with people from all walks of life, ranging from a court judge to professors and the unemployed.

Finding a suitable place for a modern *agora* has been a challenging task for Hellenic settlers in countries such as Australia. Numerous difficulties have had to be overcome, due to the fact that the division of social and geographic space and urban planning requirements had already been tailored to the requirements of earlier settlers. This means that the limits of the geographic location and architectural patterns of an *agora* have already been set out prior to mass Hellenic settlement. Finding a modern *agora* in Australia which is suitable to their perception of division of space is, therefore, a theme of interest in itself, one which often attracts much discussion among the Hellenes, when wondering where would be best to go and meet other people for a debate or to 'pass a bit of time'—as they often say among themselves. At the same time, the existence of an *agora* abroad often works as a pull force that attracts the interest of potential travellers, tourists or even additional migrants from the Hellenic world.

Upon settlement in new societies, migrants go through various processes of adoption and adaptation in the new social space before they are sufficiently equipped to be fully incorporated within the new environment. Often the starting point for their adjustment in the new environment is readily identified with earlier settlers or migrants. The speed by which migrant adjustment occurs within the broader Australian space patterns, depends not only on the host society's willingness to accept the new settlers as immigrants, but also on its readiness to accommodate them in terms of the existence of appropriate structures and policies to meet their objective and subjective cultural needs.

In light of the above, the Hellenes have had to recreate the *agora* taking account of the physical and social conditions as to what constitutes an *agora* or 'place and placemaking' in the context of their host societies. This redefinition becomes necessary since what constitutes 'place and placemaking' within receiving societies may be at variance with the 'place and placemaking' characteristics of sending societies. Modern *agoras* are found in varying forms and stylistic content in Greece and, therefore, in receiving societies. Taking Melbourne as an example, immigrants have chosen the geographic location of the Ελληνική Γωνιά ('Hellenic Corner') in Lonsdale Street to establish their *agora*, as there are some highly significant institutions surrounding this *agora* that remind them of similar environments of Grecian *agoras*. This rather modern division of space in the city of Melbourne includes the headquarters of the Greeks' major lay community organisation (the Greek Orthodox Community of Melbourne and Victoria), and the major lay community organisation of Greek Cypriots. The characteristic features of the geographic and architectural division of space of 'Hellenic Corner' constitutes, therefore, a redefinition of the Greek migrants' own perception of 'place and placemaking'.

As Pascoe observes in his study of Italians in Australia, there is an immigrant's sense of 'place and placemaking'

(Pascoe 1988: 155). This constitutes a division of urban space, in accordance with the various but consistent criteria that makes this space in some way distinctive, to suit a given immigrant group. As observed in the Italian study, the Hellenic Corner 'embeds certain cultural values in the new environment' (Ibid.).

In conceptualising the significance of people's identification with space, one needs to proceed 'by means of linguistic analysis and understanding of the meaning and division of space' through both the micro-environment and the larger-space tableaux of locality, suburb and community (Pascoe 1988: 155). My own knowledge and frequent contact with members of the Hellenic community located at the Hellenic Corner in Melbourne leads me to concur with this observation. Certain features related to division of geographic space, as well as architectural shapes and cultural characteristics as appropriated by Hellenic immigrants, reflect similarities with what constitutes the perception of 'placemaking' of an *agora*.

According to Pascoe (1988: 155–6), the division of space can be traced back to the countries of origin. Accordingly, this particular location within the city of Melbourne is one of the areas frequently used by people of Hellenic origin and serves as a traditional *agora*. This example contains within it Hellenic institutions—such as the Hellenic lay community forums, social clubs and brotherhoods—together with markets, restaurants, bookshops, bodies which administer Hellenic language schools, self-help charitable societies and churches. The *agora* allows social actors to participate in the full range of issues relevant to their lives in Australia. It is also within this environment and others like it scattered around Australia, that Hellenes present and market the icons of their cultural heritage in the form of religious and historical artefacts, books, magazines, newspapers, pictures and statues of ancient heroes which they brought with them. At the same time, it enables them to present themselves in a wide range of traditional and contemporary costumes and colours, particularly when celebrating their national days and other significant cultural events and thus engage in familiar behaviour and interactive styles.

The meaning therefore that Hellenes attach to the division of space such as the 'Hellenic Corner', is inextricably bound up with their cultural traditions and norms and enables them to enjoy stimulating and amicable interaction in a place reminiscent of home. Consequently, 'place and placemaking' both meets their subjective needs and provides for objective cultural practices. It provides the necessary space and opportunity to gather the knowledge, confidence and self-assurance that are prerequisites for extending into and interacting with the host society. The combined operation of the two—the physical and social sphere of the *agora*—functions as a stimulant and incitement to continue with their quest for the meaning of life and the concept of the 'good'. They pursue this objective through continuous dialogue, for example about politics, cultural identity and related activities enacted within the Hellenic *paroikia,* or community abroad, of Australia.

The definition of *paroikia* implies both κοινονία, or community and society, and Hellenes' perception of themselves as an ethnic population group with a distinct cultural heritage. The location of the *agora* is the appropriate place for people of migrant origin to rediscover their identity within the Australian social reality. Much of this rediscovery occurs through discussions about the *paroikia.*

Given that different ethnic population groups use different terms to refer to their own individual community, the term *paroikia* is a concept used solely by Greek-Australians to refer to their own community. Italians in Australia, according to Pascoe, use the term *comunitá.* This term is 'described in the Italian language newspapers as it also recurs in the speeches of political leaders, and in the discourse of political speech' (Pascoe 1992: 85). The term *paroikia* is used widely by the Hellenic media, academics and, generally, by Greek-Australians, although *paroikia* is somewhat different to *comunita* in that there is an interrelatedness with the *agora.* For example, *paroikia* denotes an implicit commitment to one's sense of *koinonia,* whereas the term *agora,* though overlapping with the term *paroikia,* is also used to denote what the Italians define as *comunita.*

Through debates in the *agora,* Greeks in Australia test whether they are or are not *koinonikoi,* that is, socially committed and concerned. Social commitment is tested and contested through fiery discussions that often resemble parliamentary debates among members of rival parties. Often the *agora* debates are associated with the extent to which Greek migrants adhere to the ethical codes of *koinonia.* Adherence to the ethical codes is a major theme which brings out the dimension of *koinonikotita* or sociability, as it relates to the level of attachment and loyalty to the host society and the ideals of the 'old country'.

The function, therefore, of 'place and placemaking', as a geographic and linguistically defined social space, enables individuals of Hellenic origin to participate directly in social discussions about themes derived from day-to-day experiences, a participation that has multiple benefits for Hellenes, for example it enables individuals to inform themselves about current social issues and concerns. While 'place and place-making' informs *social memory* and, generally, the *mental map*, *agora* debates help to eliminate and diffuse the tension that often occurs due to the sense of powerlessness, alienation and anxiety caused by a new social and physical environment. The placemaking of an *agora* also serves to cushion them from the harsher aspects of reality arising out of the migration experience.

Fundamental to the social mobility of migrants within their host societies, therefore, is the extent to which they are able to adopt and adapt following settlement. The extent to which they will or will not be successful depends upon a number of factors associated not only with their own value systems, but also with factors connected to the value system of the host societies. These include the different factors that led to migration, the size of the migratory group, the period and processes of settlement and resettlement and the immigration policy of the host society. All of these factors will be explored in the following chapters.

Hellenic connection with colonial Australia

The preceding chapters have outlined a migration typology, in terms of which general phases of migration can be understood. This chapter establishes that Hellenic migration had an Australian destination since the beginning of the nineteenth century.

Information about early Greek pioneers of Australia rests on scattered evidence that veers between myth and reality, which, if mixed, provide a discernible pattern for expressing significant experiences and events in ongoing life and culture through identification with traditional themes. This structure enables people to be informed about and to identify with themes which are important to them in their daily lives. The significance of this information is that myths and stories, as told from one generation to the next, can stimulate and enhance people's drive towards migration, as is evident in the accounts of many Greek pioneer settlers in Australia whose decision to migrate was, in the majority of cases, a consequence of fantasising about and romanticising accounts of other people's adventures in a remote and unknown place of the world, such as the South Land.

Events have taken an interesting turn of late. Research has recently revealed (Messaris & Koulocheris 1986) the story of Trevor Colmer's great discovery, an ancient Greek sandstone carving—in Australia. The carving, which represents Hermes, the ancient Greek messenger of the gods, was discovered by

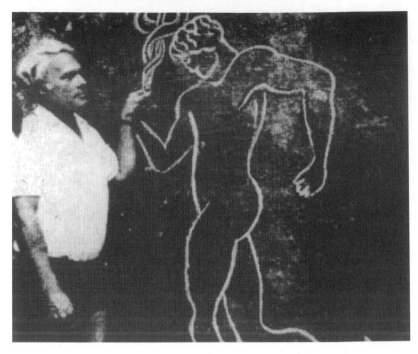

Illustration 4.1 Trevor Colmer with the sandstone carving of Hermes, in the Blue Mountains area, west of Sydney. (*Source*: Theo Koulochris and Joan Messaris.

Colmer in the 1950s in the bushland of the Blue Mountains, in New South Wales. Colmer kept his discovery secret for almost 30 years, to protect the carving from vandals, but was later encouraged by his son to make the discovery public in order to throw light on the early European presence in the continent. Colmer (who also points to the existence of additional ancient Greek artefacts in a Katoomba museum), claims that the Greeks were in Australia thousands of years ago. According to Colmer, therefore, it is beyond argument that the Greeks were in Australia much earlier than either Captain Cook or those who preceded him in the more recent period of European colonisation. Colmer claims:

> It's a Greek country . . . they were here first. After all, they were top navigators. They've been all around the world . . . the carving must date back a long time—it is not absurd to suppose that it could date back to 10–12,000BC.

Colmer does not believe that the carving of Hermes is linked to the presence of extraterrestrials and he dismisses any allusions to such ideas as expressed in the book *Chariot of the Gods*.

Archaeologist Kapitoglou from Sydney University agrees that the carving dates to Hellenistic times. There has been another important discovery that can be dated to the same period, namely a coin bearing the image of King Ptolemy IV, that was found in 1910 in a rainforest at Kuranda, in Queensland, by a farmer digging post-holes.

The conventional narrative of Hellenic migration, however, begins in the nineteenth century. In examining the corresponding social history of Italian migration to Australia, Pascoe defines the pioneer Italian migrants as 'scouts' (1992: 86). In his narrative Pascoe identifies three *generic* types of Italian migrants: the 'scout', the 'farmer' and the 'builder'. The Greek migrant settler types are at variance with the Italian in all but the first category. Unlike the Italian 'farmers' who follow the 'scouts', and the 'builders' who follow the 'farmers' (who are part of the post-World War Two mass migration), the Greek 'scouts' are followed by 'shopkeepers' and 'manufacturing workers' during the second and third phases of Hellenic migrant settlement respectively. There is a fourth phase involved in Hellenic re-settlement—the 'self employed'/ 'employer' category, which started to become the dominant category during later stages.

In an attempt to evaluate the arrival of the first Greeks to Australia, the historian Michael Tsounis argues that the early pioneers came to Australia for a number of different reasons, which single-feature explanations cannot encompass. He argues that when people are exposed to certain 'types of notions about the shape of the world', they become fascinated by them and, in their fascination, they too want to know more about the world where these stories have taken place—to experience the challenges of an outside world of which they know little. As Tsounis says, the Greek pioneers came to Australia:

> to improve their lot, to come and explore a far-away, unknown land and help pave the way for others. The very name Antipodes, if Greeks heard it, sounded curious enough, like *anapodes*, the 'upside downs' (Tsounis 1988b: 42).

Illustration 4.2 The head of King Ptolemy portrayed on a coin held by Kedumba Nature Display, Katoomba, New South Wales. Ptolemy reigned in Egypt during the Hellenistic period, from 212–4BC.

However, historical records of Greek pioneer arrivals to Australia are scant; the first Greeks to 'set foot on Australian soil are shrouded in obscurity and myth'. As the author of the first Greek book published in Australia, titled Η Ζωή Εν Αυστραλία—*Life in Australia*—stated, 'one could more easily discover the South Pole than the beginnings of Australia's Hellenism'. The author stated further that from the available information, all they could say, with reservation:

> was that about sixty years ago, there existed individual Greeks in Australia of whom most were sailors and who served in various ships. The elderly Konstantinos Argyropoulos who is still living, arrived in Australia 60 years ago . . . Argyropoulos says that while he was serving as a sailor on an English ship during the year 1854, he heard of the existence of some rich

and auriferous continent by the name of Australia, and thus decided to migrate (Cominos 1916: 87).

More recent research has partially eliminated some of the obscurity which covers the early Greek presence in Australia, and it is now known for certain that there were Greeks in Australia much earlier than the arrival of Konstantinos Argyropoulos in 1854. It is also known that some Greek scholars living outside mainland Greece knew about Australia much earlier than Captain Cook's voyage to the 'Unknown South Land' of the Antipodes. As Hugh Gilchrist comments, the Antipodes or the Unknown South Land of Australia became better known to modern Greeks as Νέα Ολλανδική Γη or 'New Holland Earth'. New Holland appeared in a map of the world in the book titled Εισαγωγή εις τα Γεωγραφικά και Σφαιρικά (*Introduction to Geographical and Spherical*), written by Chrysanthos Notaras at Padua in 1700, showing about two-thirds of the Australian coastline. Subsequently, Hellenic geography books referred to Australia as a British prison or penal colony following the initial European settlement of Australia in 1788. At the same time 'Australia appeared as a textual reference' in the book titled Γεωγραφία, Παλαιά και Νέα (*Geography Old and New*), written by a priest, Meletios, who later became Archbishop of Athens. Thus, the Greeks of the Ionian islands and those living abroad had access to more information about Australia than those living on mainland Greece, where Turkish rule prevented the free flow of information and the emergence of a Greek press (Gilchrist 1985: 2; 1992: 1018).

The Antipodes as a subject finds resonance in Hellenic themes drawn from antiquity. Based on the popular mythology handed down from one generation to the next in Greece's and Australia's Hellenic community forums or *agoras*, early pioneers to Australia maintained links with the ancient mythological tradition when telling stories of their own experiences, which, like Odysseus's adventures, went on for many years, on land and sea. The accounts the pioneers provided were often reinforced by stories told by later generations, who maintained the oral tradition of re-telling in repetitive sequence. One such story, drawn from history, refers to Nearchos' 2,000-ship expedition south of India. The story suggests that Alexander

83

the Great's fleet, under Nearchos' command, voyaged south of India for several weeks[1] and arrived in Australia in 325BC. Another account suggests that Australia was discovered by Athanasios Diakos, one of the Greek independence leaders of 1821 who was killed by the Turks. These stories demonstrate that some researchers' accounts of pioneer arrivals in Australia draw from both history and folk culture and, by mixing the two, provide explanations where myth and reality cannot be distinguished, much less separated (Gilchrist 1985; 1992: 20).

Other accounts (for example, Deliyiannis 1989: 2) emphasise Hellenic elements in the initial British settlement of Australia. For example, a Greek-Australian author, in an address to members of the Hellenic community in Melbourne, read the following: 'We have indications, although as yet not verified, that there were some Greek convicts aboard the first ship in 1788'. This view is further enhanced by generalised statements occasionally found in migration literature postulating that there were some Greeks and Italians in the first voyage (Jupp 1991). These statements have not been verified, however, firstly because of the way individual names were written in the original records—due to the practice of Anglicising foreign names—and, secondly, the probability that some names may have not been recorded correctly, thus obscuring whether they were of Hellenic or Italian origin.

Another story in which myth and reality are intertwined is that of a Greek sailor by the name of Damianos Ghikas from the island of Hydra. Legend has it that he was taken prisoner by an Algerian pirate ship in 1802, only to be recaptured later at Gibraltar by a British warship.[2] The captain of the British ship thought that he was a pirate and put him aboard a vessel that was en route to Sydney (Gilchrist 1985). There is also a version of the story in which Ghikas, after many adventures on the Barbary coast and five years in a convict settlement in Australia, finally returned home (like Odysseus) following an official request to the British government for his release by the Archon of Hydra, Koundouriotis. He 'brought with him 106 gold pounds' (Tsounis 1987: 111), a 'handsome present' given to Ghikas by the English captain in recognition for saving him, his ship and his crew from Algerian pirates.

People also speak of a legendary Greek seaman who, in

the 1850s, managed to save himself from a shipwreck by swimming some 300 miles to Melbourne. From there, he went to the goldfields in Ballarat and took part in the miners' uprisings at Eureka Hill in 1854 (Gilchrist 1985: Vondra 1979).

Similarly, in 1817 or 1818, a leading writer in the colony's first newspaper, the *Sydney Gazette*, 'allegedly noted with some chagrin that children were not safe out in the streets after dark because of Irish, English and Greek riffraff' (Vondra 1979: 28; Alexakis & Janiszewski 1988: 45; 1989: 12). It has been suggested that these Greeks had either been transported to the colony of New South Wales as common convicts or revolutionaries, or were waiting in New South Wales while searching for new berths on merchant ships trading between Australia and Europe. Some, on the other hand, may have jumped ship hoping to find a better life for themselves in the new land.

It is possible and, indeed, probable, as Alexakis and Janiszewski (1989b: 12) claim, that Greek sailors attached to British trading or naval vessels may have stayed in Sydney during the early years of European settlement. But here, again, it is impossible to fully separate myth from reality. However, practically each of the stories and myths told tends to create a link between people's present status and their past experience, irrespective of whether or not such links are of cultural or psychological significance. What seems to be most important in this regard is the fact that, in the absence of adequately documented history, myths and stories have a functional role in informing social memory.

Historical accounts provide a much more realistic picture regarding the Greek connection with Australia. For example, 'Grecian Vessels' are recorded as having utilised the coastal ports of New South Wales for 'refreshing' purposes as early as the late 1820s. According to Alexakis and Janiszewski, names which imply a Hellenic connection—such as George Greece—'are found within the colony's early chronicles' (Alexakis & Janiszewski 1989b: 12).

Turning away from myths, research has revealed that the very first Greeks in Australia were seven young men who arrived, in chains, aboard the convict transport *Norfolk*, which landed at Port Jackson on 28 August 1829 (Cigler 1988;

Gilchrist 1985; Vondra 1979: 28). Different researchers have given different accounts about the identity of these early Greeks. By some accounts they have been identified as heroes of the 'Hellenic Independence Struggle' and by others as Mediterranean pirates or Australia's first Greek convicts (Tsounis 1988b: 42).

The reality seems to be that these Greeks had been arrested on the Hellenic schooner *Heracles* in 1827 (Cigler 1988: 1459–60). *Heracles* was sailing about 40 miles from the Libyan coast on a course for Alexandria. Alexandria was then an important Turkish base which was being used to suppress the Hellenic national revolution (Tsounis 1988b: 42). *Heracles* was crewed by nine young Greek men whose ship overhauled the English brig *Alceste*, whereupon the Greeks relieved her of some of her cargo. *Heracles* was later intercepted by the *Gannet*, a British Royal Navy anti-piracy patrol vessel. The crew of the *Heracles* was arrested and taken to Malta where, five months later, they were tried on charges of piracy, despite their 'insistent claims' that they were not pirates and that they 'had acted under the cause of Greek Liberty'. It was revealed at the trial that the sailors had taken only articles which they required for personal use and no military goods (Alexakis & Janiszewski 1988: 45; Gilchrist 1985, 1992).

The trial took place in the British court at Malta and was chaired by a hero of the Greeks, Admiral Sir Edward Codrington, victor of Navarino's battle against the Ottoman Turks—which had occurred only five months before the court case began. During this battle the English navy, along with the Russians and the French, had defeated the Turkish–Egyptian fleet in the Gulf of Navarino in south-west Peloponnesos. The court acquitted two of the nine and condemned the remaining seven Hellenes to death on charges of piracy against a British ship (Tsounis 1987: 110; Gilchrist 1985, 1992). According to Tsounis, 'Patriots more than pirates were the seven Greeks, and all of them were from the revolutionary shipping community on the island of Hydra' (Tsounis 1988b: 42).

The convicted Greeks pleaded for clemency to King George IV, who reduced their sentences to transportation to New South Wales. Andonis Manolis, Damianos Ninis and Georgios Vasilakis were given life sentences. Ghikas Boulgaris

Illustration 4.3   Tombstone of Antonis Manolis, one of the seven Greek 'Pirates', who decided to remain in Australia after the British authorities granted them freedom.

(or Jigger Bulgary), Konstantinos Strombolís, Georgios Laritos and Nikolaos Papandreas were all sentenced to 14 years apiece and were transported aboard the convict ship *Norfolk* (Cigler 1988: 1459–60; Gilchrist 1985; 1992: 25). On arrival, two of the convicts were assigned to work on James MacArthur's vineyards in Camden Park near Sydney and were apparently still there in 1831 when the explorer Thomas Mitchell 'noted seeing Greek pirates at work training vines to trellises that had just been erected according to the method of their own country' (Gilchrist 1985).

The Greek convicts were freed in 1836 following negotiations between the newly-liberated Hellenic state and the British authorities. Five of them sailed from Sydney in 1837, while two decided to make Australia their new home. Four reached London and possibly Corfu and a fifth was

87

shipwrecked on the coast of Brazil (Gilchrist 1985: 6; Tsounis 1988b: 42). Of the two Greek convicts who settled permanently in Australia—Ghikas Boulgaris and Andonis Manolis—both married British women. Andonis Manolis married a local woman and lived in the Picton district of New South Wales. He worked as a gardener and vine dresser and died, childless, aged eighty. He is referred to as the very first Greek gardener in Australia. Ghikas Boulgaris became an itinerant shepherd, married an Irish woman and settled at Bombala. He died at the age of 67 and was survived by nine children (Gilchrist 1985).

People living both in Greece and Australia remember the stories of these early Greek 'scouts'. Approximately 150 years later, the elderly residents of the island of Hydra still relate the stories told by the four returnees to that island. As a Melbourne Greek radio and newspaper journalist, Rena Frangioudakis, said in an interview on 19 December 1987, these young Hellenes had returned home to Hydra following many years of struggle on the high seas and in Australia. Frangioudakis was researching 'the so-called Greek convicts' when an article published in the Athenian-based magazine *Ena* in 1985 mentioned these 'convicts' in connection with recollections by the elderly inhabitants of Hydra. Shortly after, Frangioudakis travelled from Melbourne to Hydra, 'found these lovely old people' and interviewed them. They told her several stories about these Hellene pioneers to Australia and how they got back home. These interviews were broadcast on a SBS Greek language program on radio 3EA, shortly after her return to Australia. She further stressed that:

I went to Hydra to interview some of these elderly people who recalled the stories about the so-called 'Greek convicts' of Australia, some of whom had returned home. It appeared that those young Greeks were charged by a British Colonial Court because it failed to accept their testimonies that they were not 'Greek pirates' but individuals who had the legal right to fight against the oppressors of their country the way they did, to liberate their people from the Ottoman oppression. It was evident at the time that while Great Britain was helping the Greek uprising against the Ottoman Empire, at the same time it was providing the Turks with war material to suppress the very same revolution . . . and it is for this that the nine Greeks arrested by the British navy vessel were tried. Britain was a powerful colonial power and had the capability to use force against small nations, suppress their revolutions and arrest as it did, what they called law breakers, in order to transport them to the new colonies of Australia where European population was needed . . . Anyway, those young Greeks eventually returned to their home island of Hydra, like a good Odysseus (Frangioudakis 1988).

Apart from the so-called 'Greek convicts', among the early Greek settlers known to have arrived in Australia before 1850 were Samuel Donnes (Andonis?), John Peters, Aikaterini Plessas, George Morphesis, George North (or Tramountanas) and Andreas Lekatsas. Donnes and Peters are believed to be free Greeks who settled in Australia. Donnes, the son of a sea captain from the island of Cefalonia, arrived in Australia in 1837 and married a woman named Mary shortly after his arrival in Sydney at the age of 22. Donnes was married for a second time 18 years later, to Catherine Riley. He had six children from his two marriages. He worked first as a seaman and later as a gold miner in New South Wales and Victoria and died at the age of 58, from chronic bronchitis. Peters, also a lone seaman, possibly from Samos, landed in Sydney about 1838 and married an Irish woman with whom he had 16 children. He became a gold prospector and farmer and died in Sydney in 1880. He was survived by a dozen children and 200 descendants (Gilchrist 1985, 1992). Morphesis and Andreas Lekatsas (or Lucas) were sailors from Ithaca (Cigler 1988). They were crew members of a British vessel and jumped ship on arrival at Port Melbourne in 1848. After jumping ship, Lekatsas headed for the goldfields and 'there are indications that he was in Ballarat at the time of the Eureka Stockade' (Vondra 1979: 30).

North (Tramountanas) landed at Port Adelaide, South Australia, in 1842 and worked as a seaman for several years. He then became a farmer on Eyre's Peninsula (near Venus Bay) and married an English woman named Lydia Vosper. He raised a family and died of old age in 1911 (Tsounis 1988b: 42).

There were no women among the very early Greek settlers. From the early beginnings of Greek settlement in Australia, and for many decades to come, men outnumbered women.

Illustration 4.4   Aikaterini Plessas, the first Hellene woman known to have arrived in Australia.

Gilchrist (1985, 1992) credits Aikaterini Plessas as the first Greek woman to arrive in Australia. She was from Epeiros and arrived in Sydney in 1835.

According to Gilchrist, Aikaterini and her mother were abducted by Mouktar Pasha (son of Ali Pasha), and were kept in his harem. She was betrothed to his physician, Ioannis Koletis. When Mouktar rebelled against the Ottoman Turks and was eventually executed, Koletis (who later became the Prime Minister of the newly-founded modern Greek state) broke his engagement with Aikaterini. She then fled to Messolongi, which was under the protection of the British garrison. There, she married James Henry Crummer, an Irish policeman who became a Major in an English regiment which, in 1835, was posted to the garrison of the colony of New South Wales. Crummer became a magistrate and served in Newcastle and Port Macquarie. Aikaterini bore Crummer 11 children, five of whom died young (Gilchrist 1985, 1992; Alexakis & Janiszewski 1988: 46).

The only other Greek woman who is known to have arrived in Australia in the 1850s is Diamantina Roma. From some accounts she was of Veneto-Greek descent, daughter of the Count and Countess Roma of Corfu. She married Sir George Bowen, a philhellene, who became the first Governor of Queensland in 1851. In 1847, before migrating to Australia, he had been appointed president of the Ionian University and, in 1854, he was appointed chief secretary of the Ionian Islands (Gilchrist 1985; Alexakis & Janiszewski 1988). Lady Bowen held a prominent role in society as a tireless worker for charity and her contribution to the new colony was immortalised by having the town of Roma, Roma Street in Brisbane, and the Diamantina River named in her honour (Cigler 1988: 1459–60).

According to Alexakis and Janiszewski, in 1849, moves to increase migration to Australia from Greece were being contemplated by Earl Grey, Britain's Secretary for War and the Colonies. The idea of Hellenes from the Ionian Islands (which were under British jurisdiction at the time) migrating to the Western Australian colony interested him because they would grow their native produce such as olives, vines and figs and teach the settlers from northern Europe (principally the British) how to cultivate these crops. Migration from the Hellenic world increased at this time, but not to the extent envisaged by Grey. The lure of gold, the despotic rule of the Ottomans and the myths and stories related by other travellers were responsible for this increase (Alexakis & Janiszewski 1989b: 12).

The discovery of gold in Australia brought more Hellenes to Australia. The 1850s are marked by a more regular Hellenic migration which remained small but steady until the turn of the century. About that time, what had begun as a migratory trickle became an accumulative action of individuals, which gradually increased over the years and should be distinguished from the conscious collective undertaking, a feature of later phases of Hellenic migration. Gold fever affected Greek sailors and fishermen serving on British vessels, with many jumping ship and making their way to the goldfields of New South Wales and Victoria. By the late 1850s, Greeks began to appear in the lists of ships' deserters in both the *NSW Government Gazette* and the *Victoria Police Gazette*, though many had Anglicised their names (see Appendix 4) (Alexakis and Janiszewski 1989b: 15).

According to Gilchrist, reference has also been made to John Dunmore Lang's 1852 meeting with some contemporary Greeks. One mariner was a native of Corfu returning to Europe from Sydney, the other Greek was a settler operating a Sydney coastal vessel (Gilchrist 1985: 6–7).

At the same time, other Greeks settled in Australia and succeeded in establishing themselves in their new country. Ten Greeks are known to have arrived, married local women and settled in Tambaroora, New South Wales. Researchers have compiled an impressive account of the life of an early Greek pioneer to Australia, Michael Manusu, who was one of the few successful men to leave their mark on the colonies. Manusu was a well-educated man from the island of Mytilene who spoke four languages (Greek, Arabic, Hebrew and English) and arrived in Australia in 1849. He was a ship's officer who abandoned his ship to take part in the goldrush at Aruluen, New South Wales. He married Sarah Balwin and had nine children, giving each a Hellenic and an English name. After Araluen he worked for a landowner and then bought his own farm and hotel. He appeared to be a very mobile individual, both geographically and socially. Geographically, he moved with his family from the south to the north of New South Wales and then further inland to Mudgee, in central New South Wales, where he became a wealthy grazier (Tsounis 1987: 111; Messaris 1988). According to Messaris:

In June 1862, Manusu became the third Greek to be naturalised in NSW. By this time he had settled down on a farm of 320 acres he purchased at Eurodalla, after working as a tenant farmer on the vast estate of the celebrated Thomas Sutcliffe Mort. Manusu prospered during this period. The first of his children Sarah, Amelia, Christopher, Angelina, Pericles, Achilles, and Themistocles were all born on his farm. During this time he became the owner of the Widgett Inn at Bodall and conducted a business at nearby Nerringundah. In 1865 he was listed as the licensee of the 'Grecian Inn' at Eurodalla, arguably the first Greek in Australia to run such an establishment[3] (Messaris 1988).

Like other pioneers during that period around Australia, Manusu gave his children, and also his hotel, names which evoked the memory of—and represented continuity with—the cultural mythology of his heritage. By giving each of the children two names, Manusu also demonstrated in concrete terms a tradition of openness, tolerance and respect for the rights and heritage of others.

Recent research (Wilking 1989) has revealed the story of Gerasimos Metaxas who, like Manusu and others before him, jumped ship in search of his 'luck'. According to his grandson, Lou Wilking, he deserted from the English ship in which he was serving at Port Melbourne. After abandoning his ship, Metaxas went to the Ballarat diggings where he worked for several years as a gold miner 'until he had an accident with his leg' and subsequently became a hawker. He had a kind of mobile shop that provided the gold diggers with the goods they needed. Like other surviving members of the Metaxas family, Lou Wilking believes that his grandfather was present at the Eureka Stockade and took part in the rebellion. He proudly states that:

> my grandfather must have been there during the Eureka uprising. He was there when John Myers was there. They must have started business about the same time. He has left excellent memories in our family. He was a man of self esteem and hard work. If it was not for the accident on his leg, my grandfather could have been very wealthy like the Myers family and our family would have been much better off today (Wilking 1989).

Metaxas married a local woman, Hannah Maria Perkins, who was originally from England. Metaxas' descendants have proud memories of their grandfather as a distinguished pioneer and entrepreneur, a man of high esteem, acknowledged for his integrity and dedication to his family. Metaxas died in Ballarat at the age of seventy-one.

Dr Spyridon Candiotis was another important early arrival, who is credited with being the first Greek medical practitioner to arrive in Australia. He arrived in Melbourne in 1853 and 'achieved notoriety in lawsuits at Flemont in Queensland' (Gilchrist 1985).

There were others who arrived during this time, but the first officially recorded Greeks to arrive in Australia were Nicholas Emellen and George Doikos, both from Athens. They landed in Melbourne in 1850 and 1851 respectively and went to the goldfields of Bendigo. Nicholas Emellen arrived as a teenager and later became a labourer at Port Melbourne, married an Irish woman and had three children (Gilchrist 1985: 12). According to his descendants, George Doikos headed for the diggings in New South Wales, becoming a miner and farmer. Other early Greeks such as Leonidas Koledas, Athanasios Avgoustis, George Falangas and Athanasios Cominos also made their mark during this early period. Koledas, for example, arrived in 1860 in Sydney from the island of Andros. He married an English woman and, during his struggles for progress, he:

> became entangled in a long legal case over a mining dispute which also reached Queensland's Parliament in 1884, although to no avail. He was, however, successful in a subsequent mining venture and eventually became the manager of a mine called Pluto (Gilchrist 1985).

According to Gilchrist, there were other individuals who made their presence felt in different ways within their new society. Among them were Eugenios Genetas, who served for two years with the Native Mounted Police in Queensland's outback. Genatas is recorded as singing the Hellenic national anthem at a dinner organised by the Bowens in 1862 in Rockhampton. John Doscas was a councillor at Cottlesloe, near Perth, for about 40 years. Athanasios Kaparatos was awarded

Illustration 4.5   The Carkoe (Korkou?) family in Gerogery NSW in 1906. The elder Nicolaos (centre) was born in Athens in 1829 and migrated to Australia during the goldrush of the 1860s, spending his working life in gold mines.

the Royal Humane Society's medal for his actions in saving 10 people from drowning in the Tamar River near Launceston (Gilchrist 1985: 15–16). Kaparatos, by risking his life for others, revealed himself as a *palikari* (someone who is brave, good-looking, proud, generous, humble and *philotimos*) who, like the heroes of Greece's history and mythology, upheld a strong sense of *philotimo*, worthy of a human being.

Despite the end of the convict system, the granting of partial autonomy for self-government to the Australian colonies in the 1850s and the long economic boom due to the 'gold rushes', the number of Greeks who ventured to Australia remained small. None the less, it was during this period that a number of Greeks, nearly all of them young, single men, settled in various towns around Australia and, in particular, in the goldfields of New South Wales and Victoria.[4]

Due to a lack of reliable contemporary statistics, not all accounts are consistent when trying to calculate the actual numbers of Greek pioneers arriving in and departing from the colonies. According to Tsounis, 'perhaps forty or fifty Greeks came in the 1850s and another hundred or so in the next twenty years during Australia's first great economic boom' (1988b: 42). While some made their mark and stayed in Australia, others were reported to have gone back to Greece either to settle or for other reasons, returning to Australia at a later date. In relation to Gilchrist's estimates, Messaris observes that the Greek arrivals in the 1850s numbered approximately two hundred. This total progressively increased in each subsequent decade and, by 1870, had reached between four and five hundred (Messaris 1988; Gilchrist 1992).

Only a few desired to settle in Australia permanently and they usually waited until they had established themselves in some sort of business before bringing out their wives and families from Greece. For the majority, however, Australia was a place where they could make a fortune and then return to Greece to enjoy the hard-earned fruits of their labour.

Generally, the Hellene miners rarely met each other or lived and worked together. The 'tyranny of distance' and the lack of stable and profitable employment, in a society which was showing already signs of discrimination against many non-British residents, hindered the formation of stable Greek communities. Some individuals, like those in New South Wales and Queensland, managed to signpost their presence as the Hellenic ethnic frontier of the Antipodean diaspora. By the 1870s, however, there had been a 'massive exodus' of Hellenes from Victoria due to the lack of opportunities in the goldfields. From the 1850s onwards they had been moving to South Australia and Queensland and some had ventured into the outback. A few went to Tasmania in the 1860s and several arrived in Western Australia in the 1870s. The first arrival in Darwin was in 1869 (Alexakis & Janiszewski 1989b: 15).

Of the individual Greek 'scouts' who arrived at different Australian ports and slowly made their way inland, eventually 'some . . . met and clubbed together'. As we have seen, the early settlement pattern of these pioneers was very much one of individuals independently wandering about the goldfields and elsewhere in search of rewarding work. No doubt these

In Loving Memory of

VACILLUS MACRYANNIS
DIED 12 JULY 1889
AGED 7 YEARS

ALSO
ANN BLUETT
DIED 16 JULY 1910
AGED 50 YEARS.

UR DEAR MOTHER
MATILDA MACRYANNIS
DIED 1ST OCT 1902
AGED 64 YEARS

ERECTED BY
THEIR LOVING DAUGHTERS
ELLEN & AGNESS

Illustration 4.6 In the absence of Hellene women, Hellene males married local women of Anglo-Celtic background. Old Catholic Cemetery, Tambaroora, NSW. (*Source*: 'Greek-Australians in their own Image', National Project Archives in 90th Anniversary Greek Orthodox Community of Sydney and NSW, 1988.)

pioneers must have discovered many things during their travels. As Tsounis comments, 'possibly the most exciting discovery was that there were other Greeks in the Antipodes doing much the same thing. Once they met, they clubbed together' (Tsounis 1988b: 42).

Although Greek scouts came from many regions of the Hellenic world, there were few Greek women who accompanied their menfolk. According to the Census of 1871, there were only 13 Greek women throughout Victoria (cited in Alexakis & Janiszewski 1989b: 15).

In the late 1860s some collective settlements existed in the Braidwood district, south-west of Sydney, and Arcadia in

Victoria (Alexakis & Janiszewski 1988: 45–60; 1989b: 15–16). A number of Greek miners who came from different areas of Greece, including Crete, the Aegean and Ionian islands as well as the mainland, gave rise to the so-called 'Greek Town'—in effect a 'collective' Hellenic settlement in the central western goldfields near Hill End, Tambaroora, New South Wales (Gilchrist 1985). This settlement, which consisted of approximately 20 Greek miners searching for a golden future at the diggings, represents an early account of an attempt at 'place and placemaking' with identifiable Hellenic features—it enabled them to live gregariously and in accordance with their *agora* traditions, although there was no *agora* in the complete sense of the word. In the absence of sufficient numbers of Greek women, however, like the Greeks who preceded them, they 'fathered a respectable number of Australian born children' on their English, Irish and Australian wives. Like Manusu and others, they too followed the custom of giving their children two names, one Greek and one non-Greek.

There are 14 or 15 Greek graves in the nearby Catholic cemetery of settlers who fell victim to tuberculosis, a disease which often afflicted miners (Gilchrist 1985; Alexakis & Janiszewski 1989b). As gold production fell during the 1890s, Tambaroora's population declined and eventually most of its residents, including the Greeks, departed for other parts of the country. As there were no major established Hellenic communities anywhere else in the country, geographic or residential mobility remained a prominent feature in these settlers' histories.

At the end of the goldrush, the former Greek miners from New South Wales, Victoria, Queensland, South Australia and Tasmania entered a variety of occupations, such as farming, maritime employment, labouring, small trading enterprises and, eventually, community, professional and administrative fields (Alexakis & Janiszewski 1988: 55; 1989b: 15). This period, therefore, saw the beginning of the inclusion of these early Greek settlers into diverse occupational practices across the socio-economic structure of the host society.

The material rewards gained from working in Australia enabled some early settlers to return home and, no doubt, to spread the good news. For example, Andreas Lekatsas was one of the first Greeks to arrive in Victoria during the goldrush of the 1850s. After working at different jobs for 20 years, he returned to Ithaca like a worthy Odysseus. Like Kazantzakis' Odysseus, however, who had learned to enjoy the physical and mental challenges he experienced abroad, Lekatsas wanted more excitement than his native Ithaca could provide and so he re-migrated to Australia.

During his stay in Ithaca, Lekatsas persuaded some members of his family and several other compatriots to follow him to Australia. Four of his brothers (Georgios, Antonios, Panoyiotis and Marinos) migrated and established themselves as shopkeepers in Melbourne (Tsounis 1987: 111). By his actions, Lekatsas is said to have initiated 'chain' migration—which later was to bring hundreds of Ithacans to Australia. As Price observes (1963), the Ithacans became one of the major Greek groups to settle in Australia prior to 1940.

A similar example of success and chain migration is the story of Athanasios Kominos (or Cominos), who arrived in Sydney from the island of Kythira in 1870. He worked his passage to Sydney as a seaman after hearing about the goldfields from a fellow-Kytheran called Jack Melitas who had just returned home (Price 1963; Kennedy 1976: 48). Cominos tried various labouring jobs and then worked at the old Balmain coal mine in Sydney, along with another Greek, John Theodorou, from the island of Psara, until he fell sick and lost his job. He was very partial to fish and, as he waited for his meal one day, he was 'intrigued by the ease with which a Welshman called Hughes prepared it', by simply dipping the battered fish into boiling fat. In partnership with Theodorou, he bought a fish-shop in central Sydney and did so well that he was later able to take over several oyster leases on the Hawkesbury, while Theodorou ran the restaurant (Price 1963; Kennedy 1976: 48). Cominos then extended his business activities into fish and oyster farming, earning himself the title of New South Wales' 'oyster king'. More importantly for the purposes of this study, however, his business success provoked the migration of numerous Kytherans to New South Wales (Tsounis 1987: 111), thus typifying extended migration from the same regional communities (Gilchrist 1985; Price 1963). As Alexakis and Janisjewski state:

> the characteristic feature of Cominos' successful business endeavours brought to Australia other members of his family

to join him. With his business expanding, Comino com-
menced to bring out his brothers to assist, and more oyster
saloons and fish restaurants were eventually opened. With
news of such an impressive success quickly reaching Kythira,
the 'steady stream' to Sydney of Cominos' relatives and
friends was rapidly joined by others, also eager to try their
hand in the food catering trade. Kytherian chain migration
to NSW had been set in motion (Alexakis & Janiszewski
1988: 51).

Just as the Cominos family pioneered the oyster farming
industry in New South Wales, Athanasios Avgoustis and
George Falangas pioneered it in Western Australia. In spite
of the initiation of chain migration from the Hellenic world
during this period, the migratory movement to Australia still
remained limited to a few individuals even after the 1880s,
unlike the first Hellenic migration to America, which became
a mass out-migration by the end of the 1880s (Saloutos 1964;
Vlachos 1968; Bombas 1989: 16). Greek pioneer migration to
America preceded that to Australia by many decades, mainly
because of America's more advanced European settlements and
its closer proximity to Greece. In contrast, many are said to
have contemplated the Antipodean 'gold rush', but 'searching
for their luck' in a land four or five months' voyage from
Greece proved to be too far from home (Gilchrist 1985: 21).

Apart from migrants' dream to 'amass wealth and return
home', Australia as both a country and a society had a very
low profile until well into the twentieth century. Europeans
generally tended to regard the Australian social structure as
being by and large England's 'dumping ground' for social
outcasts and criminals. The rawness of Australia, at the time,
could not have appealed to them much either, as there were
only a 'few far-flung coastal cities and towns' and a largely
unexplored and hostile interior. At the same time Australia's
population, comprising mainly English and Irish stock, did not
take kindly to the so-called 'foreigners' (Vondra 1979). Stable
Hellenic settlements are recorded in Sydney and Melbourne
in the late 1870s due to the advent of urbanisation, increased
chain migration from Greece, occupational diversification and
the creation of social and economic conditions conducive to
family life. However, it was not until the 1880s and 1890s

that organised community settlements were able to be adequately developed, while there was no organised Hellenic settlement in the Northern Territory until after 1910.

It appears that the biographies of Greek 'scouts' reflect the Odyssean adventurous mind and the willingness of modern Hellenes, like their ancient ancestors, to venture into new and unexplored territories. In their new place of settlement, being bound by what they experience, they obviously find it difficult to detach themselves from these experiences. Their inability to return home and settlement in their new land has been contained in a Kastelorizian laconic lament, composed and sung in Australia early this century. The lines which follow capture the sense of physical distance as well as longing (melancholia) and isolation from home that many Greek immigrants have felt at different times: 'Australia is an island where you can sail with ease. But once you go and settle there it's difficult to leave' (Tsounis 1987: 117).

Whatever the reasons for their decision to come to Australia, up until the 1870s Greek pioneer settlers were predominantly single men. We can gain a clearer understanding of their socio-economic and occupational distribution by examining some of their biographies and looking retrospectively at the Hellenic value system and national character. Broadly speaking, Greek pioneers in Australia followed similar social mobility patterns and made concerted efforts to improve their socio-economic status in the host society. It is evident from the biographies discussed that, in spite of the many challenges that faced them, by drawing on the rich reservoir of their traditions and culture they were better able to engage with their new society. Their cultural history, therefore, provided the base for their achievements and successful settlement within the socio-economic structures of Australia.

Whether links between these early pioneers and the Hellenic world were developed through those who went back home and the impression they made on returning (with wealth or gold), or in some other way, these links blended with the stories, legends and myths derived from Hellenic tradition to form an interplay which informed people's decision to migrate to Australia. The nature of these pioneers' social mobility, their occupational shift from mining to other industries—in which, too, they were often pioneers—their geographic mobility and

101

the degree of inter-marriage with local women each played a part in laying the foundations of Hellenism in the Antipodes. The outcome of the pioneer experiences was to create a diaspora in Australia and a bond with the Hellenic world which paved the way for the subsequent waves of chain and mass Hellenic migration that began in the 1940s. I will discuss this period in Chapter 5.

The causes of Hellenic migration

The aim of this chapter is to locate Hellenic migration in a broader historical and conceptual framework, one which is connected with the socio-economic development of the modern Hellenic nation state and it argues that this development was both a cause and effect of mass migration from Greece to America and Australia over the last century. In particular, a connection will be drawn between economic underdevelopment and underemployment in Greece, and the various waves of urbanisation, internal migration and emigration which have characterised the country's development since the formation of the Hellenic nation state in 1828. The final section of the chapter examines other miscellaneous causes of Hellenic migration.

The Greek demographer Nicos Polyzos (1947), in his historical account of the process of migration, has identified three types of Hellenic migration:

1 the 'agrarian' emigration of antiquity;
2 the 'commercial' emigration of the Middle Ages; and
3 the 'industrial' emigration of the twentieth century.

Firstly, the 'agrarian' emigration resulted from the over-population of the city-states which forced the Greeks to go abroad in search of territory, settling in places such as Asia Minor, North Africa and Sicily. Secondly, the 'commercial' emigration stretched from the beginning of the western Middle

Ages to the end of the nineteenth century. The main causes of emigration during this period were trade considerations. This emigration was directed towards destinations such as Venice, Genoa, Corsica, Vienna, Asia Minor, Egypt and Russia. Thirdly, and in contrast to the preceding two emigration epochs, the 'industrial' emigration of the late nineteenth and twentieth centuries involved the emigration of workers (including professionals, scientists and students) from Greece to the industrially advanced metropolitan centres of the Western capitalist economies. This third phase of migration from contemporary Greece has continued almost uninterrupted since Independence.

Many of the causes of out-migration from contemporary Greece were the products of an interplay between different factors which together created economic underdevelopment. Some of these factors included a lack of industrial development, lack of investment in secondary industry and lack of the cultural changes necessary to help bring about economic transformation. Government disregard for agricultural modernisation, as well as a lack of any policies directly addressing the needs of the rural population and the political conflict which undermined most forms of economic development, kept the population dissatisfied and fostered the belief that their economic problems could be resolved through migration.

The liberation of Greece in 1821 and the founding of the modern state in 1828 were not sufficient either to stop the continuing out-migration, or to encourage the return of hundreds of thousands of expatriate Greeks who were living in self-imposed exile in various overseas communities in Europe and elsewhere, due to the Turkish occupation. For many, repatriation remained but a dream, either because of the modern Hellenic state's failure to address the immediate problem of mass out-migration, or because it did not develop policies which would encourage repatriation (Vgenoupolos 1985: 38).

Following Independence, much of the nation's contemporary development was characterised by political conflict. This preoccupation has led successive Hellenic governments to either downplay or ignore most mass out-migrations from their country. During the brief administration of Greece's first President, Kapodistrias (1828–32), and the subsequent 30 years of King Otto's administration, the newly-liberated state was preoccupied with political problems. Between 1833 and 1862, Otto was busy trying to reconcile the conflicting political interest groups—the Independence leaders and the Fanariot diplomatic corps who had successfully administered the Ottoman Empire. As Saloutos observes:

> Kapodistrias proved unable to restrain the revolutionary leaders who were followed by the agricultural masses. The political orientation of the nation was unfocussed and unrealistic. Similarly, the young and inexperienced Bavarian King Otto was granted authority to control the newly liberated State whose revolutionary leaders under different conditions would have become statesmen (Saloutos 1964: 11).

Up until 1940 France, England, Germany and Russia exerted considerable political pressure on the new nation state and they regularly intervened in the running of the newly-liberated nation's political administration. Russia and Germany, in particular, placed a major strain on the new nation's internal affairs by burdening her political administration with conflicting political demands that often rendered her foreign policy provincial and contradictory (Saloutos 1964). The vested interests of European powers in the Hellenic state combined to bring about its political and economic dependency. European expansion did not take the form of extensive industrial investment in the new state; instead, it set the stage for lasting political control by establishing a patron–client relationship between themselves (either individually or in treaty) and the emerging Hellenic state. Otto's autocratic style of government had led him to ignore the Hellenic revolutionary leaders' demands in favour of the possible regeneration of a nation based on the model of the powerful and despotic Byzantine state. Consequently, in the absence of democracy, he 'was faced with political and social unrest which ultimately curbed his powers' (Saloutos 1964: 12; Svoronos 1972). With continuing political unrest the government had little time or inclination to deal with internal economic problems.

The country's development was denied the social changes which the Industrial Revolution had brought to western Europe. The Greeks of the diaspora contributed towards a cultural renaissance of the Hellenic Republic, although the 'brain-drain' that had taken place during Turkish rule had left their country without the intellectual resources necessary for speedy development. The newly-established University of Athens was influenced by the revival of the ideas of the Greek Classics in Europe. It took only a few decades after liberation for this institution to become the spiritual centre of all diaspora Greeks (Svoronos 1972: 91–101).

Difficulties with land distribution and agricultural and industrial development were central to internal and external Hellenic migration during the first half of the twentieth century. All three were exacerbated by political instability and disastrous investment policies. In 1833, of an estimated 120,000 farm families, only 20,000 were proprietors and, in 1842, of an estimated 5 million acres of land, two-thirds remained uncultivated (Vgenopoulos 1985: 38). The Hellenic government did not honour its promise to distribute free land to the landless peasants who had fought for the liberation of that land during the Independence struggle. Instead, the *Donation Law* of 1835 gave them 'the right to purchase small plots by annual payments over 36 years. This law was not very popular and its implementation proceeded at a snail's pace' (Mouzelis 1986: 39).

It was not until 1871 that the first effective landownership policies of Premier Koumoundouros were established. These policies allowed the residents of Peloponnesos to purchase small land holdings, thus becoming private owners. The second major land reform laws were implemented in 1923, more than 50 years later, by Premier Venizelos. By this time, however, out-migration to America was occurring on a mass scale. To highlight the desperate poverty of life in rural Greece at the time, Vlachos quotes from a letter sent by a potential migrant, who outlines the reasons for his desire to migrate to America. The words of this person undoubtedly epitomise the thoughts and feelings of many who chose to migrate to other destinations, including Australia:

> Why remain to struggle for a piece of bread without any security for the future, without honour and independence? . . . Why not open your eyes and see the good that awaits you? . . . Harden your heart and seek your fortune abroad,

where so many of your countrymen have already made theirs
. . . Or are you waiting to cultivate the barren lands? . . .
Have you not seen how much progress you have made thus
far? (Vlachos 1968: 54).

Land reform laws involved the government gaining access
to large estates that had been previously controlled by a
handful of individual landlords and distributing it to repatriated
Hellenes. These reforms were a result of the government's
desperate attempts to accommodate 1.5 million Hellenic refugees from Ionia (that is, Hellenic Anatolia), and 18,000
refugees from East Romelia, following the eruption of Balkan
nationalism and Greece's defeat by Turkey in the 'Catastrophe
of Asia Minor' in 1922. Meanwhile, special treaties already
signed with Turkey safeguarded the land rights of Turkish
Chiflik owners in the central and northern provinces of Greece,
even after liberation was completed in 1913. These treaties
were injurious to the Hellenic peasants who were the true
owners of the land, but who never achieved ownership because
they did not have control of the political administration of
their country. As a result, many preferred out-migration to
starving on land they could not call their own (Saloutos 1964;
Vgenopoulos 1985; Mouzelis 1986). By 1936, land reform
laws had led to the distribution of a total of 425,000 acres to
305,000 families. These laws were unpopular with the large
property owners, but then helped to slow down the out-migration of rural peasants (Filias 1967: 128).

The problems caused by the slow implementation of land
laws were exacerbated by the almost non-existent rural welfare
policies. Farmers throughout the country lacked such basic
social welfare measures as government planning to increase
arable and irrigated land and a bureau to offer advice about
agricultural production (Malliaris 1982: 335). Consequently,
in spite of a partial economic improvement, many chose
out-migration in order to escape a degrading life of poverty.
In the absence of welfare incentives, migration from rural areas
became a necessity. Migration became necessary also because
many peasants owned plots that were too small to support
them or because much of the land still remained under feudal
ownership. For example, as Filias observes, of the 2,658
villages of Thessaly, Macedonia and Epirus, 1,422 belonged

to powerful landlords (Filias 1967: 113). The government gained control of the liberated estates following Independence but, according to Mouzelis, refused to sell them by auction, and its stand on the issue was a serious hindrance to land reform (Mouzelis 1986: 39).

Agriculture was pivotal to the country's future because of its interrelatedness with demographic distribution, skills, economics and migration. This element is highlighted by the fact that almost 50 years after the War of Independence, approximately 82 per cent of the population lived in small communities of fewer than 5,000 inhabitants. Despite rapid urbanisation, in 1928 the peasant class still comprised 67 per cent of the total population and in 1950 almost 50 per cent of the Hellenic population still lived in rural communities. According to Price, during this first period of contemporary mass out-migration to America (the 1880s–1920s), so many people migrated that many villages were left empty or half-empty (Price 1963: 115). This migration had such a great impact on the remaining population that cultivated land was either converted to pasture or abandoned altogether (Svoronos 1972: 100–3).

Price (1963) stipulates that another factor was the phylloxera disease in the wine-growing areas of Europe:

> A currant crop failure due to phylloxera in Dalmatia and France in the 1880s caused a shortage of wine, which resulted in farmers all over Greece pulling out century-old olive trees to plant vines. In the short-term this led to high prices for wine and the consequent increase in the export of Greek wines and currants (Price 1963: 115).

The long-term consequences for Hellenic agriculture were dire. In the 1890s the French changed to grafting classic stock onto phylloxera-proof American roots, leading to the recovery of the French market. The demand for Hellenic wine weakened and this, along with the uprooted olive trees (which take at least fifteen years to reach commercial size), greatly undermined the largely agricultural base of the Hellenic economy. The French went further and imposed protective tariffs which literally legislated Greek currants out of the market; Russia adopted a comparable policy (Saloutos 1964: 29). Both the massive out-migration of 1890–1906 to the United States and the increased numbers of Hellenes departing for Australia during these years can be attributed to the decline in the price of currants, the major export crop (Kennedy 1976: 45; Saloutos 1964: 29).

Capital investment in the agricultural sector continued to be insufficient, depriving rural communities of the opportunity for economic growth. In spite of positive recommendations and, in 1929, a substantial injection of funds by the Agricultural Bank to the rural community the situation did not improve (Filias 1967: 116). By the beginning of the Second World War, agriculture remained underdeveloped because capital investment was being directed towards other sectors. In a nation whose economy remained largely based on agriculture, in 1939 there were only 1,578 tractors for farming and the use of chemicals and fertilisers remained severely limited as small farmers were not able to afford them (Filias 1967). Because government investment in farming remained practically non-existent, farming methods remained largely archaic and feudal in structure.

Along with poor agricultural development, inadequate government policies failed to foster industrial development and economic growth in secondary industries. Between 1840 and 1860, for example, industrial development in Greek foundries was non-existent. In addition, most of the industrial goods consumed in the Hellenic state were imported from overseas, so that while the skills to make simple metal objects such as pocket-knives could not be found locally, the same goods 'were sold so cheaply in Paris' (Tsoukalas 1977: 262). Economic improvement was taking place at a snail's pace and, by 1876, the nation's 'industrial sector was still in an embryonic state' (Rodakis 1976: 31, 36). At this time the country's first official statistics revealed the dearth of industries: 89 small manufacturing industries employing 4,959 men, 1,230 women, 627 boys and 524 girls—many of whom were the employers' families (Tsoukalas 1977: 36). Even by 1885, both industry and agriculture were still in a 'primitive state' (Svoronos 1972: 100). Ironically, however, due to a lack of urban development, there was a shortage of industrial workers for the moderately expanding modern industries (which could have led Greece to social change). As a result, the Hellenic economy relied even more on greater returns in trade.

Migration was also the product of the continuous imbalance in capital investment allocated to different industries. Between 1880 and 1890 the only industries, other than banking, which had expanded their activities, were merchant shipping and trade. In spite of this expansion, however, these industries were faced with increasing competition from other countries. It was these industries, along with the building industry, which emerged as the market leaders within the expanding Hellenic cities, while the secondary or heavy industry sector stagnated. This imbalance in economic development has been an important feature in Hellenic migration. Investment in areas such as the merchant marine tended to encourage expansion in the tertiary sector, but not in the secondary industrial sector, which was necessary in order to generate more employment opportunities.

Conflict between rival political parties during the 1880s and 1890s further aggravated the socio-economic disorder of the state and contributed to the deteriorating living conditions of the poor and landless. As a consequence, many chose migration as an escape from hardship and desperation, a state of affairs that lasted from 1880 to 1920. Premier Trykoupis was a capable politician who dominated the Hellenic political arena for 15 years. His policies for development and industrialisation were, however, both cursed and blessed by the rising middle class: cursed because they were expensive, and blessed because they supported modernisation and road construction policies, public works programs, the setting up of the substructure for industrial 'take-off' and restoration of the balance of payments incurred from army expenses during the 15-year annexation of Thessaly (Svoronos 1972).

Initially, Trykoupis' reforms were opposed by the conservative forces. The conservatives (represented by Koumoundouros and then by Deliyiannis) were supported by King George of Greece, leader of the ruling oligarchy (who once curbed the powers of Otto but strengthened the position of the 1864 constitutional reform) and were a strong opposition who were more concerned with politics than with economic reform. These conservatives were an old urban class who clung to power, but they continually failed to recognise the country's urgent need to industrialise, and thus keep pace with the related developments in other European states (Svoronos 1972: 100–5).

Following the socio-economic changes of the 1880s and, more particularly, the 1890s, some industries flourished while others failed. For example, there was a rapid growth in banking. Apart from the Ionic Bank, the National Bank largely controlled the government's financial activities and several other bodies were established at this time. These included a number of banks and insurance–finance organisations (Svoronos 1972: 101). The sharp rise in banking investment occurred during the period of Greece's economic crisis—between 1880 and 1910—when the balance of payments was very high. It rose from 46.9 million to 337.2 million drachmas by 1910, thereby increasing its initial capital seven times (Svoronos 1972: 255).

In the same period, Greece as a nation remained capital-starved. While banking was booming, returns from farming remained small and tenuous. Increased interest rates imposed yet another burden on the rural population. Many lenders were extracting interest rates of 10 per cent upwards. Such businesses proved so profitable that villagers who had returned to Greece from the United States often became money lenders while capital investment continued to favour the traditional industries such as shipping (Saloutos 1964: 1–30).

Opposition to the conservative class increased in intensity and political and social unrest spread throughout the country. This unrest produced many new political parties and factions which contributed to the political instability of the country. Trykoupis himself held office on five occasions, three of which lasted from five days to a few months. His expensive public works programs, involving the construction of many sea ports, the opening of the Isthmus of Corinth and the extended railway line and road construction, transformed the country within ten years (Tsoukalas 1977: 246–50). However, the unstable political climate, together with the client–patron activities of Greek governments with other European states, forced the country into an economic crisis, with national bankruptcy being declared in 1893. Bankruptcy only intensified the economic and political crisis and its after-effects caused a massive exodus of people to trans-oceanic countries—principally to the

United States but also to Australia (Malliaris 1982: 1–15). Premier Trykoupis was held responsible for allowing extended foreign banking and large borrowings in the name of 'Public Works', when in fact a very small proportion of these loans (about 6 per cent) was used in productive works. The rest was directed to improving the National Bank and the Bank of Epirus–Thessaly and to repaying internal loans (Svoronos 1972: 104).

The national bankruptcy of 1893 and its socio-economic aftermath led to what has been described as the 'tragic' defeat of Greece in the Graeco–Turkish War of 1897, which finally put Greece's economy under the jurisdiction of International Financial Control (Rodakis 1976: 3). The cost of the war—together with the previous expensive public works program—led to the imposition of higher taxes. Loan repayments absorbed 40–50 per cent of government earnings. From a loan of 639,739,000 francs, only 359 million was granted to Greece as a net total between 1879 and 1890. The rest was used to service loans—the costs of which were obviously greatly disproportionate to the net loan ultimately received by the country. The outcome of the defeat was to disturb public calm and set in motion public inquiries into the affairs of the government—all of which undermined political stability and the economic credibility of the state (Rodakis 1976: 104).

In contrast to difficulties related to government borrowings, the last quarter of the nineteenth and the beginning of the twentieth century saw an influx of foreign and Hellenic diaspora capital which, despite its extremely exploitative character, made a significant contribution to the revitalisation of Greece's economic development (Mouzelis 1986: 8). For the first time in the country's history, the diaspora formed a financial alliance with the local Greeks. According to Tsoukalas, this meant that capital was concentrated in the hands of a few and profit-making operations that ultimately impacted on the government's approaches to economic management were encouraged (Tsoukalas 1977: 246). It is equally significant that the main sources of capital investment in the country were Hellenic (including the Hellenic diaspora).

By 1914, increasing investment in the merchant marine had placed Greece in tenth position among the nautical powers (Svoronos 1972: 102), and, by the end of the Balkan Wars, second only to Norway in the proportion of its merchant marine to its population (Tsoukalas 1977: 330). This industry reaped high profits—ranging between 15 and 25 per cent—and, in periods of national economic crisis such as 1890–1910, these profits could double and often triple (Tsoukalas 1977: 265). This meant that Hellenic shipping capital underwent a very sharp growth from the 1880s onwards, as the industry expanded into countries such as Turkey, Russia, Egypt and the Balkans. Such a move was aided by the famous 'Independence Loans' that ironically brought about the economic subordination of Greece to its lenders, namely England, France and Germany (Malliaris 1982: 365). Unfortunately, this investment in and expansion of the shipping industry provided minimum employment in proportion to the volume of investment. With the exception of some coastal cities, where it generated significant numbers of jobs, the industry did not provide a major employment base even though many administrative, technical and financial management services depended on the merchant marine (Malliaris 1982: 326).

With the collapse of the rural economy and the consequent national urbanisation, the building industry increased, but expanding cities failed to develop proportionate industrialisation, becoming instead current market places for consumers, which in turn created employment for dealers of tertiary goods. Profits were so significant that even during national bankruptcy the consumer industry flourished throughout the first quarter of the twentieth century, absorbing large numbers of workers and making large capital gains (Tsoukalas 1977: 255; Saloutos 1964).

During this time, class disparities were aggravated by the apparent arrogance of the educated and privileged urban dwellers towards the neglected and 'downtrodden' peasantry. Crippling government taxation had become a paramount concern of the rural classes, who found it extremely difficult to make their payments. Despite the lodging of frequent petitions to the government, protesting against the primitive methods of taxation, reform proposals were rejected. As late as the 1890s, the rural class, hardest hit by government taxation, comprised approximately 75 per cent of the working population (Saloutos 1964: 13). Government taxation amounted to a tenth of the gross national product during the nineteenth century and this revenue was now being collected from the rural classes by private contractors. This practice contributed to the general restlessness, causing a substantial evacuation from the countryside to both the cities and abroad in search of better living conditions and rewards (Saloutos 1964: 1–30). By the end of the nineteenth century, economic and political instability had produced a country in which it was, at least for rural groups, difficult, if not impossible, to live.

The first 20 years of the twentieth century was a period of transition and social change across a number of socio-economic indicators. For the first time, various pressure groups were forming among both professionals and peasants. The Thessalean uprising of the propertied classes during 1905–10 had attracted national interest (Saloutos 1964: 11–14) and, for the first time since 'Independence', the middle class had grown to half a million. These were significant developments in a country which had initially failed to develop a sufficiently large and thriving middle class which would be capable of reinforcing the developing social forces required to bring about social change.

Economic confidence was gradually renewed during this period, especially following the re-valuation of the drachma, and increasing industrialisation and trade contributed to the higher profile of the middle class. However, despite the fact that the economy was now on the road to recovery, the slow pace of industrial development and the depression of 1911 precluded any rapid improvement in living conditions (Filias 1967: 115; Fairchild 1911: 81). It was not until 1913 and, more significantly, the beginning of World War One, that internal trade and multiple industrial investment began to flourish (Tsoukalas 1977: 61).

Overall, the socio-economic circumstances of these three decades (1890–1920)—including a drought and the currant crisis—and the lack of the appropriate protective policies that would have made the agricultural economy competitive operated as push factors, which prompted Greeks to leave their homeland. Consequently, in the first 20 years of the twentieth century 402,000 Greeks made the decision to emigrate, mainly to the United States. The number of Greeks arriving in Australia also increased significantly, when compared with arrivals recorded in the second half of the nineteenth century

(Price 1963; Tsounis 1971; Gilchrist 1985, 1992). Out of this group, 90 per cent belonged to the 15–40 age group, which was considered the most important sector of the working population for industrialisation. Such emigration prompted Fairchild to say that 'Greece has always been a splendid place to go away from to make a fortune' (1911: 9). The young and able were exhorted to leave for trans-oceanic countries like America and, for some, Australia.

During the 1920s and 1930s industry in general continued to expand but, due to the lack of development in heavy manufacturing, urban centres often became the forums of people's transition from the rural communities where they grew up to their subsequent trans-oceanic migration destinations, rather than as permanent dwelling places (Filias 1967). By the Great Depression in the 1930s, after 50 years of development in manufacturing, Greece had not yet managed to build a strong secondary industrial infrastructure that could expand and eventually absorb more labour. The new industries lacked both technical innovation and the necessary private and government protection measures (Malliaris 1982; Filias 1967). As a consequence, market competition with other countries ended up crippling the national economy (Malliaris 1982: 1–10).

Modernisation produced neither the industrial capacity nor the directives that would solve the main unemployment problems, with the number out of work rising from 75,000 in 1928 to 150,000 in 1935 (Filias 1967). For example, between 1911 and 1938, approximately 600 proprietary limited companies were established; however, these were mainly small textile and food-producing firms. The tertiary sector continued to dominate development, due largely to the nationalism of the 'Young Turks' who forced residents of Hellenic origin living in countries under Ottoman rule to return to Greece. Many of these refugees transferred their capital to Greece, where it was invested in manufacturing and banking and, at the same time, they stimulated the tertiary industry, because, as refugees, they had additional consumer goods needs. As investors they managed to secure very high interest rates—ranging from 30 to 40 per cent per annum, but this compounded the plight of the poor peasant borrower (Saloutos 1964). Merchant shipping, which had almost 67 per cent of its carrying capacity destroyed during the Great War, experienced a very sharp rise in development (Svoronos 1972: 131). The growth of this industry depended upon the ongoing devaluation of the drachma, low-paid labour and some protective governmental policies that ultimately penalised the consumer.

The Great Depression had a devastating impact on the national economy and its public works programs. Between 1923 and 1932, total borrowing was 1,654 million gold drachmas; in spite of the tax burden this reached 114 gold drachmas per head in 1928–29, (compared with 29.1 in 1920). At the same time, a minority that controlled the financial integrity and independence of the Hellenic state through overseas borrowing, imposed their own terms on the state (Svoronos 1972: 130). Despite improved measures in the industrial sector, national bankruptcy was declared once again in 1932 (Svoronos 1972: 101). Even when the economic crisis of the early 1930s had passed and business and living conditions had returned to normal, the value of trade dropped from 172.05 to 87.05 gold drachmas per head between 1931 and 1939. Despite some reduction in the balance of payments, the budget continued to show a deficit. Exports were only 50.65 per cent of imports in 1921–30, and only rose to 54.81 per cent for the period 1931–39 (Svoronos 1972: 101).

In the 20 years between 1920 and 1940, politics and military conflict, as distinct from economic conditions, were responsible for both internal and external migration. Migration continued throughout the period, although in somewhat smaller numbers than the previous 20 years and with many returning home after a short stay abroad. Of the 200,000 Greeks, or 5 per cent of the workforce, who emigrated between 1920–40, approximately half had returned to Greece by the late 1930s (Malliaris 1982: 365).

Both internal and external migration continued up to the beginning of World War Two—despite the large re-migration taking place, the expansion of the country's national borders and increasing industrialisation, all of which played important roles in partially slowing down migration by 1917. The annexation in 1864 of the Ionian Islands, of Thessaly in 1913–14 and of Western Thrace and Epirus in 1920, encouraged significant numbers of people to return to Greece. Almost half of all males who had migrated to the United States between the 1880s and 1917 returned home, while many returned home from Australia to fight in the Great War. Australia continued to experience a significant increase in Hellenic migration. One reason for this increase was that chain migration between Greece and Australia was already in operation, following the increased settlement of Hellenes in Australia. The expansion of national borders coincided with a population density increase, despite mass out-migration. Population levels grew from 34 people per square kilometre in 1889 to 37 in 1920. Although this increase is statistically insignificant, its importance lies in the fact that it was the first time such an increase had been noticed since Independence (Filias 1967: 115; Saloutos 1964: 260).

The 1930s were characterised by social unrest and workers' strikes and a noticeable increase in available workers (see Table 5.1). These developments coincided with widespread political upheaval, the rise of an active militant left-wing movement, the rise to power of the anti-communist regime, the 1936 dictatorship of Ioannis Metaxas and the development of a plethora of unions. For example, in 1928 there were 1,199 workers' unions in existence and their membership had reached 269,000 by 1939 (Svoronos 1972: 131). The Metaxas military regime forced many to leave the country for various destinations and, as Petropoulos has argued, thousands of Greeks were forced into self-exile—as either political dissidents or refugees—in European and overseas countries, including Australia (OECD 1988).

The issue of migration was overshadowed by the tragic consequences of World War Two. Between 1940 and 1949 one million people, approximately 8 per cent of the population, died as a result of the war, the subsequent internal political troubles and the Civil War of 1946–49 (Iatrides 1981: 1–36). In less than a decade, Greece faced the most acute population crisis of its modern history. This unprecedented state of affairs was beyond the reach of governmental controls, and placed a terrible pressure on the country, both economically and socially. These bloody events and the destruction of the country's social, cultural and economic networks, prompted Greek demographer Nikos Polyzos to predict, in 1947, that massive migration from Greece would be underway from 'all social levels of society, unless drastic social and economic structural changes were implemented' (Filias 1967: 119).

Table 5.1   Improvements in industrial performance of Greece
             1877–1938

Year	Number of Factories	Number of Manufacturing Workers	Manufacturing Industrial capacity in C. V.
1870	170	7,300	n.a.
1889	145	n.a.	1,967
1917	2.213	35,000	70,000
1938	4.515	140,000	277,000

Source: (Svoronos 1972: 101, 102, 130)

By 1950, Greece was politically and economically in ruins, making migration the almost inevitable choice for many of her inhabitants. Agricultural production had been reduced by more than 70 per cent. The merchant marine had once more lost more than 70 per cent of its total carrying capacity, and the state's socio-economic and industrial structures were in ruins (Svoronos 1972: 145). This destruction caused a decade of unprecedented national hunger and poverty, leading to social disturbance on a scale that shook the roots of the nation's traditional culture and values system. The volatile situation attracted the interest of several foreign powers—initially the British and then the Americans—who successfully 'seduced' important members of Greece's administration into pursuing personal or individualistic interests (Clogg 1985). This 'seduction' undermined the nation's sovereignty, inhibited the exercise of its full rights and unrestricted foreign policies, destroyed its self-determination and made it almost impossible to establish a clear focus for future political directions (Iatrides 1981: 1–36).

The Americans, who had taken over the 'de facto rights' granted to them by the British in 1947 in defending Greece against communism, played a decisive role in shaping the country's postwar political and economic future. Under extensive assistance granted under the aegis of the Truman Doctrine both during and after the Hellenic Civil War, the United States encouraged modernisation and supported centre-right political administrations. According to Mouzelis (1986: 135), the conservative nature of Hellenic–American patron–client networks weakened the 'social pact' by creating exclusivist or more direct control of Hellenic society's affairs and systematically excluding people who were supporters of the centre-left factions from government decision-making. As Mouzelis states:

> The communist party was outlawed, and all left-wing sympathisers kept out of the state apparatus and public life, through an intricate system of legal and illegal means (Mouzelis 1986: 160).

By the mid-1960s, economic and political developments in Greece were steadily undermining the traditional system of political control and state administration. The growing socio-economic inequalities due to poverty and the massive population shift to the cities had created a high level of discontent, which, when articulated in the political arena, threatened the stability of the democratically elected system of government. At the same time, there was increasing discontent among the working class, which was more or less directly linked to the growing inequalities of capitalist development and the electoral decline of the right. One indicator of the level of unrest was the extraordinary increase in strike action. As Mouzelis (1986: 138) observes, the number of working days lost per 1,000 workers doubled from 48 between 1959 and 1960 and reached 271 in 1963 and 519 in 1966. In 1964, the Centre Union Party, under the leadership of the political veteran George Papandreou, triumphed over the traditional conservatives, winning an unprecedented 53 per cent of the vote (Mouzelis 1986: 138).

The social, political and economic order of the Hellenic democracy ended when the 'Colonels'-led army became alarmed at growing popular support for George Papandreou's agricultural and educational reforms and united to prevent him returning to power. This was an American-funded and approved military coup but it was upstaged by a lower-ranking group from the IDEA, the Secret Band of Hellenes, established in 1944 by officers who were hard-line anti-communists (Mouzelis 1986).

The coup was headed by Colonel George Papadopoulos and a number of military officers who, with American and Israeli backing, staged a coup on 21 April 1967 and presented the King with a *fait accompli* (Mouzelis 1986: 144). The Junta administration that followed was characterised by political repression and persecution, especially of communists. The collapse of the Junta, in June 1974, was brought about both by the uprising of Athens Polytechnic students against the military and the failure of the Junta-directed coup in Cyprus against the Makarios administration. Petropoulos (OECD 1988) has estimated that approximately 100,000 Greeks fled as political refugees during the Junta's seven-year military administration of Greece. The Junta's collapse was followed by political repercussions which ultimately led to the subsequent Turkish invasion and occupation of almost 40 per cent of Cyprus. Almost 200,000 individuals were evacuated from Cyprus and many thousands of Hellene-Cypriots outmigrated to Australia, Canada, England and elsewhere during the years that followed.

By destabilising the political and social life of Greece and, at the same time, offering opportunities for out-migration, foreign intervention was a major causal factor in contemporary Hellenic out-migration. This migration had a major and unprecedented impact on the nation's demographic composition. Between the end of the Axis occupation and the beginning of the Civil War, Hellenic out-migration again began to rise to very significant population proportions. As Polyzos (1947) had predicted, this time it was not only the landless peasants who were emigrating, but also artisans and educated people. Greeks were migrating not only from deprived areas, but also from advanced ones (Polyzos 1986; Saloutos 1964; Filias 1967).

Unlike the trans-oceanic nature of turn of the century out-migration (which accounted for 75 per cent of the total population movement), the most distinctive feature of post-World War Two out-migration (particularly from 1954 onwards) was its mainly European orientation. Emigrants were attracted to the industrially advanced societies of western Europe; for example, between 1955 and 1974, 728,756 migrants, or 61.8 per cent of all migrants, sought work in European Economic Community nations (Vgenopoulos 1985: 42). Trans-oceanic migration accounted for only 406,195 migrants (or 35.3 per cent) for the same period, with Canada the country of popular choice (with 214,068 or 18.16 per cent), the United States second and Oceania (chiefly Australia) third, absorbing 174,565 or 14.81 per cent of the total. These figures do not include migration from established Hellenic communities outside the geographic borders of Greece, such as Romania, the Soviet Union, Egypt and the Middle East (Price 1975). Hellenes also migrated to various Mediterranean countries, as well as South Africa and Asian countries (the last being mainly after 1965).

Post-World War Two Hellenic migration has been described by several authors as the *greatest massive exodus* of modern Hellenic history. According to Mouzelis, this exodus was so massive that in the course of these two decades (1950s and 1960s) 1.5 million people, out of a total population of 9 million left the country (Mouzelis 1986: 138). Between 1955 and 1974 alone, permanent migration reached 1,179,076, and temporary migration 966,744 (Vgenopoulos 1985: 42). In this period annual permanent migration averaged 58,954 persons, so that between 1955 and 1960 migration exceeded natural population increases in Greece by 32.8 per cent. The same phenomenon occurred during the peak migration years of 1963, 1966, 1969 and 1971 (Malliaris 1982: 356). Permanent migration from Greece culminated in a record number of 117,167 in 1965, with another sudden upsurge in 1970–71. As Malliaris (1982: 356) observes, it was, by any reckoning, an impressive record for a small country like Greece.

Overall, the same economic factors which had caused the urbanisation and mass out-migration during the period leading up to the Great War were again in operation during the post-World War Two period. According to Mouzelis (1986: 115–60), migration had its roots in the inter-war agrarian reforms which had partly eliminated the big landowners in favour of small, independent landholders. Land fragmentation often prevented the consolidation of labour units[1] that could have led to more efficient mechanisation, modern cultivation methods and the 'regeneration' of labour employment. The most striking feature of economic development in Greece at this time was the dramatic drop in agricultural production which, after a somewhat brief upward trend, decreased its share of the GNP from 29.7 per cent in 1954 to 23.9 per cent in 1964 and ultimately to 16.1 per cent in 1973, a drop of 13.6 per cent in only 20 years. In real terms, despite urbanisation and out-migration, agricultural production and

121

industrial production both doubled between 1952 and 1972, but these reforms failed to slow down migration. The mountains of Greece, that once symbolised glory, security and freedom and also supported more than half of the Greek population, had by the 1950s dramatically changed their image to that of backwardness and deprivation, with a marginal and problematic economic status. Similarly, social justice and welfare considerations enshrined in the lives of the peasants were inadequately addressed. The merchant marine reached its prewar heights under Greek and foreign flags, claiming third place internationally (Wagstaff 1985: 10). In real terms, however, secondary and manufacturing industries did not show an increase, but rather a decrease. In 1951, 450,400 people, or 14.2 per cent of the nation's active workforce of 3,189,400, were employed in secondary industry, in contrast to 484,400 or 13.2 per cent of 3,671,400 in 1961. During the decade from 1951 to 1961, the country's labour force increased by 15 per cent, but secondary industry absorbed only an annual average of approximately 7.1 per cent (Filias 1967: 123), demonstrating that the employment situation did not improve (Vgenopoulos 1985; Mouzelis 1986). As a consequence, unemployment and internal and external migration continued to feature throughout this period.

Another feature of the changes during this period, that further hampered the exploitation of arable land, was the rapid increase in rural land sales. In 1959 there were 59,500 blocks of land sold—by 1964 this had risen to 103,000 blocks. The sales did not coincide with the creation of larger properties that could have led to more efficient farming units and increased production. On the contrary, these land sales took place during a period of mass migration when cultivation was being drastically reduced. The new landowners were 'urbanites', whose only interest in land acquisition was speculative (Filias 1967: 130). These figures do not include the thousands of smaller blocks of land, in some of the country's top locations, sold to tourists from the late 1960s until the present day—properties which previously had been important to small landholders as cultivated land.

Between 1951 and 1961, as well as the labour shortage problem and loss of available land, there was also a demographic crisis. During this period, the rural population recorded a 10 per cent increase in only 31 out of 147 rural residential localities or *oikismoi*; at the same time, the urban population increased by 25.5 per cent. The urban and semi-urban populations, which together amounted to less than 27 per cent of the country's population in 1920 and less than 47 per cent in 1940, had increased to 56.2 per cent by 1961 and by 1971 had risen to 69 per cent. Rural localities were left with 35.1 per cent (3,081,731 people) of the total population and these people lived in some 19,933 residential rural localities of fewer than 2,000 inhabitants. By the mid-1960s population centralisation reached the point where one-third of the total population was settled in 5 per cent of the land, and another half in 15 per cent (Filias 1967: 13, 115–21).

Out-migration, urbanisation and rapid industrial growth led to dramatic changes in the distribution of the labour force during this period, with a relative decline in agricultural labour. The occupational structure of the country eventually became similar to that of the developing countries of South America (Mouzelis 1986: 140). As before 1914, the out-migration of skilled labour further hampered the development of some industries, particularly those which depended on the establishment of local technician networks (Filias 1967). Rural migration also weakened the development of socio-economic structures which, in turn, caused faster evacuation of people from the countryside. In the single year 1963–4, for example, the nation lost 150,000 persons to migration. Migration itself became a cause of further migration, which in turn led to labour shortages (especially in agriculture) that became apparent as early as 1965. Subsequently, labour shortages became a characteristic feature of practically every sector. As Wagstaff comments:

> The migration of the more active people in the population has produced an actual shortage of agricultural labour and thereby retarded the spread of various high-value but labour-intensive crops, such as citrus and vegetables (Wagstaff 1985: 19).

The cycle of post-World War Two migration was completed in the mid-1970s when, for the first time in the postwar period, repatriation exceeded out-migration by a mere 172

Illustration 5.1   Hellenes came to Australia on board several Hellenic-owned ships such as *Kyrenia, Patris, Ellenis, Australis* but also on board a number of British, Italian and other ships. Above, at the port of Pireas, is pictured Maria Andreaki, centre, (with her brother, parents and sister), just prior to the moment of departure, the moment of their 'separation', ready to go on board the Italian passenger ship *Flaminia* in June 1959, en route to Melbourne, Australia. (*Source*: Dimitra Temelcos)

individuals (this being the difference between 24,448 persons to 24,276) (Malliaris 1982: 39). This trend, where repatriation exceeds out-migration, continued from the mid-1970s until 1987, with re-migration averaging 40,000 persons per year (*Neos Kosmos,* 5 June 1988: 1). None the less, the mass migration and settlement of Greeks in Australia between 1947 until the mid-1970s, prompted the Melbourne writer Vondra to state: 'no wonder that it is often said that there are more Greeks living outside Greece than within it' (Vondra 1979).

Out-migration and remittances sent home by those working abroad remained an 'exclusive' method used by modern Hellenic administrations to tackle the unemployment problem and a substantial proportion of their cash economic needs (Vgenopoulos 1985). Migrant and seaman remittances were influential in economic development, accounting for 13.9 per cent and 9.7 per cent of exports in 1955 respectively, figures which had risen to 24.4 per cent and 19.2 per cent in 1971 (Vgenopoulos 1985: 64–6). In 1991, remittances or migrants' investment—from the United States, Canada, Asia and Australia to Greece—totalled approximately 690 million dollars. Of this total, 14 million dollars came from Australia (National Bank of Greece 1990).

Hellenic migration to places like Australia, however, cannot be understood without an examination of non-economic and non-political factors. As discussed in Chapter 4, the nation's cultural forces, traditions and the history of Hellenic migration itself, together with the continual waging of wars, have both inhibited economic improvement and encouraged modern Hellenic migration. A variety of other intrinsic and extrinsic factors, operating either singly or in combination to alienate or disempower people from taking part in policy-making affecting their own destiny can be viewed as forcing migration to distant lands.

It has often been argued that the Hellenic value system requires individuals to make immense psychological and material sacrifices to the demands of the family unit and society. Many people migrated to distant lands such as America and Australia because of a commitment to their family's values and beliefs. One such value has been the concept of *philotimo*, that has remained a core concept of Hellenic language, cultural ideology and history, and influences people's ways of behaving within different social circumstances. The concept implies both individual and family pride, self-esteem, honour, faithfulness, altruism, individuality, progress, prosperity, freedom of choice, democracy, fairness and much more. People migrate to make a fortune for their families; that is their *philotimo*. Large sums of money have been sent back to Greece by sons who migrated to assist towards the purchasing of dowries for sisters and the education of relatives. Conversely, re-migration has also been linked to the concept of *philotimo*. In fact, it has often been argued in *agora* settings that it was Odysseus' *philotimo* which brought him back to Ithaca after many adventurous years abroad.

Single men and, especially, single women, often migrate to avoid family humiliation connected with the marriage system. That this humiliation has a direct or indirect association with economics or cultural practices, such as the dowry system, cannot be doubted. Before the 1980s, when the PASOK (PanHellenic Socialist Movement) government finally passed legislation that overruled dowry requirements, many families migrated in order to be able to finance a dowry. This legislation removed a great burden from many families who would otherwise have suffered economic hardship. Presumably, under the new legislation, people do not have to comply with the obligations of the dowry system because of family self-esteem, honour or family *philotimo*. However, the custom remains, under a new name. Instead of using the term 'dowry', people simply define the new situation as a 'financial start' or 'family assistance' for the newly-weds. This help or assistance again can be conceptualised as people's *philotimo*. *Philotimo* in this case is encapsulated in the traditional Hellenic philosophy of child-rearing, that requires the Hellenic family, and society as a whole, to provide the newly-weds with sufficient support for them to devote themselves to their children. Part of family commitment, therefore, entails upholding the traditional belief that a 'newly-established family' is entitled to have as much time as possible for child-nurturing and parent–child inter-action.

Philotimo, along with other related cultural values, is also directly connected to institutional education (Dimitreas 1981). In many cases, education received by family members while abroad has led them to seek permanent residency in their host societies, following the completion of their studies. Education has, therefore, led to a Greek 'brain drain' of intellectuals who have left to pursue their careers in different countries around the globe. In fact, education is traditionally regarded as the most important value, after health, in the hierarchy of national values and aspirations of the Hellenic culture. Accordingly, education *per se*, or even the failure to qualify for admission into tertiary education in Greece, has caused much internal and external migration, often of either the student or the entire family. Much of this migration appears to be due to both the lack of radical reforms in educational policies and also the absence of universities or other further education institutions within the rural areas of the country. The existence of such institutions in rural areas might have helped to slow the continuous process of urbanisation and encouraged the decentralisation of urban population. Education is particularly important when considering the fact that those involved in farming and its related occupations suffer from a low status profile (Tsoukalas 1977).

The Hellenic system of land inheritance has also been implicated in emigration. A farmer's land is normally divided between his sons and daughters. In situations where the daughters have not been provided with marriage dowries they receive land and a home for themselves. This inevitably leads to holdings becoming smaller and smaller holdings, or perhaps reduced to infertile mountain land, unless one or more of the sons migrates (Kennedy 1976: 45). Other alternatives to inheriting land could be found in the acquisition of a traditional trade or in tertiary education. However, employment opportunities for people with such skills were limited and high enrolments in law or medicine by people seeking to escape the hardship of agricultural work created a surplus of qualified people in such professions. As Saloutos comments: 'Perhaps the hardship of rural life accounts for the incentive to improve working skills. Small wonder then, that in 1907 Greece had one lawyer for every 888 people' (Saloutos 1964: 8).

Migration does not only occur because of abstract value concepts such as *philotimo* and the way such concepts are interpreted and applied in every-day human transactions. There are other cultural phenomena that relate to the physical world, such as the geographic location of countries. In fact, when people decide to migrate, both subjective and objective social and cultural dynamics are usually in operation. Some authors stress the importance of particular aspects as having exceptional influence on people's behaviour. In a Hellenic government publication about Greece's geographic location on the world map and its social effects on people, the authors state:

> Hellenes are sea people ever since the country was inhabited. The Aegean islands, where some of the earlier advanced civilisation appeared, exist very close to each other. This helps travelling, movements (mobility, migration) and inspires the imagination of the traveller to find out about other countries. It is the Hellenes' islands through which the first Greeks passed to go across to Ionia (Hellenic Anatolia) (General Secretariat for Greeks Abroad 1985: 13).

Similarly, Andrewes' work on the history of Greek society comments on how travel is encouraged by the social space and geographical location of the many islands of Greece. The need for people to travel from one island to another is described as a natural phenomenon in people's daily activities. This view is reinforced by the Greek climate, that allows people to enjoy their conversations and share their experiences in the open air, under the sun and the trees. In Andrewes' words:

> Greece itself is deeply penetrated by the sea, and there were sailors in the Aegean already in Neolithic times . . . But for very many Greeks the sea was an essential element of life, never far out of mind as it is seldom long out of sight. Their poets at all times rejoiced in the sight of a fine ship, and even Hesiod, though he hated to leave the land, still felt obliged to include a section on sailing in the poem of instruction which he composed for farmers. The Greeks were inevitably led out into the Aegean (Andrewes 1984: 2).

Andrewes further stresses the importance of human interaction and behaviour within social gatherings which, he believes, are both influenced by the prevailing climatic conditions in Greece:

> The social effects of the climate must not be forgotten. For most of the year, the Greek could work and eat and talk in the open air, somewhat scantily clad, seeking the shade rather than the sun; and this had a large effect on his way of life. Farming left some time to spare, even for industrious Hesiod, and the ancient Greek spent most of it talking with his fellow-farmers, as his successor does today in the village cafe . . . Consequently, the Greeks lived a very public life. The pressure of the community on the individual was greater than it is in climates where man must shelter indoors for most of his leisure time. It was harder to hide from disapproval, more essential to display what might earn praise (Andrewes 1984: 14).

The climatic conditions of their physical environment enabled the Hellenes to establish communal interaction and eventually to build the *agora* culture, through which they learned about society, politics and economics, philosophy, the arts and the world outside. The impetus, therefore, to migrate, willingly or otherwise, has also been associated with other physical environmental forces. Mountain terrains (which constitute 70 per cent of the total land mass) are not easy to cultivate—due to high elevations, steep slopes, thin soils, and snow in some areas above 1,000 metres—which makes these regions economically less productive (Wagstaff 1985: 10). Various types of natural disasters, such as earthquakes and floods, have also contributed to rural hardship and the desire to migrate. For example, a statistical survey of buildings erected between the years 1801 and 1978 shows that the average number of buildings destroyed in Greece as a result of earthquakes was 900 per year with approximately 50 deaths per year (Malliaris 1982). Saloutos has also emphasised the importance of earthquakes, quoting an observer's rather astonishing account of the experience:

> within the twelve months passed or little more, she has rounded a full cycle of calamity and earthquake well nigh destroying Zante, a constitutional crisis, national insolvency or the next thing to it. And now, in the very throes of her economic distress, she is prostrated by a fresh visitation from heaven (an earthquake), which is without parallel in her modern history. It has shaken the solid core of Greece from Isthmus to Thermopylae, as well as the great island of Evoia rocked it up like a ship in an angry sea (Saloutos 1964: 32).

More recent earthquakes have resulted in large-scale population migration. Earthquakes caused major destruction on Kefalonia in 1954 and Kalamata in 1986. Both these disasters were accompanied by significant population shifts. Kalamata, for example, whose population prior to the earthquake was about 52,000, lost 10,000 inhabitants to other areas of Greece and to other countries such as Canada, the United States and Australia (Interview, Committee members for Kalamata Appeal, Melbourne, 26 January 1988). Migration has also been influenced by volcanic activity which has forced the populations of the Lipari Isles of north-east Sicily, Thera and Lesbos in the Aegean and Ithaca in the Ionian Sea (Price 1963: 25), to seek homes elsewhere.

People also migrate in search of adventure, or when they are encouraged by 'chain letters' from earlier emigrants already established in an overseas destination. Greek peasants, lacking adequate information, formal education and material wealth, read letters sent from abroad by friends or relatives, or listened, fascinated, to the stories of Australian prosperity those who returned home had to tell. Stories often told were of gold from the diggings and of unimaginable wealth, even streets paved with gold. Less exaggerated stories told of increased opportunities to acquire wealth, enviable salaries and working conditions and also the openness of the Australian social structure.

Hellenic migration to Australia, especially during the latter half of the twentieth century, has been influenced by both the chain of letters and by the individuals returning home. In the nineteenth century, Lekatsas recounted, for example, on his return to Ithaca in 1870 after 20 years in the goldfields, stories of wealth, wonderful adventures, and success in the Antipodes that, by the 1880s, had resulted in the emigration of large numbers of his relatives and their friends (Kennedy 1976: 45). The chain of letters sent by Greeks from Australia boosted the country's image, making it look like the everlasting 'lucky country'. The effect of twentieth-century letters and stories is very similar. Photographs depicting colourful clothing, TV sets and well-furnished lounge-rooms stimulated people's interest in and desire for migration. They coveted motor bikes and other commodities portrayed in the glossy snapshots. Loved ones who returned to visit their families also gave vivid accounts of comfort and success and rarely, if ever, showed the contrary images which reflected the reality of the frequently exploited migrant workers, who spent their working lives on the factory floor.

Colourful advertising campaigns also disturbed social harmony and manipulated the masses because they made promises to people that were rarely realised. Although it is impossible to measure exactly how effective these advertising campaigns were, it is certain that representatives of host societies had correctly identified and portrayed the dreams and aspirations of the lower socio-economic groups in Greece (Interviews with Grambas and Trahanas, 11 September 1991). As the following interviewees stated in regard to advertising in Greece:

> through successful advertising in Greece, trans-oceanic long distances, especially to Australia, were made to appear short,

and the journey comfortable, exciting and romantic . . .
Travel agents and other authorities such as Government
officials spoke about journeying by passenger ships across the
seas as one of the most unforgettable experiences . . . Life
upon passenger ships were said to be a continuous dream of
a great life that involved great meetings of people of all social
backgrounds . . . The journey itself was made to appear as
a part of an exotic scenery in an adventurous paradise, while
stopovers and related experiences in the sea ports of the East,
were made to sound interesting, safe and, the 'most unforgettable' experience one could imagine, and the Indian Ocean,
was discussed as a mystery journey with the most exciting
and romantic events (Interviewees, Grambas, Trahanas,
11 September 1991).

The Hellenic state, by encouraging emigration as a routine
way of containing its unemployment and underemployment
problems, continued to play the part of Pontius Pilate. It
permitted the mass media to convey the propaganda of private
capital in receiving countries. The owners of passenger ships
and the travel agencies all contributed to the creation of
unrealistic views and myths of the migration experience that
simple peasants accepted unconditionally, just as they had
during the period of Greek migration to America leading up
to World War Two (Vlachos 1968; Saloutos 1964).

International organisations operating in post-Second World
War Greece were also responsible for encouraging migration
by offering advice, seminars and free passages to prospective
migrants. For example, the role played by the Inter-Governmental Committee for European Migration (ICEM) as well
as the various church organisations in selecting, training
and funding individuals to migrate cannot be under-
estimated. Through their operations such organisations,
particularly ICEM or DEME (Διακυβερνητική Επιτροπή
Μεταναστεύσεως εξ Ευρώπης), as it became known in Greece,
played an instrumental role in fostering migration on a national
level, with its representatives visiting rural towns and selecting
potential recruits who were willing to migrate to Australia in
search of work.

Political upheavals were responsible for sudden large-scale
population movements (Saloutos 1964; Price 1963: 116).
Threats to civil and political rights, such as freedom of

131

expression, were at the core of much Hellenic migration abroad. The birth of Turkish and Balkan nationalism during the last quarter of the nineteenth century resulted in religious conflicts between Moslems and Christians, and by 1912, fears of reprisals prompted many thousands of Greeks to migrate before the 'catastrophe' of Asia Minor. As discussed, many others (approximately 1.5 million) migrated as a result of the defeat of the Hellenic Army in 1922 in Smyrna and the Turkish retaliations which followed, or because the Turkish government imposed restrictions on the commercial activities of islanders, thus forcing them to flee. Many of Australia's Greek families from Smyrna and other towns in 'Hellenic Asia Minor' migrated when, in 1947, the Turkish authorities expanded extended military service to include Christians. Other political acts of aggression, such as the so-called 'pogrom' in 1956 against the Hellenic population of Constantinople, forced more than 250,000 Greeks to seek refuge in other countries. Similarly, Ankara's abuse of the Lasagne Treaty of 1923,[2] forced the native inhabitants of the Greek islands of Imbros and Tenedos to flee their homes and seek refuge in other parts of the world. The Turkish invasion of Cyprus in 1974 caused more than 200,000 Hellene-Cypriots to migrate to various countries, including Australia.

However, even in Greece itself, the unstable political situation often had undesirable social consequences and forced many people to migrate, even when they did not have economic reasons to do so. Economic and political factors often overlapped, making the distinction between the two difficult to establish. In fact, according to the social investigator Nicos Petropoulos' report on OECD (1988), when studying Hellenic migration, political migration from Greece can be seen to occur in three distinct periods: firstly, the dictatorship of Ioannis Metaxas in 1936–40; secondly, during the Civil War of 1946–49; and, thirdly, 'the dictatorship of the colonels' under the leadership of George Papadopoulos in 1967–74. The Civil War made life politically intolerable and unsafe both in the *agora* as well as in the private arena. Lack of personal safety was a product of anti-communist campaigns and restrictions on freedom of speech, as well as the use of direct and indirect scare tactics, made many individuals fight or flee to foreign lands, while others who were already abroad often made the ultimate choice not to return home to Greece due to the undesirable political climate. The OECD document states:

> While there are no statistics on the number of Greeks who emigrated as a result of the dictatorships, it is commonly known that large contingents of Greeks in Sweden, Germany, Canada, and the United States were political refugees of the 1967 dictatorship. The Civil War itself was responsible for the departure of some 100,000 Hellenic political refugees (including 25,000 children) who found themselves in the socialist societies. The third type of Hellenic political emigration was the outcome of political transformations in Eastern Europe, Asia Minor, and Africa (revolutions, movements of independence, nationalist movements, etc.) which compelled an indeterminate number of Greek descendants from earlier periods of emigration to take refuge in Western countries (OECD 1988: 2–3).

Migration from Greece, therefore, has been inextricably bound together with political and economic developments. These two factors—combined with small and mountainous land holdings, the waging of continuous wars and the paucity of natural resources—have, along with Hellenic cultural forces, contributed to the development of a domestic political system which inhibited industrialisation and encouraged out-migration.

Internal and external migration were products of political and economic underdevelopment, coupled with the need for agricultural reform and the absence of a middle class powerful enough to enhance industrial expansion. One of the major obstacles to economic development was the lack of capital investment in both agriculture and the manufacturing industries. The main reason for this situation was that capital investment remained concentrated in industries which generated high profits and minimum employment (Filias 1967: 115). This situation made migration an attractive proposition, in spite of the generous capital contributions made by Hellenes of the Diaspora. Neither classic nor neo-classic theories of economic development which encompass the view that migratory inflows and outflows have a balancing effect regarding the economic development of underdeveloped and developed economies (Kindleberger 1958: 436) have solved Greece's underdevelopment problems. In addition, the implementation of such theories has failed to provide sufficient employment to curtail Hellenic migration in over 160 years of modern Hellenic history.

Partly because of the intervention by other European powers and partly because of the political developments within the new Hellenic state, there were both domestic and external limitations upon the political and economic development of the new state. The essence of migration can be attributed to the immigrants' personal motives or choices but more so to action taken by the state. In this context, it makes sense to classify Hellenic migration by its causal effects such as economics and politics which matter more in understanding out-migration. However, despite the contributions by the neo-classic schools to explain migration, by reducing the massive migration exodus to the individual's personal choice this model fails to provide a complete picture and understanding of the causes behind out-migration. Similarly, Marxist explanations ignore other alternative explanations of migration. Thus it has been argued that an understanding of the complexity and strength of the forces behind migration is central to classifying Hellenic migration. It is equally important to understand that today's division of the world into mutually exclusive territorial authorities is an added factor with which the nation state has had to contend, one that crucially influences the trends and patterns of migration currents between other nation states within a global economy.

It is within this division of the world that out-migration from Greece has been justified—by the hope that remittances will be sent back home, both to compensate for the loss of human labour and to provide the starving economy with much-needed capital. Traditionally, it is through remittances that Greece has both resolved unemployment and achieved national development by exporting real human resources. In theoretical terms, remittances have meant that Hellenic migration in the context of classic and neo-classic economic theories has been considered as a 'blessing' by conservatives or right-wing government administrations, and a 'curse' by restrictionists or those sections associated with the centre and left of the political spectrum. Supporters of conventional right-wing views have held out the hope that, in the long term, migration would contribute to the revitalisation of economic development and capital investment. In view of increasing unemployment and underemployment and the obvious need of developing nations like Greece for capital investment and foreign exchange, the conservative forces have accepted an easy and short-sighted solution to solving the problem—migration. Further, it has been claimed that, even with population growth at a high rate, large-scale migration may produce real income for the remaining population if the rate of remittances sent back to the home country is considerable (Kindleberger 1958: 434–8). At the same time, it was hoped that the effects of migration would improve the long-term trade of the sending country and that re-migration would contribute to its development through skills returnees learnt while abroad. This type of exchange was taken for granted both in the earlier and more recent periods of migration, even though nationalistic preconceptions are regarded as outdated in light of the new entities—for example, a United Europe—that have become a reality since the 1960s (Vgenoupolos 1985: 40).

As well as the economic and social developments of the modern nation state being responsible for shaping the patterns and trends of Hellenic migration currents, it is the complexity of the Hellenic past that reinforces the present. There are 3,000 years of culture and philosophy of life that, having left their mark upon this nation, continue to influence the modern Hellenic national character. The glory of antiquity and the many struggles for freedom by the new state, together with the persistent efforts of Greek migrants for socio-economic achievement and social mobility, are obvious forces behind migration to 'remote lands' such as Australia, as will be shown in subsequent chapters.

Australia's immigration policy and Hellenic migration

This chapter focuses on the arrival of Greek migrants to Australia in the context of Australia's immigrant history and formal attitudes towards Hellenic settlement during the twentieth century. Specifically, an outline of Australia's immigration policy is provided in the context of the nation's socio-historical development. Any investigation along these lines must include a consideration of the changing criteria for immigration policies and, from the perspective of this present study, how these policies have affected southern Europeans, particularly Greeks.

As discussed in Chapter 5, the discovery of gold brought an influx of immigrants to Australia, mainly from Great Britain and New Zealand, but also from America, Germany, Poland, Scandinavia and Hungary. According to Borrie: 'Three-quarters of the increase of the population in the decade was due to net migration' (Australian Immigration and Population Council 1976: 23). The discovery of gold did not, however, bring significant numbers of Greeks to Australia, even during the subsequent decades of the goldrush period. The few Greeks and other southern Europeans who arrived at that time were mainly seafarers, adventurers or 'scouts' (Gilchrist 1985). During the goldrush of the 1850s, white Australian society became increasingly diversified as a result of the accumulation of wealth by various individuals. For the first time in the country's history cities boomed as trade centres, and an economically powerful middle class began to challenge the social and political supremacy of the large landowners. This diversification led to the formation of discrete socio-economic groups which, in turn, fostered the attitude of an independent spirit intent on economic success. At the same time, immigrants from Britain and Ireland succeeded in blending into this new society through inter-marriage, thus forming the new ethnic identity that, by the late 1860s, was 'ready to claim the continent as its heritage' (Borrie 1954).

It can be argued that from the outset Australia's immigration policy traditionally gave preference to the selection of certain national groups over others. One way in which this preference was clearly manifested was the provision of fully-paid passage assistance schemes to Australia. This formal preferential treatment was subsequently reflected in Australian attitudes towards and treatment of its immigrant groups. Upon Federation in 1901, when immigration and its associated policies became a Commonwealth responsibility, preferential treatment was reflected in the enactment of the *Immigration Act* and what became known as the 'White Australia Policy'. The implementation of the White Australia Policy, the Dictation Test and the subsequent suspicion of southern European migrants, were all connected with the host society's need to insist on immigrant adaptation to Australian living standards. The separate states continued to provide their own assistance schemes to migrants, a course in line with the provisions of the Act, until 1920, when immigration became the sole responsibility of the Federal government (Borrie 1954: 9, 16).

Assisted immigration could be said to have been a key feature of Australia's settlement history, beginning in 1788 with the landing of the first reluctant contingent and ending in 1981 (Kern 1966: 31; Australian Immigration and Population Council 1976: 23–9). Even before transportation to the mainland ceased, in the 1830s, much of the labour supply to the colonies had been in the form of assisted migration. Between 1810 and 1820, 42,000 assisted immigrants arrived, compared with only 10,000 non-assisted immigrants. Although Tasmania (Van Diemen's Land) remained the exception, with transportation continuing until 1850, there was, never the less, 'a rapid increase in free migration after 1830' (Kern 1966: 14; Australian Immigration and Population Council 1976: 23–9). While non-convict and non-British immigration was encouraged from 1810 through to the late 1820s, the number of southern European immigrants, including Greeks, remained negligible until the late 1830s. The population grew spasmodically until the 1850s; initially, it comprised convicts and military personnel, then it was augmented by free settlers. For example, in 1828, convicts constituted 40 per cent of the population of New South Wales. Some 601,000 immigrants arrived between 1850 and 1860, many of whom were assisted, and the total non-Aboriginal population grew to 1,145,000 (Borrie 1954: 14; Australian Population and Immigration Council 1976: 23).

It is the kind of assisted migration, that is, the payment of both passage and accommodation costs, which historically distinguishes Britons and northern Europeans from the immigrant waves of southern Europeans. The nature of this assisted migration gradually changed from coercive to non-coercive. Hellenic migration to Australia, therefore, can neither be sufficiently understood nor defined outside the context of Australia's formal attitudes towards both British and southern European migration, from early colonisation to the present day.

According to Borrie, the formation of national unity and pride, that emerged towards the end of the nineteenth century and was expressed in strong Australian egalitarian feelings, eventually spread the seeds of democracy within the colonies. However, despite this democratic dimension, Australia's social evolution remained, by and large, restricted in that it took place within the 'bounds' of the British Empire (and later the British Commonwealth of Nations), and owed its allegiance to a common crown, which was never true of the European and American experience in the nineteenth century. For example, the French Revolution placed its emphasis on liberty, equality and fraternity, while the American War of Independence expelled the British and established a democratic Republic. Australia's physical isolation from the ferment of such social and political ideas served to sustain the British connection until well after 1945 (Borrie 1954: 13).

Australia's Immigration Policy and subsequent internal social, economic and political developments have been deeply rooted in these experiences from the nineteenth century. In particular, during the initial period of British colonisation, the perception of Australia held by some employers was that of a plantation settlement that drew cheap coloured labour from the Pacific and, to a lesser extent, from Asia. The introduction of cheap labour brought Kanakas to work in the cane fields, Indians as pastoral workers, Afghans as camel drivers and Chinese to the goldfields. This period, namely the second half of the nineteenth century, was one of sustained migration, which varied in response to socio-economic changes. Borrie notes that the impact of cheap labour upon Australian society was significant, in that it changed the perceptions of political and economic democracy:

[The effect of cheap labour was to strengthen] the egalitarian tendencies of Australian democracy which demanded a fair cut of the national product for the wage-earner and the small property-owner. The sharpness in the antagonism between employers and employees which was characteristic of Australia in the latter half of the nineteenth century was in part the product of the very simplicity of the social structure. It was a case of every man thinking himself to be as good as another, if not, as once was said, twice as good as another (Borrie 1954: 15–16).

A major consequence of these perceptions was that sentiment about constraining immigration began to strengthen. The Chinese were the first ethnic group to experience major constraints. As early as 1854, public opinion forced the Victorian colonial government (constituted three years earlier) to pass the *Chinese Restriction Act*, thus imposing limits on the entry of Chinese to the colony. By 1887, all the other colonies had followed Victoria's example (Australian Population and Immigration Council 1976: 5, 23). By the 1880s, popular and formal attitudes towards Chinese immigration, coupled with opposition to the Kanaka labour force, led to the development of a racist ideology and the operation of a White Australia Policy within the colonies (Borrie 1954; Jupp 1991).

The antagonism towards the Chinese was due to both racial and economic causes. The Chinese were considered culturally incompatible with Europeans in terms of their obvious difference in appearance, their social organisations and their cultural activities. The white Australian population was fearful that the Chinese were different in so many ways that

139

they would never fit in with the rest of society. There is evidence that Queenslanders, in particular, feared that the Chinese, through their diligence and hard work, could soon gain significant economic power. Also, as the numbers of Chinese immigrants increased, the fear emerged that they might take over vast unsettled areas of the colony, and so 'swamp the white population' (Australian Population and Immigration Council 1976: 5, 23). Legislation restricting the Chinese followed, and:

> [as] Chinese numbers also began to increase in north Queensland, there were riots on the remote Palmer goldfields in 1877. The immediate response was the passage of Queensland legislation restricting Chinese access to those goldfield areas which had already been worked over by Europeans (Jupp 1991: 45).

Initially, the government's goal was restriction and not prohibition of the Chinese, but once the former was established the latter was inevitable. This process was illustrated by the reaction to attempts in the 1880s to introduce Indian labourers as pastoral workers. Again, the fear was that the Indians would abandon their designated occupations and drift into competition with European labour, eventually dragging down wage levels and living standards for all workers. Both liberal and trade union opinion opposed the drift for the same economic reasons (Jupp 1991: 45).

Host society attitudes towards non-Britons were connected to measurements of living standards—as these were interpreted by organised union labour and by white Australian employees generally. Popular and organised labour attitudes were, therefore, a key determinant in shaping Australia's immigration policy both prior to and after Federation. As Borrie observed:

> This was undoubtedly the hard core of labour policy, but how far this concept of protection of economic standards was intermingled with suspicion on racial, social or other grounds was seldom, as far as white migration was concerned, put to a test; for assisted and free migration from Britain and Ireland continued to flow in quantities sufficient to meet the country's economic requirements (Borrie 1954: 16).

Table 6.1   Hellenic migration to Australia 1860–1900

Year	Number of people
1860	400
1880	600
1900	1000

Source: (Price 1963: 3, 4, 5; Gilchrist 1985: 13)

According to the Australian Population and Immigration Council (1976), the Census in the year of Federation (1901: 23–4) showed the non-Aboriginal population to be 3,773,801, of which more than 77 per cent had been born in Australia and 18 per cent in the United Kingdom. For the period 1851–1900, assisted migrants totalled approximately 575,000, or about one-third of the total arrivals, with unassisted immigration between 1861–1900 adding another 766,000 (Borrie 1954: 9).[1] There had also been net settler losses during the economic depression of 1892–99. Up to this point southern Europeans, including Greeks, were not included in the colony's assistance schemes—as argued in Chapter 5—and, as shown in Table 6.1, the number of Greeks in Australia remained rather small until Federation.

Following the 'Immigration Restrictions against Asiatics' after 1888 and the Premiers' Conference of 1896, each colony enacted a 'Restriction Bill' applicable to all races. By these activities, the colonies had already decided the future form of the White Australia Policy that was to be implemented by the Commonwealth in 1901.

Because of the racial implications of the White Australia Policy, the British Imperial authorities suggested an alternative package, which included the so-called 'Dictation Test' and which applied to all non-British individuals. This legislation, which had a precedent in the immigration laws of Natal (Borrie 1954: 6), prohibited the entry into Australia of any person who, when asked to do so, failed to write out on dictation a passage of not less than 50 words in any European language. As Jupp stated:

The language [on which the dictation test was based], did not need to be one understood by the immigrant. The object

141

of the test was entirely to facilitate exclusion (mainly racial), rather than to ascertain whether immigrants were literate. A 1905 concession allowed testing in non-European languages but this was never implemented. The test could be applied to Europeans if there were reasons for excluding them (Jupp 1991: 48).

The legislation remained the keystone of the restrictive aspect of Australia's Immigration Policy until it was abolished in 1958 and there were no exceptions to this rule, other than in the case of Japan. Concessions were granted to Japanese immigrants in response to their government's criticism of the selective bias imposed by 1901 legislation. The test was applied at the Immigration officers' discretion.

The conception of Australia as an outpost of western civilisation in Asia was reinforced by the assistance schemes run by the different colonies—which had brought to Australia 40 per cent of the 1.3 million immigrants from the British Isles who arrived between 1860 and 1919, at which time medical examination of new immigrants was transferred to the Commonwealth (Appleyard 1971: 1). During the first 40 years of this century, there were two periods when assistance was again offered to prospective settlers (the scheme having previously been largely abandoned because of the country's economic instability between the 1890s and 1906). Firstly, between 1905 and 1914, population gain from net immigration was 282,000, of whom 162,000 settlers received assistance. This assistance consisted of free or part-paid passage and free land offered to British immigrants (Sherington 1980: 113; Australian Population and Immigration Council 1976: 22–9). Secondly, the Empire Settlement Scheme operated between 1921 and 1930 with the aim of distributing the white British population throughout the Empire's colonies through migration. Australia was one of this scheme's main participants, bringing a further 215,000 assisted immigrants into the country—out of a total net immigration of 313,000 (Australian Population and Immigration Council 1976). Both schemes were based on the White Australia Policy which continued to serve as an agreement reflecting selection priorities of potential groups who wished to migrate to Australia.

Up to 1945, the Australian states and, later, the Federal

government, distinguished between northern and southern Europeans, providing assistance only to Scandinavians, Dutch and Germans, for example, as alternatives to Anglo-Celts. The Assistance Scheme did not extend to southern Europeans, because northern Europeans were regarded as more likely to assimilate within the Australian social, cultural and labour market structures than southern Europeans (Borrie 1954). Of the main southern European groups, the 15,000 ethnic Greeks and 40,000 Italians estimated to have arrived in Australia by the outbreak of World War Two, had, in the main, paid for their own passages and accommodation (Price 1993a, 1993b; Tsounis 1989b: 3; Vondra 1977). They achieved this largely on the backs of earlier immigrants, with Hellenic migration, in particular, largely shaped by the personalities of those pioneering migrants, as well as on family and local ties (Price 1963: 133; Kern 1966: 61–2). According to Price, often the first-comers not only persuaded others to emigrate but also paid their travel and accommodation costs and, in addition, found or offered them employment. Alternatively, potential emigrants sold their land or borrowed to raise the money. But, in either case, the Greeks, like the Italians and other southern Euuropean migrants, did not benefit from government assistance. This, then, was the main pattern of southern European migration up to 1945, with more than 80 per cent of southern Europeans estimated to have entered Australia in this way (Price 1963: 62, 134, 248). This system of chain-sponsoring relatives distinguishes the mainstream of southern European immigration from those of Britons and northern Europeans. Initially, apart from sailors, the only ones who could afford their ticket were:

> businessmen, migrants who had once gone to America and saved enough, soldiers receiving accumulated pay on discharge from the army after WWII, and peasants able and willing to sell enough land to cover their expenses (Price 1963: 98).

Again, only 7 per cent of southern Europeans during this period arrived independently of associational migration and the 'chain of ties in this period' (Price 1963: 109).

143

Occasionally, Australian employers brought out a few unskilled or skilled labourers from southern Europe, but this practice did not become common before 1945 (Borrie 1954: 46–7).[2] Unlike most migrants, whose employment depended entirely on whatever jobs British-Australians were willing to offer them, the Greeks created their own paths to employment and prosperity. This became increasingly evident between 1890 and 1920, when there was an expansion of Hellenic ownership in the restaurant, fruit-growing and fishing trades (Price 1963).

Yet, while Greek-Australians were returning to Greece to fight in the wars, many more arrived between 1910 and 1920, with the total reaching around 6,000 persons by 1921. According to Borrie: 'Up to three-quarters of the arrivals must have come to settle in Australia, because the 1921 census shows 3,650 Greeks born in Australia' (Borrie 1954: 45). However, in the absence of figures giving departures by nationality or birthplace, the pattern of return migration to Greece is unclear. From different studies (Price 1963; Tsounis 1971a), it appears that Hellenic immigration increased rapidly after 1920, although migration from Australia's previously traditional Hellenic sources, the islands of Ithaca, Kastelorizo and Kythera, declined even when immigration restrictions were lifted in 1920. There was an increase in intake in 1923 but re-imposition of the restrictions in 1924 led to a corresponding decrease in the quota for southern Europeans in that year (Price 1963; Kennedy, 1976: 5).

In 1925, the *Immigration (Amendment) Act* was put into practice, imposing further restrictions on southern Europeans who wished to enter Australia. This legislation was based on Canadian law, but was first replicated by the United States Immigration Authorities in 1924. The American restrictions were successful in reducing southern European and, especially, Italian intake to the United States. The Australian restrictions that followed suit, however, produced a reduction in the number of southern European immigrants—with the exception of Italians. The Italian immigration almost doubled from 3,200 to 6,000 persons, while Greeks numbered only 700 and, like Yugoslavia, Malta and Albania did not fill their quota of 1,200 individuals per year between 1925–27, with southern European migrants coming from only a few Hellenic and Italian localities. Migration for this period reached its peak in 1925 (Price 1963: 90–2).

In the light of cultural discrimination, as well as organised labour's economic discrimination against non-British migrants, the Federal government was forced to prohibit entry to any alien who did not possess a written guarantee regarding his or her employment prospects and accommodation support from compatriots following settlement. Once again, guarantees of economic independence during the resettlement period were required. The imposition of restrictions on southern European immigration was partly based on estimates of unemployment among Italians, Greeks, Maltese and others in Australia. This requirement created a hurdle for prospective migrants similar to the 1901 *Immigration Act*'s discriminatory Dictation Test. Consuls in Europe were also requested to discourage persons with inadequate English from migrating to Australia, by refusing to issue them with passports or visas (Price 1963: 88–91; Borrie 1954: 46).

The guarantees of economic independence, high percentage of unemployment in Australia at the time and the distance and expense of travelling to Australia combined to place the burden of migration costs solely onto the immigrants' shoulders, or the shoulders of their relatives already settled in Australia. Greek-Australians were wary of accepting this role of providing support to their relatives who wished to join them abroad.

Unlike the preferred British migrants who were granted various privileges including favourable conditions for bank loans and the best plots of land, southern Europeans, even those who were British subjects, received no assistance at all. As Peter Alexander, a Greek migrant from the British Protectorate of Cyprus, who arrived in 1923, recalls:

> You fought battles on your own. I couldn't afford to pay any other fare because I didn't have any money. I went to a Greek family staying in the city; I had only one address of a Greek club which was run by a Greek Cypriot. After a week or ten days I got a job on a farm that was run by a Greek, not far from the city (Interview with Alexander 1987).

Another elderly participant, John Black (Mavrokefalos), who came to Australia from the island of Ithaca, described the economic situation awaiting him on his arrival:

145

We learned that there was no chance for us to get free land, even though it was promulgated overseas that the government here in Australia was helping adults, at least males, by 1926. That is, those who wanted to go onto the land, with both land and with loans to cultivate it, until it became ready to produce, and so start the loan repayment. That was done only for the returned servicemen of WWI. I came in 1926 with an uncle of mine who was 50 years old; he went back in three months. We learned that there was no chance for us to get free land or anything, so I stayed in Sydney for two years. My first job in Sydney was in a cafe (Interview with Black 1987).

Archival material for the period shows that the situation of newly-arrived Greek immigrants had been a matter for serious concern to the Greek Consul General in Sydney. According to the Athens-based newspaper *Ithaki* (1 May 1928), the Consul reported to the Ministry of Foreign Affairs in 1928—providing a graphic account of newly-arrived Greek immigrants' socio-economic status in the context of the socio-economic conditions of the host society. The newspaper commentary claimed that the Consul's report:

paints the condition of Greek immigrants there [in Sydney] with gloomy colours, providing relevant information for the first nine months of the year ending in 1927 when 1,202 Greeks migrated as in contrast to 248 for first nine months of 1926 (*Ithaki*, 1 May 1928).

As indicated in Table 6.2, migration from Greece to Australia shows a steady decline during the second half of the 1920s, with newly-arrived Greek and Yugoslav adult males totalling only one-third of the reduced quota in 1929–30.

According to Price (1963), although it is not evident in Table 6.2, in reality departures exceeded arrivals when the number of settlers returning to Australia after visiting their home country along with dependent children (and other non-quota persons) from Europe are added. During this period arrivals of both Yugoslavs and Greeks reached only about two-thirds of their quotas. According to Price: 'Quite clearly factors other than reduced quotas were involved' (Price 1963: 92–6) The Labor government continued to impose restrictions

Table 6.2   Southern European migration 1929–1930

Nationality	Males	Arrivals / Departures Females	A/D*	Arrivals	Departures
Italians	2,804	3,856	72.7	1,367	432
Yugoslavs	504	947	53.2	260	98
Greeks	497	873	56.9	215	118
Maltese	201	457	44.0	68	20
Spanish	99	105	94.3	47	28

Source: (Price 1963: 93) * Arrivals as proportion of departures.

and, in 1928 and 1929, it halved the quotas for southern Europeans in response to increases in the unemployment rate and, in 1930, it completely prohibited the entry of southern Europeans except close relatives of existing settlers who had considerable financial resources (Appleyard 1978: 11; Price 1963: 91). As Price has indicated, of the 40 Greek islands from which migrants had come to Australia, 'only thirteen became major districts of origin for further migration' (Price 1963: 96). The other 27 who also had representatives in Australia by 1924 and could have increased their numbers under the sponsorship system, did not take advantage of their already settled compatriots in Australia. The islands of Dodecannesos, Kasos, Kythera, Ithaca, Kastelorizo and Lesbos had hundreds of representatives in Australia, but due to the economic situation reduced their rate of immigration between 1924 and 1932 (Price 1963: 96).

The Lyons United Australia Party government, which gained power in 1932, adopted similarly restrictive policies towards southern European immigration in the light of Australia's slow economic recovery. These changes affected even British immigration, though to a much lesser extent, as the government ceased to offer assisted passages until 1938 when the Empire Settlement Scheme was renewed with migration from Britain on a passage-loan basis. A year later, however, immigration to Australia was halted by the events of World War Two.

Meanwhile, Australia's immigration policies towards southern Europeans remained highly discriminatory. In 1934, the Lyons government required independent migrants to provide

147

Table 6.3   Net immigration by nationality 1921–1940

| Year | Northern Europeans | | | Southern Europeans | | |
	German	Scandinavian	Italian	Greek	Yugoslav	Total Net
1921–5	194	1,213	13,582	3,391	412	179,668
1926–30	1,184	507	10,446	1,774	2,116	124,650
1931–5	152	−128	1,523	−194	−39	−10,886
1936–40	7,302	108	7,650	3,478	1,600	43,128

Source: (Borrie 1954: 39)

a financial guarantee of £500. As socio-economic conditions improved, this sum was reduced, in 1936, to £50 and only applied either to dependent migrants or to those intending to enter occupations in which there were vacancies (Sherington 1980: 92). These new measures were aimed at keeping the number of new adult arrivals at a manageable level. In practice, 900 Greeks, 3,000 Italians, 400 Yugoslavs, 100 Albanians and 100 Maltese arrived between 1937 and 1939, which constituted a considerable increase in southern European immigration, in spite of the fact that, during the economic crisis (1929–35), almost 35 per cent of all Greeks who had come to Australia left for unknown destinations (Price 1963: 90–6).

Up to 1936, four-fifths of new settlers were British, while between 1936 and 1940 other European immigration rose to two-thirds of the total net increase (Borrie 1954: 37). During this time, European immigration to Australia went through its first major change in composition. Although there was no evidence to suggest a change in formal attitudes or race and ethnic relations, none the less, for the first time in Australia's immigration history, there was an impressive shift in migrant intake from northern towards southern Europeans.

The trend was in favour of southern Europeans until 1940, in spite of both economic and social trends in Australia in the opposite direction. Between 1930 and 1940 Greeks were Australia's second-largest non-British ethnic population, after Italians (Price 1963, 1993: 40; Borrie 1954; Vondra 1979: 24). However, despite this, the demographic composition of Greeks did not change very significantly and, as in the nineteenth century, was one of excess of single males, with only few females venturing to travel to Australia. Greek-born males outnumbered Greek-born females almost four to one, and Italians three to one: 'two-thirds of southern Europeans before 1940 were male' (Price 1963: 113–14). Over time, there was only a moderate change in terms of the sex ratio for Greek immigrants—in 1921 there were 16 Greek females to every 100 males, by 1947 this ratio had increased to 35:100 (Price 1963: 35). Inter-marriage with British-Australians was not as frequent for southern Europeans as for Scandinavians, who seemed to inter-marry and assimilate into the broader Australian society earlier, perhaps because like the early Greek 'scouts' who inter-married successfully with local women, they were few in number and did not pose a threat to the status quo. Price (1963) and Tsounis (1971a) have suggested that most Greeks appear to have left their families in Greece, with the intention of returning when they had saved enough money. Along with their families waiting for their return, they were also influenced by the myths and legends of the Hellenic culture linked with stories of returning home, and the concept of the *agora* of their home country, where they could take part in the stories told and share their own experiences abroad to act as pull factors on those who stayed at home. These factors combined to make Greek migrants behave differently from other European settlers. Their cultural make-up, and the lack of inter-marriage with local women operated as discouraging factors towards further Hellenic immigration. However, as the sex ratio started to become more balanced, immigrant settlement also began to mature, with changes in immigrants' employment orientation. As Price comments: 'Jobs for easy earning give way to jobs offering greater security following permanent immigration' (Price 1963: 113–14).

Until 1945, besides the *Immigration (Amendment) Act* of 1925 and some short-term restrictions imposed by the authorities, there were other serious obstacles to the full participation of southern Europeans in the cultural, economic and social life of the host country, although host society attitudes demanded that immigrants should assimilate. The degree of assimilation achieved by migrants often became a cause of discrimination against their national origins and such discrimination came from both the authorities and popular attitudes.

The events of World War Two led to a radical change in migration policy, when Japan's threatened invasion revealed

Australia's vulnerability to outside intruders and led Australian politicians to advocate an increase in population—through immigration—as a means of defending the country. Prime Minister Curtin had been instrumental in bringing about a change in policy but, by the end of the war, the main advocate had become Arthur Calwell, the Minister for Immigration. To the national security rationale, Calwell added that an increase in immigration would stimulate economic development, especially in view of Australia's low birth rate since the turn of the century. Although he estimated an intake of 2 per cent of the total population to be the optimal migration figure—for a while this became a yardstick for future planning by both government and private enterprise—he did not have a clear policy or even a perception as to what was to occur in terms of changes in immigration policy in later years. The natural increase in immigration had proven to be only half this figure, having averaged 1 per cent over the previous five years (70,000 in 1945 when the population was 7 million) (Australian Population and Immigration Council 1976: 24; Hugo 1986; Castles & Miller 1993).

Up to 1977, rapid population expansion took place through preferential immigration, with priority given to migrants from the United Kingdom. Calwell had responded to the demands of sectional interests—the unions, employers and public opinion—by paving the way for increased migration with selective immigration. In outlining this preference, he expressed the hope 'that for every foreign migrant, there will be ten people from the United Kingdom' (Calwell 1972: 35), a hope which found concrete expression in the two Assistance Agreements entered into between Australia and Britain in 1946 and 1947, which provided for free and assisted passages for Britons who wished to immigrate to Australia.

According to Calwell (1972), by 1947 there were over 400,000 Britons anxious to settle in Australia. However, despite his desire to commence migration *en masse* and his success in convincing the British that his priorities were more vital than theirs, Britain was unable to provide the necessary shipping and 'the program was in danger of collapse'. Under these conditions, Calwell turned to non-British areas—the government's selection priority being northern European countries—and, in 1947, he officially announced a preference for displaced persons to fill labour shortages and to help to rebuild Australia's industry after the war. Applicants were selected on the basis of age and skills. After contacting the International Refugee Organisation (IRO), Australia agreed to take 12,000 Baltic immigrants and, subsequently, 170,000 (out of 1 million refugees or displaced persons) were settled in Australia between 1947–54, with the IRO providing transport (Sherington 1980: 133). Britain's inability to provide the numbers and types of immigrants required forced Australia to sign further agreements with the Netherlands and Italy (1951), Malta (1952) and West Germany (1952). Although the British migration program continued to grow, non-British immigration had come to stay, thus breaking away from the official and customary attitude towards southern Europeans: namely, that they simply 'came to make money and go home'. Thus, in August 1952, the acting Minister for Immigration announced not only that the annual immigration intake would be halved, but also that only half the quota would be British. Not only would the wives and children of southern Europeans already in Australia now be admitted, but schemes to assist non-British migration would replace the Displaced Persons Scheme (Australian Population and Immigration Council 1976; Sherington 1980). This decision formalised the acceptance—for the first time—of non-British Europeans as assisted migrants and is regarded as a milestone in Australia's immigration history (Appleyard 1971).

This change in Australia's policy was reflected in her membership, after 1951, of the Inter-Governmental Committee for European Migration (ICEM), which was established to provide transport and financial assistance to potential immigrants from non-British countries (see page 131). Through ICEM, Australia entered into informal tripartite agreements with Austria and Greece (1952), Spain (1958), Belgium (1961) and other European countries (Australian Population and Immigration Council 1976: 26). All immigrants, including the displaced persons of 1947 to 1953, were selected on the basis of age, occupation, education, health and employment or business prospects.

The 1952 Agreement with Greece was based on the Australian government providing assistance to Greek immigrants on the basis of a two-year contract. For its part, the

Hellenic government refused to share the costs of assisted-migration schemes involving ICEM which, as an organisation, was responsible for the selection and dispatch of many thousands of Greek migrants to Australia. The Greek–Australian agreement of 1952 granted assisted passages to heads of houses and single males who, in many cases, were individuals selected by the ICEM travelling teams of recruiters. Appleyard claims that this provided a rare opportunity, for working-class Greeks in particular, to emigrate to Australia without either a personal sponsor or the immediate cash for the fare. Through an empirical study of Greek migrants, he presents a positive picture in relation to the role and process of migration through IECM (Appleyard 1971: 12–20).

According to two interviewees, Trahanas and Grambas, for some migrants the scheme was more or less a modern form of slave labour, designed to fill the factories of the industrially expanding countries:

> [it] was a migration which had clear intentions on behalf of the industrially developing countries and that was to drive, as it did, people who needed work from the rural areas and villages of Greece to the middle of nowhere, across the oceans of the world, simply to exploit their labour for the sake of profit. It did this by converting them from agricultural workers into industrial robots overnight with no consideration of the risks of those workers' lives, and the impact on their families for the sake of international capital controlled by the elite class of the world (Interviews with Trahanas and Grambas 1991).

Grambas, who, like Trahanas, migrated to Australia after the Second World War, stressed that this migration was unprecedented in the history of Hellenism, in that:

> it was ironic to think that instead of moving the factories to Greece, that is, to the country where the workers were, the international elite, the international capital, through the successful propaganda machine of ICEM for migrant recruitment, entangled governments and people in . . . the biggest deception in the history of Hellenism, by removing indigenous people away from their social and cultural roots, away from their homes, away from their families, away from the social

and physical environments in which they had lived for
thousands of years and knew how to cope with their sur-
roundings and [how] to stimulate their lives, find happiness;
that is, they knew how best to organise themselves and get
on with their lives. Instead, with this migration, they were
transferred to the most remote of all countries in the world,
to Australia, where capital and human investment were taking
place at the time. It is also ironic that this uprooting of the
Hellenes and also of other people from their homes, contemporary economists, especially, *the neo-classical economic
rationale define not as forced but voluntary migration* (Interview
with Grambas 1991, author's emphasis).

According to Grambas ICEM or DEME represented Australian government interests in its attempts to select the best
migrants. It often propagated and manipulated public opinion
in Greece in order to achieve its objectives by recruiting as
many young Greek immigrants as possible. He also asserted
that ICEM was one of the Australian authorities' most intel-
ligent schemes for the recruitment of young Greek workers.
Its role was to select the best and the fittest Hellenic labouring
hands for the newly-developing Australian manufacturing
industry of the 1950s and 1960s.

These immigrants were mainly young females and males,
between 17 and 35 years of age, who were not given sufficient
information to help them develop a mature decision about
migration and life abroad. The stories told by sailors and the
few returned migrants about their adventures or the chain of
letters sent from abroad usually provided accounts mixed with
the legends and myths drawn from their traditional culture
and related to immigrants' successful lives in unknown lands.
In reality, potential migrants from Greece had little, if any,
specific information about the world outside other than the
images created by the stories told in the *agora*. The stories of
the *agora*, combined with a thirst for adventure and their youth
and inexperience, excited young Hellenes about life outside
the boundaries of their own *agora*.

According to various participants, one of the worst aspects
of ICEM's role as an organisation of migrant recruitment was
the function performed by its appointed Hellenic agents who
were employed to assist in the recruitment of Greek migrants.
Some of these individuals were interpreters, with 'inside'

153

knowledge of Hellenic culture. These staff were not used for interpreting purposes alone, but as instruments for propaganda—according to the instructions of Australian officials. For example, in telling young Greeks about the great occupational and financial opportunities available in Australia, interpreters contributed to the propaganda stories and helped ICEM to achieve its objectives. During the campaign to recruit potential migrants, ICEM showed various films and displayed colourful portraits and photographs, presenting Australia's glamorous geographical wonders which were shown extensively throughout the nation in order to appeal to the youth by presenting images of the endless beauties of Australia. In doing this, Australian officials in Greece never told potential migrants what really awaited them after their arrival in Australia, such as the real picture of the migrant reception camps like Bonegilla and Tatura, Greta or the kinds of jobs they were going to be assigned to, as labourers in factories and on construction sites. The Australian representatives did not show the prospective migrants what a factory looked like, or explain what it meant to work in a factory, if you had not worked in one before. As Grambas, and also Trahanas (Interviews 1991), described:

> by 1954, ICEM officials were going from town to town searching for the healthiest, the strongest, and those who it was thought, were determined to work (not that anyone suspected what factory labour was, as it became known later). They were checking everything, our social activities, and whether we were on the right or left of the political spectrum. In selecting potential immigrants, they were doing so as if people were horses and not humans . . . they checked our legs, feet, spine, eyes, ears, head, arms, hands, and so on, to see if we were one hundred per cent healthy, fit and muscular. When examining people's health status, they checked our teeth, and occasionally suggested that we should take one or two teeth out, *so they will not have to bother about it if we came to Australia* . . . Those who had the slightest health problem were rejected . . . ! Unfortunately, all this happened in a period in which Greece itself was experiencing an economic stagnation and was searching for a new future following the end of World War II and the Hellenic Civil War. As a result, our *Ethniko Kentro* [National Centre],

through its silence, contributed to the evacuation of the countryside and the migration of some of our better talented and most productive youth (Interviews with Grambas and Trahanas 1991).

During the period 1946–52, before the formalisation of the large-scale assistance scheme, only 8,962 permanent settlers—the excess of arrivals (10,325) over departures—came from Greece. Most of the Greek immigrants during the earlier postwar years were Greek-Egyptians and Greek-Cypriots, whose numbers had risen to 5,988 and 4,670 respectively between 1946 and 1954. The bitter civil war in mainland Greece at first limited departures from there (Tsounis 1975: 24–6). Many of these earlier arrivals were family members of the 15,000 Greeks who had come to Australia before World War Two, that is, before or after the Great Depression. Some families had been waiting for a long time. As one Greek woman, who arrived in 1951, stated:

My father came to Australia in 1927, when he waś eighteen years old. He worked for a few years and returned to Greece in 1937. My mother and young brother came to Australia in 1951. My father sent us the money (quoted in Sherington 1980: 142).

During the first four years of large-scale migration between 1947–51, 310,000 assisted migrants out of a total of approximately 500,000—of whom almost 40 per cent were British—arrived in Australia. Besides the displaced persons from Europe (170,000), there were 120,000 British, 10,000 Maltese and 10,000 others (including many Dutch from Indonesia). In the same period, there were 160,000 unassisted immigrants, including 70,000 British, 30,000 Italians, 15,000 Jewish and other refugees, 10,000 Greeks and Cypriots and 10,000 Dutch (Australian Population and Immigration Council 1976: 25). This trend, whereby non-British arrivals exceeded British arrivals, continued until 1965. This means that post-World War Two immigration never met its planners' targets: net immigration fluctuated above and below the projected 1 per cent annual growth. Government priorities had to change, due to the nature of immigration sources—refugee status,

Table 6.4   Assisted and unassisted Greek immigrants, 1945–82

Year	Assisted	Unassisted	Total
1945–48	1	2,199	2,200
1948–49	6	1,485	1,491
1949–50	25	1,696	1,721
1950–51	3	2,224	2,227
1951–52	8	2,671	2,679
1952–53	494	1,485	1,971
1953–54	3,368	1,993	5,361
1954–55	9,593	3,292	12,885
1955–56	3,972	7,226	11,198
1956–57	3,060	6,649	9,709
1957–58	1,911	4,634	6,545
1958–59	2,074	3,362	5,436
1959–60	2,184	4,466	6,650
1960–61	2,085	5,921	8,006
1961–62	2,763	9,458	12,221
1962–63	3,052	9,726	11,778
1963–64	2,646	13,417	16,063
1964–65	3,518	14,378	17,896
1965–66	2,723	13,306	16,029
1966–67	3,031	7,482	10,513
1967–68	4,491	5,210	9,701
1968–69	6,397	6,030	12,427
1969–70	6,490	5,357	11,847
1970–71	6,406	4,551	10,957
1971–72	3,148	3,637	6,785
1972–73	1,278	1,994	3,272
1973–74	632	3,283	3,915
1974–75	5	2,502	2,507
1975–76	0	1,632	1,632
1976–77	4	1,852	1,856
1977–78	1	1,314	1,315
1978–79	1	909	910
1979–80	8	1,058	1,066
1980–81	10	1,334	1,344
1981–82	8	1,533	1,541
TOTAL	68,990	154,715	233,654

Sources: (Immigration Department statistics, quoted in The Australian Government Commission of Inquiry into Poverty 1975: 20; Australian Immigration: Consolidated Statistics No. 13, 1982, Canberra, 1983.)

economic recession in some countries and the postwar reconstruction of the 1950s and 1960s in others (Sherington 1980: 140). In broad terms, of the approximate total of 5 million people who arrived in Australia between 1947–80, only just over 3 million settled, with approximately 33 per cent of them coming from Britain and Ireland. Northern Europeans totalled 9 per cent, while the remaining 58 per cent came from over 100 countries, with Italy contributing 8.8 per cent, Greece 5.2 per cent and Yugoslavia 4.2 per cent (Price 1981: 4). The picture changed dramatically (Tsounis 1975) when the Commonwealth Assistance Scheme came into operation in 1952 in order to initiate new and large-scale migration. This was achieved by granting assisted passages to several thousand heads of Hellenic families, in order to 'ensure' settlement by family migration and to reinforce earlier increases in chain migration. Table 6.4 tells part of the story, with the periods 1953–55 and 1967–71 representing the highest Hellenic intake under this scheme. This increase in Hellenic migration to Australia coincides with periods of political instability in Greece. This instability, as argued in Chapter 5, worsened during the second period (1967–71), when the military regime curtailed political freedom in Greece.

Under the Commonwealth Assistance Scheme, Australia received a total intake of 29,444 Greeks, 16,933 of whom had been assisted, between 1953 and 1956. As shown in Table 6.4, between 1945 and 1959 there were 63,423 'permanent and long-term arrivals' from Greece (excluding Greeks from Cyprus and Egypt), of whom 24,515 were assisted by the Australian government.

The total intake of immigrants peaked in 1958–59 and again in 1964–65 when it reached 17,896, with over 50 per cent of immigrants being assisted in the period 1965–82. Assisted immigration had almost ceased by 1982, although some of those not assisted by the Australian government before 1967 may have received interest-free travel loans from the World Council of Churches (Henderson 1975: 20).

In contrast to Greeks, 85 per cent of British settlers and 60 per cent of Germans, Yugoslavians, Maltese and eastern Europeans arrived under the Assisted Passengers Scheme between 1947 and 1974. Southern Europeans—particularly the two major groups—Greeks and Italians—were significantly under-represented in the Scheme; only 34 per cent of Greeks and Cypriots, and 20 per cent of Italians were assisted immigrants. In fact, according to Henderson's report on poverty, for the whole of the period 1947 to 1972, only 72,449 out of a total of approximately 214,304 Greek immigrants received government assistance; the rest were sponsored (Henderson 1975). Furthermore, of the 239,723 Greeks registered between October 1945 and June 1982, only 74,447 (31 per cent) were assisted, compared with 66 per cent of settlers from the United Kingdom, and 62 per cent of settlers from the Netherlands. For Italians, only 16 per cent were assisted up to 1964 (Collins 1988: 31; Appleyard 1978: 12; Stoller 1966: 21).

The Scheme's discrimination against the Hellenes and other southern Europeans, both before and after World War Two, as manifested in the distinction made by the Immigration Department between assisted and non-assisted northern and southern European migrants, can be traced to the White Australia Policy, which remained in place until 1966. Even after arrival, the discriminatory immigration policy was reflected by the type of accommodation provided to assisted immigrants by the Australian government, thus setting the pattern of social stratification from the very beginning.

Many began their lives in their new country in migrant reception camps, for example at Bonegilla. The majority of the first large group of assisted Greek migrants, consisting of approximately 30,000 people who arrived during 1952–8, passed through the Bonegilla camp rather than hostels or other better-class accommodation. Bonegilla was an ex-army camp that was located near Albury, on the borders of Victoria and New South Wales. The camp was converted to hostels in order to accommodate the 170,000 Displaced Persons who arrived in Australia between 1947 and 1952, and it continued to provide the 'neat' solution to the Australian government's problems and, as the government used to argue, to the problems of the migrants themselves. Such reception and training centres provided Australian governments with bargaining power in respect of employment and with practical solutions for immediate southern European accommodation and subsequent settlement.

The immigrants who passed through Bonegilla have their own version of life in that place, one which often conflicts with the official view. In an article entitled 'Bonegilla, that's how we started', the editors of *Parikia-Greek Australian Monthly Review* wrote:

Illustration 6.1   Bonegilla settlement camp, where non-British migrants, and especially southern Europeans, were segregated. (*Source*: Christos Mourikis)

From what the memory holds, Bonegilla covered a land size of 400 acres and had the capacity to provide, in its 400 [corrugated iron] camps, housing for up to 3,500 persons. The whole army camp was used as a reception centre mainly for southern Europeans. The Anglophones were sent to hostels in the large towns and cities. For the length of time an immigrant stayed there, s/he was given free meal, [and] in addition, a single person was given 30 shillings and a married one with children 50 shillings as pocket money . . . The whole of the Bonegilla camp was organised in a military way . . . with individual [and very small housing] blocks as . . . The blocks were numbered and the newcomers were sent there on the basis of predetermined arrangements: There were the men, and there the women. There were the Hellenes, there were the Italians, and there the northern Europeans . . . (Mourikis 1985: 20, 26).

According to another inmate:

In Bonegilla certainly we did not have the appropriate [housing] infrastructure because of the mass immigration . . .

159

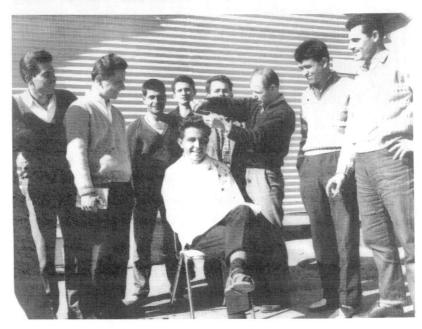

Illustration 6.2   A single haircut in the open space at Bonegilla enabled Hellenes to gather and pass their time together while waiting for employment offers to come. (*Sources*: Christos Mourikis; *Parikia-Greek Monthly Review*, Dec. 1985: 21.)

As it is known [in Bonegilla] immigrants resided temporarily immediately after arrival in Australia. In 1954 I lived in Bonegilla for 36 days. As many people from the Hellenic Community know, the conditions of living there were frightening. When it was cold we were freezing and when it was hot we were asphyxiated. It is only when one lives in a [tin!] hut that one understands what migration and refugeeism is all about (Messinis 1992: 10).

In a letter written to the editors of *Parikia-Greek Australian Monthly Review*, Trahanas stated that:

Unforgettable will be for me the way by which people were distributed to [potential] employers. The distribution was done by the office according to the needs and the demand. While some were being taken by the employers themselves, others were sent by buses and trains to the various jobs. The

Illustration 6.3   English classes at Greta NSW in a government hostel camp in January 1955. Pictured are Vassilios Rekaris and Stephen Themelios along with other Hellenes from various regions of Greece with their two English-language teachers (in the printed shirts). These migrants arrived at the Port of Sydney in December 1954 by the Hellenic passenger ship *Kyrinia*; shortly after, they were taken to Greta by train. (*Source*: Dimitra Temelcos)

length of residence in Bonegilla varied according to the conditions prevailing in the country. However, those who remained in the military camps for months were not few. And this provoked insanity to many . . . as it happened with Nikos . . . he was sent to Melbourne . . . and later we heard that our compatriots collected money and sent him back to Greece (Trahanas 1986: 4).

For the Australian government the advantages derived from providing cheap accommodation and stipulating a two-year contract were obvious from the beginning. Governments and employers were able to place migrants in jobs which they wanted them to do without the newcomers being able to negotiate fairly (Calwell 1972: 13; Mourikis 1985: 26–7).

Once in Australia, Greek migrants, like many others, felt restricted by the contracts which they had signed in Greece,

161

without being fully aware of the implications, should they decide to break these contracts. The participants I interviewed on this question had ranging recollections of the contracts. Some 'feared' being punished or penalised by the government authorities if they ran away from designated jobs and remained there until their contract expired. Others claimed that once they were designated to a job, although they worried about being caught, they still ran away from their employers and were never prosecuted because the authorities were not trying too hard to find them, while others claimed that if they were found by the authorities, they were returned to their initially designated jobs.

According to the editors of the *Parikia-Greek Australian Monthly Review*, Bonegilla, as a government reception and training centre for immigrants, enabled the government to pre-determine migrants' experience in Australia for the first two years of occupation and settlement, since agreements had been signed between migrants and government authorities. However, many of Bonegilla's inmates schemed to escape from the camp and some did escape. This escape was regarded as an escape from 'containment', an escape towards 'freedom', and indeed, a necessary step, so that migrants could take 'responsibility in their own hands' (Mourikis 1985: 26–7).

In contrast to those who were housed in what the Hellenic media have traditionally called the 'concentration camp' of Bonegilla, other migrants were sponsored or, at least, aided by other Greeks in Australia, a pattern which continued to dominate Hellenic and Italian migration after World War Two. In the late 1940s, the sponsors were generally settlers who had arrived prior to the war. This pattern was the salient feature of immigration from Greece between 1947 and 1966 (Price 1966: 22).

Three-quarters of all assisted settlers who arrived between July 1947 and September 1964 were family groups. Greeks and Italians were not well represented in Australia before 1945 and, since only some of the new migrants were assisted by the government or other organisations, for example the Church, they in turn started their own chain migration (Price 1963: 279). While sponsored migrants depended almost entirely on their sponsors for accommodation and employment, those who came by the ICEM program were often the first from their village to settle in Australia and, therefore, had no pre-existing village associations or settler links to help them adjust to the new country. For various reasons, these individuals found limited support from the general Hellenic community. In part, this reflected the uneven sex ratio of Greek immigration in the early postwar years (up to 1964), which had seen predominantly male workers migrating from rural Greece to urban Australia, particularly to the industrial suburbs of Sydney and Melbourne. As a result, in some cities, considerable social problems were created among these immigrants. The imbalance between the numbers of Greek men and women was a cause for concern to the community at large and led to the initiation of sponsored fiancees and marriages by proxy, as one interviewee attests:

> The migration of young Hellene women in mass numbers from Greece was a political as much as an economic and population question as far as Australia was concerned. The Australian authorities adopted this view on the advice given to the Prime Minister, that if Hellene females were brought to Australia in sufficient numbers, this would be the only way to offset remigration and to keep the Hellenes in this country. Even Greek advisers were used to provide their point of view to the Australian Prime Minister at the time to whom it was suggested that unless you brought enough Hellene women to Australia, Hellene males will either return to Greece, or remain bachelors for good and they will keep sending their money to their relatives in Greece. These advisers based their view on the Hellenic American experience, where mass migration during the first twenty years of the century, had shown that almost half of all Hellenes who migrated there had returned home to marry, often in older age, or remained bachelors mainly in the United States. So Australian authorities seemed to have listened to their Hellene advisers that Hellenes once married to their kind of girls, will settle in Australia, raise families and produce children which was what Australia was after anyway (Interview with Grambas 1991).

Under these circumstances, the government introduced a new immigration program, designed to reduce the imbalance between the sexes and to satisfy the many critics of proxy

163

Table 6.5   Male and female arrivals, 1945–71

Year	Males	Females	Total
Oct.1945–June 1948	874	948	1,822
1948–9	614	689	1,303
1949–50	1,178	862	1,040
1950–1	1,034	612	1,646
1951–2	1,279	786	2,065
1952–3	955	650	1,605
1953–4	3,366	1,723	5,089
1954–5	8,639	3,888	12,527
1955–6	7,431	2,856	10,287
1956–7	3,729	5,039	8,768
1957–8	1,848	3,662	5,510
1958–9	3,516	3,252	6,768
1959–60	4,349	3,729	8,078
1960–1	3,658	8,576	12,234
1961–2	5,508	5,760	11,268
1962–3	8,861	8,693	17,554
1963–4	8,128	7,821	15,929
1964–5	5,413	5,059	10,472
1965–6	5,063	4,840	9,843
1966–7	6,241	6,038	12,279
1967–8	5,931	5,607	11,538
TOTAL			202,334

Source: (Australian Immigration, *Consolidated Statistics,* Canberra, 1971)

and 'wharf side' marriages. The Scheme became known as the Single Greek Workers Scheme and favoured a much larger intake of females than males (*Parikia-Greek Australian Monthly Review,* February 1986).

During 1945–49 the ratio of females to males was greater (see Table 6.5 above); thereafter, the male ratio increased again, until 1956. The females who arrived during 1945–49 were priority immigrants, since they were mainly the wives of Greeks who had settled in Australia before 1940, whose reunion had been prevented by World War Two and the Civil War in Greece (*Parikia-Greek Australian Monthly Review,* February 1986: 39). By 1956 the overall ratio of males already in Australia was double that of females, being 25,470 men to 13,014 women. After 1957, many more females than males arrived as privately-sponsored immigrants, thus offsetting the imbalance in the sex ratio.

Illustration 6.4 Arrival of the Chandris Line's *Patris* in 1951 with a shipload of young Hellene migrants, with waiting compatriots on shore. (*Sources*: Christos Mourikis: *Parikia-Greek Monthly Review*, Feb. 1986: 44.)

Many men returned to Greece to bring brides back, or had them sent over by friends or relatives. After this, steps were taken by the ICEM and the Immigration authorities to equalise the numbers between the sexes, as seen in Table 6.5.

165

Illustration 6.5   In the top photo, the Chandris Line's *Australis* anchored at the Port of Melbourne in 1965, after emptying its cargo of many hundreds of Hellenic souls. Below, the *Tasmania* with its load of 850 brides arriving at the Port of Sydney in October 1958. (*Sources:* S. Raftopoulos; Christos Mourikis; *Parikia-Greek Monthly Review,* Feb. 1986: 39.)

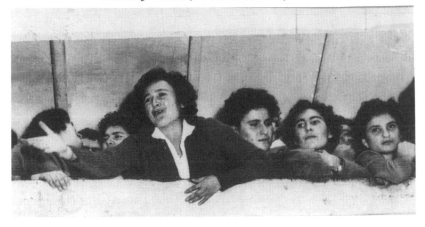

By 1962, the shiploads of single male migrants, travelling under the aegis of the ICEM scheme, had metamorphosed

Illustration 6.6 Shiploads of brides were supplanted by airloads of brides. Here Hellene brides brought out under the auspices of ICEM are welcomed at Melbourne's Essendon Airport by Father George Loutas in June 1968. (Source: *Parikia-Greek Monthly Review*, March 1986: 50.)

into 'shiploads of brides'. Thereafter passenger ships carried large numbers of both men and women.

By about 1967, Turkey, too, had become a major source of immigrants as a result of the dwindling supply of other European labour. By this time moves to dismantle the White Australia Policy had begun. In 1972, the policy was finally abolished by the Whitlam government. During this period, the numbers of Hellenic migrants, along with those from other southern European countries, were steadily decreasing. Greece's role as a supplier of labour to the industrialised nations had exhausted her (and, indeed, she had started to take in migrant labour from other countries for her own industrial needs). In addition, with the end of the Assistance Scheme in 1981, mass immigration from other European nations also ground to a halt and, although Hellenes continued to migrate to Australia, the number of arrivals in any one year has not risen above the low hundreds ever since.

The decline of Australia's manufacturing boom in the mid-1970s and the end of the White Australia Policy, posed new demographic challenges for the nation due to an increase in non-European immigration which was never anticipated by the architects of earlier immigration policies.

At times, however, Australia's new point system—introduced to monitor immigrant selection on the basis of immigrant skills, qualifications and availability or not of sponsorship in Australia proved inadequate to monitor large numbers of people (Hitchcock 1990): it was a system that had been systematically refined over 20 years so that selection of immigrants best served the national interest. For example, the annual arrival of 10–15,000 Indo-Chinese refugees or 'boat people' between 1978–82 operated outside the point system, while through subsequent chain migration and family reunion, the numbers of Indo-Chinese immigrants increased significantly. By the 1980s, 40 per cent of Australia's immigration intake included individuals from previously excluded backgrounds, such as Chinese, Filipino, Malay, Indonesian, Indian and Vietnamese (Castles & Miller 1993; Freeman & Jupp 1992).

According to Castles and Miller, the postwar increase of Asian migration was linked to Australia's foreign policy and her historical obligation towards the Indo-Chinese arising from her involvement in the Vietnam War on the side of the Americans (Castles & Miller 1993: 102). The demographic change that ensued as a result of Asian migration generated strong reactions from both ordinary Australians and conservative academics, such as sociologist Bob Birrell and historian Geoffrey Blainey. These reactions culminated in the 'Blainey debate', that stirred up immigration issues throughout the 1980s.

As opponents of family reunion, Birrell and Blainey argued that a more generous family reunion immigration policy would bring many low-skilled migrants to Australia (Birrell & Birrell 1981: 273–5). Although the views of such academics had a strong impact on Australia's immigration 'debate', their often racist remarks against Asians in Australia were not well received by the general public, particularly since they emphasised the values of a homogeneous British culture, while opposing immigration on family reunion grounds. Many other academics regarded Birrell's and Blainey's views as a serious setback to the immigration debate. Birrell and Blainey were condemned by their peers as anachronistic or assimilationist since, in reality, such views were reminiscent of the White Australia Policy (Markus & Ricklefs 1985). The Ethnic Communities Council (which included the Hellenic community) also opposed Birrell's and Blainey's views because such views undermined Australia's multiculturalism that non-British migrants had struggled so hard to establish (Federation of Ethnic Communities Council of Australia (FECCA) 1984).

Although Birrell's views in favour of selective skilled migration found some support on the basis of environmental costs, they had little influence on the shaping of immigration policy because of the outlay they would necessitate for social infrastrucure and micro-economic considerations. In contrast, the 1988 FitzGerald Report on immigration had argued for a substantial intake increase—especially of skilled immigrants—in order to boost productivity and economic growth in a period of high unemployment. Since the late 1970s, the Ethnic Communities Council has, for the first time and in consultation with governments, been an active participant in the making of Australia's immigration policy and the Council has consistently argued in favour of the rights of migrants to bring out immediate members of their families. This view was strongly supported by the Hellenic community because Greeks knew that family reunion was vital for many immigrants who had left their families behind, if they were to settle permanently in Australia.

By the late 1970s, the Hellenic community—along with other ethnic communities who became embodied by FECCA —was participating in the immigration debate and this constituted a radical departure from the pre-1970s practices, when immigration policy was determined by politicians and bureaucrats, according to employers' interests (Collins 1975, 1986; FECCA 1984). Ethnic communities' participation in the immigration debate contributed to the development of a less discriminatory policy by obtaining a widened scope of legal limits, with a 'broadened focus for migrant economic skills', while 'preserving the overriding commitment to family reunion' (Freeman & Jupp 1992: 9).

In summary, then, Australia's immigration history has moved from one of coercive and discriminatory immigration to one in which selection criteria are based on migrants' skills and abilities and measured by a point system. While migrant intake has remained strongly grounded on the economic benefits of immigration, at the same time it has enabled organisations and individuals—other than unions and employers—to participate in the immigration debate. This participation included the views and opinions of ethnic communities which, prior to the 1970s, had been excluded from participating because the proponents of the White Australia Policy regarded Greeks and other non-British migrants as 'lucky to be here' and, consequently, they were not invited to share their views on immigration.

Australian society's attitudes towards Hellenic settlement

The pre-Whitlam years

This chapter will explore how the social, economic and cultural structures that emerged from Australia's pro-British immigration policies affected Australian attitudes towards the settlement and subsequent social mobility of non-British migrants. In particular, it will trace the social mobility of Greeks in the context of the host society's formal and popular attitudes during the inter-war and post-World War Two periods, and indicate how social mobility was connected with the process of integration or assimilation and the economic and political participation of migrant population groups.

Some of the determinants of the host society's attitudes towards new settlers have been: the size of the particular ethnic population group; the extent to which migrants were perceived to threaten the existing occupational and residential profiles; the ratio of endogamy to inter-marriage; and the level of fluency in the English language. According to Price (1963), none of these factors has been constant in Australia, particularly in regard to southern Europeans since, over the years, the official attitude has mattered less than the everyday behaviour of locals at any given time. As Price observes, 'in some places British-Australians were either comparatively favourably disposed or indifferent, especially where numbers were small and inter-marriage occurred. In other places feelings at times became most hostile' (1963: 208).

Price's study on the social history of southern Europeans in Australia has traced the tradition of social conflict in early incidents between British-Australians and southern Europeans. He cites the case of two adjacent goldfield towns in Western Australia as being illustrative of the friction between British-Australians and Italians, Slavs and Greeks after the discovery of gold in 1894:

> [They were employed as] either miners or as timber-cutters providing wood for pit-props or furnaces; accompanied by a number of Ithacan, Kastellorizan and other Greeks of whom some mined or cut timber, but others followed a few Italians and Slavs in opening restaurants, hotels and clubs. Before long, British-Australians became incensed at alleged agreements whereby employers brought southern Europeans to Australia under contract to work at less than standard wages. Southern Europeans were also accused of insanitary habits in the mines, aggravated by their different way of life and their carelessness with explosives in the mines as a result of their inadequate English. These events led to the appointment of two commissions to investigate the charges (Price 1963: 208–9).

Attitudes towards southern Europeans—including the Greeks—fluctuated and often depended on government policy, including immigration policy. At times, governments bowed to popular or employer demand and, in an attempt to avoid social unrest, imposed regulations permitting only those with some knowledge of English to work in the mines. They also banned the contract system of working for lower wages. Social and political pressure was often so intense that it resulted in a proposition for a Bill aimed at compelling mining employers to limit the number of their alien employees to 10 per cent of their workforce. This position was an attempt to force the alien workers to assimilate and so 'cease evading the provision concerning the learning of English and taking up duties of full citizenship'. The Bill was passed at all stages in the Lower House, but was rejected by the Legislative Council (Price 1963: 208). Throughout Australia's labour and industrial relations history, the measurement of living standards in material terms goes a long way towards explaining the White

Australia Policy. Both official and public opinion were based on the view that:

> if the migrants were prepared to conform to the industrial laws of the country relating to hours, working conditions and wages, their introduction was easily tolerated by organised labour. This was the hard core of labour policy. But how far the concept of protection of economic standards was inter-mingled with suspicion on racial, social or other grounds was seldom, as far as the white population was concerned, put to a test (Borrie 1954: 13–20).

Through their control of economic and political power, British-Australians were able to demand the acculturation of all immigrant groups by accepting little if any transculturation. Suspicion about non-British migrants (with the exception of the early Chinese settlers) was not aroused until the arrival of increasing numbers of southern Europeans, especially once they started forming noticeable groups—by about 1910. By then, whether they were Greek or not, migrants had to fit into existing organised labour structures to avoid further racial and ethnic discrimination. In fact, by 1915, British-Australians had gained a significant victory when the government required all miners to join miners' unions and accept laws regarding labour and working conditions. Even though the new settlers con-formed to the industrial laws, conflict was not always prevented.

Price maintains that, in 1916, there was an outburst of xenophobia against the Dalmatians, who, though mostly anti-Hapsburg, were from Austria-Hungary, and therefore tech-nically treated as 'enemy aliens'. Similarly, Greeks experienced racial hatred because, although the Greek government was always officially on the 'right side' of the Allies, King Con-stantine had taken a pro-German stand (Price 1963: 209; Tsounis 1971a; Gilchrist 1985; Vondra 1979: 19).

It was during the same year that the first Hellenic book in Australia—entitled *Life in Australia*—was published in Sydney. Tsounis (1971a) has noted that the 10,000 copies published exceeded by far the number of Greeks in Australia at the time, which was, as reported by the Commonwealth Census of the same year, between 2,500 and 3,000. In its opening section, the book addressed both the Greek and Australian governments and societies and carried the message that, above all, Greeks in Australia had been 'progressive, industrious, and law-abiding citizens' (Cominos 1916). As also noted in the introduction, Kosmas and Emanuel Andronicos, George Kentavros and John Cominos, the 'oyster king' as he was known in Australia—who had paid for this 'expensive publication'—wanted their readers to avoid political conflict and concentrate instead on their business operations, because King Constantine's well-known pro-German orientation meant that Greeks were in danger of retaliation from anti-German Australians. Greeks had witnessed 'the smashing of Greek shops in Sydney in 1915 by Australian soldiers sensitive and hostile to a pro-German Greek king' (Tsounis 1971a: 60). There were many other situations where Australian soldiers entered Greek restaurants in Sydney, ate and left without paying. In one case they reduced a number of restaurants to 'glass and nails' (Tsounis 1988c: 41).

This unrest motivated the Orpheus Hellenic Club of Melbourne to call a general meeting (Tsounis 1971a). Subsequently, the club's committee sent a telegram expressing sentiments of support to Greek Prime Minister Venizelos and to the British government, as a declaration of loyalty to the Allies. There is no evidence to show that Greek-Australians were divided into pro-royalist and pro-Venizelist factions to the same extent as in Greece and America (Saloutos 1964). Indeed, it is likely that they were more concerned about reprisals on their shops than Greek politics. The main exception was that several Greek consuls in Australia owed their appointment to their affiliation to certain political parties in Greece (Tsounis 1971a: 60, 99, 100), as did many others in subsequent decades.

By 1916, the mounting suspicion of foreigners led to a national investigation, a *Secret Census*, of all Greek immigrant activities (*Secret Census* 1916). Police were requested to collect detailed information from Greek migrants, including their names, addresses, occupational practices, social practices, movements and associations, as well as political preferences for Greece's political parties. Interestingly, only seven Greek royalist supporters were found, out of 2,500 immigrants surveyed in the *Secret Census*. The results of the *Secret Census*

Illustration 7.1   The Heads Cafe in Swanston Street Melbourne, 1910—
one of the many hundreds of such establishments
owned nationally by Hellene-Australians. (*Source*:
S. Raftopoulos)

enabled Australian authorities to divert attention from the
Hellenic community and instead concentrate their efforts on
the activities of German immigrants, whose country was at
war with the Allies.

By the time the *Secret Census* was completed, *Life in
Australia* had been published (Cominos 1916). The book
identifies approximately 250 Greek-owned shops out of the
625 shops or businesses alleged as known to be owned by
this ethnic population group nationally. Their distribution
across the states is largely proportional to the size of Hellenic
settlement in each state. There were some 300 in New South
Wales (of which 130 were in metropolitan Sydney and 20 in
Newcastle); 120 in Victoria (70 in metropolitan Melbourne);

175

Illustration 7.2. The owners and serving staff of the Heads Cafe, 1917.
(*Source*: S. Raftopoulos)

120 in Queensland (only 20 in metropolitan Brisbane); 80 in
Western Australia (mainly in Fremantle, Perth and Kalgoorlie);
four in Adelaide; and one in Hobart (Tsounis 1971a: 59).
These shops were usually family businesses, while some, like
the Freeleagus family shops in Brisbane, were quite large and
employed upward of 30 Hellenes, as well as offering significant
employment opportunities to non-Hellenes. According to the
authors of *Life in Australia,* only a few Hellenes worked for
British-Australian, rather than Greek-Australian, shopowners.
This view is verified by the information contained in the files
of the *Secret Census.*

The prevailing socio-economic conditions, as well as the
cultural ideology of Australian society, were the major reasons
that led many Greeks to shopkeeping occupations. At the same

time, self-employment enabled Hellenes to continue their gregarious and homogeneous gatherings and thus maintain their cultural traditions. Living within a network of friends and compatriots and sharing with them a common social and cultural life was important in a society which still wanted to keep migrants firmly in their place by tacitly imposing segregation, via an uncompromising adherence to the dominant British-Australian culture. It was important for southern European migrants to work in similar industries and share the experiences of the unionised British-Australian work force, although the Greeks were careful not to upset their hosts. As Tsounis observes:

> partly because of their occupations, partly because of their other conspicuous features, Greeks were not insensitive to the moods of their host society. Community leaders frequently admonished their compatriots to cultivate good public relations, reminding them that they were 'guests in a hospitable land', and that any wrong behaviour would be detrimental to all Greeks and to Hellenism (Tsounis 1971a: 61).

In practice, however, no one person's advocacy of the need for good relations between migrants and their host society could be sufficient. The host society's xenophobia against southern Europeans came to a head in August 1918, when returned soldiers, incensed at the death of a comrade during a brawl with North Italian wood-cutters and miners, demanded the deportation of all Italians from the goldfields. Trade union officials eventually halted the looting and damaging of Italian, Slav and Greek clubs, shops and hotels, but by then many southern Europeans had already been forced to flee into the bush (Price 1963).

Greeks were often mistaken for Italians and the more extreme British-Australians made no effort to distinguish between them. An entire ethnic population group could be held responsible for the transgression of an individual. Hatred of or discrimination against non-British migrants was more severe in some areas than in others. Tamis's (1988) research on Macedonian Greeks in Australia found that the Western Australian government did not give Macedonian Greeks the legal right to purchase their own home. Pascoe and Bertola (1985) found that:

> The Italians and other non-British minorities entertained no hope of taking up land in the southwest, but instead took up bushworking. The expression, 'The mines or the Bush', became the catchcry of immigrant Italians in the interwar era (Pascoe & Bertola 1985: 13).

The absence of housing and appropriate government organisations and the lack of welfare provisions and services forced a number of Greeks and other southern Europeans throughout Australia to seek refuge at Salvation Army centres. These centres offered them food, shelter and protection from an intolerant host society (Interview with Tamis 1988).

Unlike other southern Europeans, such as the Italians, who found the Catholic Church already established by other Catholic migrants who had preceded them, the Orthodox Greeks found no established church or social organisations to which they could attach themselves (Price 1963: 210). They faced the contempt and prejudice of British-Australians for setting up their own formal and informal types of organisations and entertainment—churches, social organisations, lay communities, brotherhoods and Sunday or language schools. Often, discrimination was the result of Hellenic reaction against the host society's attempts to Anglicise their culture. Out of ignorance, British-Australians resented the Greeks for attempting to keep their own culture, language and value system. This is evident in the way the editors of the first issue of the *Hellenic Herald* addressed their readers in English instead of Greek, stating their aims in an apologetic tone and style:

> Our aim in inaugurating this journal is primarily to enlighten our fellow-countrymen, the Greeks, in this noble country, and particularly those who have not had the advantage of long residence on its shores . . . Our sole aim is to enlighten and educate. We are absolutely and sincerely non-partisan. We neither support nor condemn any particular party, and our watchwords will be Truth, Right and Justice to all (*Hellenic Herald*, Tuesday, 16 November 1926: 1).

Hostility towards Greek migrants continued throughout the

inter-war years and, with many unable to find suitable employment, they became the obvious targets of discrimination. Greeks seeking work outside the Greek community were often rejected. Raftopoulos maintains that before establishing themselves in some sort of small business, many Greeks had suffered employment discrimination and hatred, simply because they were Greeks. In discussing his experiences in Australia, Raftopoulos recalled the following:

> I remember the late Floros Demetriades in 1924, when he went to McIlgraith. It was a large steam shipping company and it was seeking somebody who knew French and other languages. So Floros went there for an interview. He was welcomed by the manager there and had a long talk. He was asked if he spoke French sufficiently and was told to begin work on Monday. He said goodbye, and as he was stepping out of the door . . . the manager asked, 'By the way, where did you come from?' Floros at the time was a young man, with blond hair, very good-looking and educated. He said 'I'm a Greek from Cyprus', and then the manager turned to him and says, 'No Greek will ever work in this establishment' (Interview with Raftopoulos 1988).

On the rare occasions employment was offered outside the self-contained Hellenic shopkeepers' community, Greek employees could not easily negotiate their employment rights, nor were there any appropriate government employment agencies to help newly-arrived migrants find work. As Price (1963) was the first to point out, Greeks had to help other Greeks to find both work and accommodation. As Peter Stevens (whose given name was Panagiotis Tsirginis and who migrated from Promario, Mitilini in 1925) put it:

> I came to Australia in 1925. I went to a place in Ipswich. I found an oldie, a gambler, who used to gather at the coffee shops. I actually stayed at the beginning for six months in Sydney and then I went to Brisbane. He wanted to send me to pick up cotton. But this oldie gambler said to me 'I'll send you to a village where you gonna work. But don't ask for too much money because things are very bad.' Twenty-five shillings a week was the wage (Interview with Stevens 1987).

179

Australian government authorities often dealt with southern Europeans by monitoring their activities and ordering inquiries into their activities. For example, in 1925 Commissioner Ferry investigated the socio-economic practices of migrants in North Queensland. This report made 'scathing remarks' about Greek lodging-houses and cafes. It claimed that 'Greeks did not engage in agriculture', and that 'socially and economically this type of immigrant is a menace to the community in which he settles, and it would be best for the state if his entrance were altogether prohibited'. 'They engage in no useful work that could not be better performed without their assistance' (Ferry 1925: 76).

Ferry's views were challenged by the findings of a report prepared by the Hellenic Society of Northern Queensland, which denied that Greeks were only city-dwellers. Greece's Consul General wrote to the *Daily Standard*, asking the newspaper to publish the report, which stated that of 250 Greeks in the 'Innisfail district, 200 were employed in farming' and only 50 were employed in business. Other nearby towns, the report stated, had more Greek agriculturalists than the Innisfail district. Ferry's remarks were based on xenophobia rather than systematic research (*Daily Standard*, 29 June 1925: 12).

Following Ferry, Lyng (1927) overtly discriminated against southern Europeans by showing a marked preference for northern European migrants, who he describes as 'well-to-do immigrants' because they were farmers, carpenters, mechanics and educated, clean-living industrious people (Ferry 1925: 76; Lyng 1927: 141–3). In contrast, however, Lyng claimed that the 'Greeks are the least popular foreigners' and that Australia does not need this type of immigrant, because:

1   they live mainly in low-class lodging- and boarding-houses and, occasionally, in restaurants owned by Greeks;
2   with the exception of a few, most are city-dwellers; and
3   when they have become well-to-do, they generally return to Greece.

Lyng's criticism went beyond the immediate socio-economic status of Greeks in Australia by attacking the political order of Greece. Yet his conclusion contradicts his earlier findings when he states that the 7,000 Greeks settled by 1927 had been absorbed into Australia's social mainstream 'without any unpleasant incident', adding patronisingly that 'we will miss the Greeks if they leave us' (Lyng 1927: 141–3).

Unlike Ferry and Lyng, Price (1963), Alexakis and Janiszewski (in GOC 1988) and Gilchrist (1985, 1992) all indicate that there were historical and economic factors in operation that forced migrants to behave in particular ways in order to ensure their economic survival in Australia. In addition it can be assumed that because many Greeks left impoverished agricultural conditions in Greece, they would try to avoid farm work once in Australia. The urbanisation of Greek migrants that followed the end of goldrush, constituted the beginning of a new era with many immigrants now seeking to raise families in a more stable social milieu. As Greeks were getting out of goldmining and waterfront jobs, they were moving instead into cafes, restaurants, shopkeeping and oyster-farming—occupations in which they can be counted pioneers. While social groups formed in the cities, Greeks had no intention of forming ghettos: indeed, by the 1930s, only half of all southern European immigrants were living in cities and this figure remained steady throughout the following decades (Price 1963).

Price shows that prior to 1947, out of a total of 15,000, there were only about 1,000 Greek settlers in each of the bigger cities of Sydney and Melbourne, with a lesser concentration in parts of central Brisbane, Adelaide, Perth, Darwin, the mining towns of Boulder-Kalgoorlie and Broken Hill and the industrial fishing town of Port Pirie. 'Southern European migration, therefore, was not markedly rural-to-urban before 1947 as it had been to the United States', and even as late as 1947, Hellenic settlement in the cities was still only 55.7 per cent (Price 1963; Tsounis 1971a). From the evidence available, it is not possible to conclude that concentrations of people from the same Hellenic region ended up in the same region of Australia, although this was true in the early years when 'regional loyalties and support were necessary as a starting point' (Price 1963: 161).

Unemployment, especially from the mid-1920s to the mid-1930s, led to many, sometimes violent, incidents of racism and discrimination against foreigners. Greek labourers were used in undesirable or provocative jobs in the labour market. One such instance of violence in Melbourne was an attack by

181

British-Australians on the Acropolis Cafe in 1928. More than 100 unemployed Greeks took on work at the Melbourne waterfront while the wharf labourers were on strike, to the outrage of union members, who were insensitive to the financially degrading position of non-British migrants. The union members viewed the participation of unemployed Greeks as scab labour. As a consequence, many Greeks were physically attacked and, on 1 December 1928, a bomb blew up the cafe, injuring 15 people. Five British-Australians, including one trade unionist, were charged and sentenced to 15 years' imprisonment (*The Age*, 5 December 1928: 3, 4)

The socio-economic situation in Australia prompted Mr Hrysanthopoulos, Greek Consul General of Sydney in 1928, to request his government to intervene and reduce Hellenic migration to Australia. There is little doubt that the prevailing socio-economic conditions had become almost intolerable for both the host Australian society and the newly-arrived immigrants, especially those individuals from non-British countries. As the Athenian newspaper *Ithaki* commented at the time:

Ever since [1926], there has been an observed increase in the migration influx. As a result of this trend, the observed lack of employment in Australia and the hatred against foreigners, the majority of Hellenic immigrants completely lacking language and/or occupational skills, go about the streets or remain without employment in the Hellenic *kafeneia* [coffee houses], which operate under the constant surveillance of the police authorities. Sydney's Hellenic newspaper *Hellenic Herald* published an article in which it describes the tragic conditions of these young immigrants who, as it says, in the flowering of their age, full of life and energy, are going about ragged and hungry in search for employment in vain. The Greek newspaper attributes the immigrant influx to ignorance about the [socio-economic] conditions in Australia on the one hand and on the other to the deceitful methods of some shrewd travel agents. The Greek Consul General suggests that Greek citizens must be informed so that they would not migrate to Australia unless firstly, they have secured employment. He further suggests that in this case Greece needs to take disciplinary measures [restricting and prohibiting migration to Australia] (*Ithaki*, 1 May 1928).

Conflict often erupted without consideration of costs. The 'anti-dago' riots in the Boulder-Kalgoorlie region in 1934 are such an example. Following the death of an Australian footballer who had been killed after refusing to pay for his beer in a local hotel, British-Australian miners overpowered the local police, looted a number of southern European shops and burnt to the ground at least five Italian, Greek, and Slav hotels or clubs and over 50 houses. Many southern Europeans panicked and fled to the bush (Price 1963). In their analysis of the social history of white men's settlement at Kalgoorlie, Pascoe and Bertola maintain that the 'rhetoric' of the 1934 riot was certainly economic. 'An Italian bar-tender accidentally killed a local Anglo-Australian sports hero: the rioting which ensued became crystallised into a set of industrial demands by organised labour' (Pascoe & Bertola 1985: 23). Government interference led to enforcement of a law which, from then on, required all mine employees to have an adequate knowledge of the English language (Price 1963). In 1969, Tsounis interviewed Peter Manos, a victim of the riots, about the events of 1934 and was told about Greeks and others who had lost more than 100,000 pounds in property damages, but received only a maximum of 10,000 pounds in compensation (Tsounis 1971a; Tsounis, Interview with Manos 1989). There was no significant reaction by Australian organisations to the events, with the exception of the Communist Party of Australia (CPA), which was one of the few organisations to see the violence as a product of capitalist economic relations. Shortly after the riots, the CPA distributed a leaflet to all members of the community, in which it put forward its view of the matter. The leaflet was written and distributed by Ted Docker, just before a general gathering of miners at Kalgoorlie and read:

> The Communists stand four-square for unity amongst all workers irrespective of racial, political or any other differences. Had the policy been adopted, no bloodshed or burning of workers' houses would have occurred (*Tribune*, 14 June 1980).

Many more, albeit milder, events of this sort have been reported both before and after the large-scale postwar immigration, particularly in the inner-city and working-class suburbs

183

where these migrants often lived. There were few sympathisers to whom victims could turn in moments of need, as racial prejudice came from both members of the public and formally organised forums. Lack of social justice and equal opportunities in the job market, coupled with either the indifference or active prejudice of general society organisations, led many Greeks to either tacitly support or openly join radical political organisations such as the Communist Party of Australia (CPA).

With the exception of the CPA, the other political parties excluded non-British migrants from their lists. In contrast, a 1922 CPA membership list showed that 28 per cent of members were from non Anglo-Saxon backgrounds. A list of 150 names of known communists, handed over to the New South Wales Parliament on 23 December 1931, revealed that at least 30 individuals were from non-British backgrounds— Russians, Jews, Germans and Greeks (Parliamentary Papers, NSW, 1930–1: 465–7).

Although the actual extent of Greek membership of the CPA is not known for the period leading up to the Second World War, it is estimated that the CPA had a higher incidence of southern European participation than any other British-Australian organisation. Unlike other parties, such as the United Australia Party and the ALP, the CPA, with its ideology of uniting different nationalities on an equal footing, welcomed membership from across the social and racial strata of society.

According to George Georges (whose given name was George Georgouras), an Australian ex-senator who joined the CPA after being a member of the Eureka Youth League, there was no racial discrimination in the League as in the other political parties of Australia. When asked if he faced racism in the Eureka League, he spoke of an all-embracing mentality that existed among the members of the League. He said:

> Not in the Eureka Youth League, not in the young socialist groups and that's where Socialist groups have the advantage over other groups, they differ from the Labor Party. Strangely enough even though I have forced myself to the top in a way that I can use in the Labour movement, there is still that 'you're a nice fella' patronising about it. But in the early days in the ALP, it was very apparent and I think you couldn't succeed and get very far on contacts and I had to

make a very hard decision to shorten my name . . . Of course there was that blatant racism in the Electorate. 'He's just a bloody wog' (Interview with Georges, 1987).

Another veteran member of the CPA, Peter Stevens, when asked whether he faced any kind of racism in the CPA responded that it was 'very good. No problems. Well, problems existed but minor ones, and we solved them with discussion' (Interview with Stevens, 1987).

Despite the fact that Greeks have a strong tradition of political culture, Australia's Greeks, as Tsounis (1971a: 99–101) observes, were more concerned about non-party political activities than party politics in Greece or Australia. The majority of Greeks in Australia were generally focused on their own Hellenic community life and practices and preoccupied with the development of their *koinotites* (Hellenic lay communities) and Church politics in Australia, a trend which continued for several decades (Tsounis 1971a; Interview with Tsounis, 1989). As Georges recollects:

> you have to realise that Greeks were still separated and they weren't in any way integrated or assimilated. They had their close community built around them . . . and it was within that community that young people started to stir and rebel against the close traditions of the community which held them apart, through arranged marriages and the rest . . . (Interview with Georges, 1987).

By the end of the Depression in 1933, the number of Greek-born unemployed was up to 33 per cent, as against 20 per cent for the general Australian population (Commonwealth Bureau 1933). The few available jobs in non-Greek-owned businesses were offered to British-Australians and the immigrant quota was not filled for about ten years. Almost 5,000 Greeks left Australia for destinations unknown due to the economic crisis (Price 1963).

> Many suffered due to the socio-economic situation and some ended up gambling. Approximately 50 per cent remained permanently, often separated from Greece and from each other within Australia by the tyranny of distance, without

185

ever managing to return home (Interview with Raftopoulos, 1988).

Gambling was one aspect of degraded Hellenic life during the Great Depression. Many migrants felt excluded from their ethnic culture and led lonely, rugged lives. These views are highlighted in the work entitled Κάτω Από Ξένους Ουρανούς (*Under Foreign Skies*) by the playwright Alekos Doukas (1963). Doukas, who arrived in Australia in 1927, provides a vivid biographical account of life during the Depression, for both Hellenes, other migrants and native Australians. He shows how many spent years wandering through country towns and cities, engaged in a fruitless search for work.

Doukas' work is ideologically grounded within a Leftist framework and is noteworthy for its socio-historical importance in understanding the Depression era. The author argues that the employers (who he calls αφεντικά) keep the workers divided by using employment 'preferences' within the reserve army of labour. 'This preference was in favour of the local labour as against the foreign-born. The same way they had bought many labour leaders. The same way they had bought Judas with thirty coins . . . few are the those who cannot be bought even with all the gold of the world . . .' (Doukas 1963: 155). Those who cannot be bought are παλικάρια (*palikaria*—good hearted, brave and generous), that is, with a strong sense of *philotimo* (Doukas 1963).

Doukas' discussion of the social problems caused by increased unemployment looks at its effect on society as a whole rather than on migrants alone. He describes life on the farms and in the country towns and argues that the banks provided no credit to local farmers to help them sustain a living on their farms. As a result, many farmers became 'refugees' within their own country, by migrating to the cities in search of work (Doukas 1963).

The Depression increased local resentment against foreigners because many still thought that 'we take their jobs' (Interview with Raftopoulos, 1988). Life was extremely arduous for the Greeks who arrived in Australia during the economic crisis of the 1930s (75 per cent of whom were single men). Many migrants took almost four years to pay off their passage fees (Price 1963). According to *Paroikia*:

> Many Hellenes [as late as the 1930s] were forced to wander about the country as seasonal workers, or woodcutters and quarry workers, working in the lime pits, often crossing long distances, because the Collier's government in Western Australia did not grant migrants permission to work in the cities (*Paroikia* 1995: 38).

During this period, with few migrants able to find a job in Australian-owned businesses, Greek businesses provided the solution for many of their compatriots. For example, according to the Greek bulletin *Paroikia*, the tobacco industry owned by Petros Michelides in Perth employed mainly Greek workers, because British-Australian employers did not want to employ them. If they did employ migrants 'the Anglo-Celtic employees went on strike' (*Paroikia* 1995: 38).

Although Greeks offered work to other Greeks, this often created an unequal relationship between the employee and the 'boss', both of whom had different expectations of each other and, by the nature of their status, already had different material interests. Doukas distinguishes at least four categories of Hellenes during this period: employers, employees, unemployed and those who, due to the prevailing poverty in society, led degraded lives. The last category were seen as Hellenes who had failed and were excluded from both the general and Hellenic communities. Doukas ironically categorised those who owned shops, or managed some kind of small business as the 'bosses', yet he recognised that they worked under inhuman conditions in order to earn their living. Many suffered from having to spend 'endless hours' on their feet or were involved in 'dirty' and 'unhealthy' jobs, such as cleaning fish-shop environments. There were a few who saw themselves as rich because they had been successful in establishing a business. They hated all those Greeks who voiced nonconformist views or subscribed to progressive ideologies; consequently, they informed local authorities about the activities of such Greeks. In addition, there were those who worked long hours for a meagre wage, thus often being exploited by their own compatriots who had employed them to work in their shops.

According to Doukas, this situation was a direct result of the decline of the farming industry and 'the farms now looked like sterile cows whose udders went dry' (Doukas 1963: 164). In the absence of sufficient employment, those who were lucky enough to have a job had no choice but to work up to 50 hours over and above the national union labour standards. Doukas, who in his play is represented by his hero Stratis Mourtzos, says:

> Stratis was getting paid 30 shillings a week. He knew very well that the wage was 85 shillings for a 48-hour week. He worked 75–80 hours a week for 30 shillings . . . one day Stratis asked for an increase . . . [the boss responded] . . . if you don't like the work look for another . . . [job] (Doukas 1963: 165).

> But mostly detrimental was the monotony of this life [in the shops], that was killing Stratis who remembered . . . life in the farms under the full sun in the company of others (Doukas 1963: 164).

Although Greeks posed little threat to British-Australian employment prospects, local misconceptions about cultural and linguistic differences continued to exacerbate the situation. As Price (1963) observes, although economics has always been the main source of friction between members of the host society and immigrants, hostility was evident even in areas where economic competition had been minimal, for example in areas where British-Australians had never shown much interest, market-gardening, retail, deep-sea and scallop fishing and oyster farming. These were areas where Australians enjoyed the benefits of southern European goods and the seafood caught by the fleets of southern Europeans operating out of Port Pirie and Fremantle (Price 1963: 213).

Many Greeks were caught between their dreams of Australian prosperity and their inability to fulfil the obligation of the Odyssean journey by returning home to their loved ones. Many Greeks who 'stayed behind' in mobility terms, often also failed to return to Greece. The effects of failure to return home can be understood in the context of the Hellenic sense of *philotimo*. Greeks regarded returning home without wealth or other resources acquired while they were abroad as *entrope*, that is, 'an inward sense of shame' (Interview with Raftopoulos, 1988). Their senses of *philotimo* or *entrope* often undermined their *eudaemonia* (their virtue, their happiness). Failure to return home due to *entrope* had serious ramifications for individual migrants and their families in Greece who were waiting to join them. This is highlighted by the fact that, in Hellenic culture, *philotimo* and *entrope* are linked to the individual debates which take place in the *agora*, thus forming part of the collective perception of κοινονία (*koinonia*) society, and vice versa. In other words, going back home like a good Odysseus implied some form of success. It was often preferable for a migrant to postpone returning home until he succeeded, either economically or socially, in order to avoid either personal humiliation or their extended family's shame in 'the eyes of *koinonia*'. However, there is no evidence to suggest that, if migrants remained in Australia, success would be forthcoming, or that they would face less humiliation, particularly since they remained excluded from the full range of occupational and social opportunities of the host society.

Throughout the inter-war years, discrimination against foreigners took on various forms, whether the precipitating factor involved culture, linguistic, occupational or economic differences. Migrants' lack of fluency in English would often be sufficient to precipitate conflict between the locals and the newcomers. When questioned about racism during the 1920s, Stevens recalled the following event:

> Oh yes, I had bad experiences. In those early days if you didn't know how to speak proper English they look at you as a stranger. I went to drink a beer and without saying a thing someone punched me. There were three other blokes there too you know (Interview with Stevens, 1987).

According to Peter Alexander, 'many Australians, in those days treated Hellenes as inferior, as if they were lower than second- and third-class citizens. Since there were no educational facilities like they have today' (Interview with Alexander, 1987). Similarly, ex-Senator George Georges stated that many immigrants were considered as a 'sort of semi-lunatic because they couldn't express themselves in English'. People 'shouted' at his father to try and make him understand:

it wasn't because he couldn't hear, it was because he couldn't understand, so it was terribly difficult in those days . . . I resented that, I had to fight against it, it was one of the things I had to fight against. That in a sense developed militancy, it was hurtful. There is no doubt of the hurt one feels at being considered inferior (Interview with Georges, 1987).

The outbreak of World War Two did not improve local perceptions of migrants, especially since British-Australian xenophobia continued unabated. When the government of the Commonwealth instigated 'Aliens Control' in 1940, Greeks were not excluded (Commonwealth of Australia, *Certificate of Registration of Alien* 1940). As Raftopoulos recalls:

we queued inside and outside police stations. It was an unforgettable and painful experience especially when some of us had been here for many years and had worked very hard, while others like myself were raised in this country and attended local schools . . . The whole thing reminded one that we are undesirable settlers who cannot and should not be trusted when it comes to the security of Australia. Yet there was no evidence for such suspicions (Interview with Raftopoulos 1988).

Even when Greece had joined the Allies, Hellenes in Australia still suffered from local hatred. Hostility and suspicion toward 'aliens' increased and few attempts, if any, were made to differentiate between 'allied' and 'enemy' aliens, so entrenched was Australian-British xenophobia. Although both Italy (in 1915) and Greece had joined the Allies in the Great War, Greeks and other non-British migrants were still viewed with suspicion by their hosts. In contrast to the Italians, who were placed in internment camps because their government had allied itself with Germany, the Greeks were on the side of the Allies fighting against the expansion of fascism, both in Europe and in the Middle East. For the second time in 30 years, Greeks, Australians, New Zealanders and British were fighting together, with some of the most decisive battles for the outcome of the war taking place on Greek soil in Crete in 1941 (*Paroikia*, May 1986: 34; June 1986: 34).

In the retrospective commemoration of these events,

Illustration 7.3 Pte N. Raftopoulos with Theodore Spyrakos at Tocumwal, 1940. Two of many young Hellenes who served in the Australian Armed Forces during WWII. (*Source*: S. Raftopoulos)

191

Illustration 7.4 'Ohi (No) Day', 28 October 1944, Newcastle NSW, commemorating Hellenic Resistance to the German occupation of their homeland in 1940. (*Source*: S. Raftopoulos)

Australia's Hellenic media reminded its readers that those battles were battles against fascism, against the powers of darkness. The Hellenic media has repeatedly emphasised that those battles helped build a historical bond between Hellenes and Australians because both were fighting for freedom and democracy, in order to preserve the dignity of humanity. As the editor of the *Paroikia* wrote, 'this was a test for the strengthening of existing relations between the Allies at a crucial moment of history' (May 1986: 34).

> In a moment of contemporary history—the most critical for the fate of humanity—Hellas and Australia came so close to one another and found themselves fighting from the same positions, had the same motives towards the ideals of freedom and democracy (*Paroikia*, May 1986: 34).

According to Raftopoulos, the battles against fascism were a useful lesson for those who did not know Greeks well:

> Hellenism had shown Australians and Americans and generally to the allies that Hellenes are democratically minded people and with our historical *OHI* (NO), we had made it clear to the AXIS forces of Mussolini and Hitler in 1940 that Hellenes fight for freedom, and Independence at all costs. We ignored Mussolini's threat when he said to the Hellenes that he had eight million bayonets, an equivalent number to the population of Greece at the time. Hellenes like other Australians also had occasional quarrels with Italian Australians who tended to support Mussolini. There was a significant difference in the way we felt as Hellenes of Australia and the world and the way Italians and Germans did . . . and it is because of this that Hellenes were suddenly treated with less contempt by Australians in comparison to the suspected Germans and Italians who were placed in three or four concentration camps like Tatura. We instead concentrated all our efforts to provide assistance to the Committee for Australia's War Effort (Interview with Raftopoulos, 1988).

To avoid brawls similar to those which took place during the Great War when Greeks were often mistaken for Italians, the president of the Hellenic Orthodox Community, Antonis Lekatsas or Lucas, together with the Hellenic Consulate of Melbourne, issued a bulletin requesting all Greek shop proprietors to inform the general public that Greece was Australia's ally. Small posters bearing the Hellenic Royal Crown at the top and also the words: 'the owner of this establishment is a Greek Ally', were attached to the windows of Greek shops (Interview with Raftopoulos, 1988). Raftopoulos further stated that:

> we placed them on the windows of every one of our shops then, so they won't think we're all Italians and thus have the same luck as the rest of our compatriots of 1914–16 (Interview with Raftopoulos, 1988).

In contrast to the Hellenic experience in Australia, thousands of British, New Zealanders and Australians in Greece were given a great welcome, warm *philoxenia* (hospitality) and protection by Hellenic families. 'Many individuals risked their lives to protect the Allies.' This behaviour towards the Allies was indicative of the Hellenic determination to make Allies feel at home away from home. It was ironic that the opposite was happening to Greek migrants living in Australia. The tendency of Greek immigrants to form organised groups incited members of the host society to various forms of control, including violence. As Raftopoulos recalls:

> I remember an instance outside Yiannopoulos' bookshop in Lonsdale Street in the city of Melbourne. We were a group of Hellene-Australian soldiers and had formed a circle and were speaking in Hellenic. We all were of Hellenic origin serving in the Australian Army. As we were speaking in Hellenic and also making certain physical communication gestures, another group of British-Australian soldiers was passing by, dressed in khaki similar to ours with the same crown on the uniform . . . but because we spoke in Hellenic, they attacked us and we were caught by the arms, although we were all the same kind of soldier, and all of us were struggling for the same cause, the same purpose (Interview with Raftopoulos, 1988).

Despite the Hellenic stand in the war, hostility towards Greeks was only partially defused (Saloutos 1964; *Paroikia*, May 1986; Interview with Raftopoulos, 1988). There is no evidence to suggest that Greeks were encouraged to participate in mainstream social and occupational activities any more frequently than other southern European population groups. Although the declaration of Greece on the side of the Allies provided relief for many Greeks living in English-speaking countries, including Britain, the United States and, especially, Australia, social mobility within the wider socio-economic and institutional structures of Australia still remained closed to foreigners. Raftopoulos argues that Australia remained a racist society which excluded non-British migrants from entering diverse mainstream social and occupational practices (Interview with Raftopoulos, 1988).

However, over many years, through diligence, hard work and related values attributed to their understanding of *philotimo* and progress, Hellenes came a long way towards establishing themselves in business. Because of their practice of using Greek workers in Greek-owned businesses, unlike most other southern Europeans Hellenes posed less of a threat to British-Australians in the job market. Yet the average British-Australian did not distinguish between those who opened up new avenues of employment that posed no threat to the living standards of the locals, and other groups who were a threat (Price 1963: 161; Borrie 1954; Kennedy 1976: 51). Raftopoulos emphasises the high percentage of self-employment among Hellenes by the 1940s. He maintains that, by 1945, the Hellenes in Melbourne who were not employed in a Hellenic-owned business numbered less than 30 people. He adds that:

> myself, Kostas Trilivos, Floros Demedtriades, Odysseus Kostopoulos, Jim James . . . we all sat down and calculated at the time the number of Hellenes who were not employed by Hellenic-owned enterprises and found that they did not exceed the number of 30 individuals. This may sound unreasonable but it was true (Interview with Raftopoulos, 1988).

Similarly, according to Commonwealth censuses of two contrasting periods during the inter-war and immediate post-war years, the number of self-employed Greeks increased significantly. According to the 1933 Census, 43 per cent of Greeks were employers or self-employed (18 per cent and 25 per cent respectively), despite the Great Depression's negative effect on the national economy. By 1947, this percentage was even higher. From a total of 8,730 members of the workforce who were born in Greece, 55.5 per cent were either employers

Illustration 7.5   The Taifalos brothers clearing land for sugar cane in Queensland, 1946. (*Source*: S. Raftopoulos)

(2,729) or self-employed (1,917) (Commonwealth Bureau of Census and Statistics 1947).

Self-employment was the vehicle that enabled Greek migrants to work in independent occupations and, at the same time, spread themselves across the country, offering their services to Australian customers in the shops that fed outback Australia. Reflecting on their childhood, Dow and Factor claim that, 'In those days, the best eating places in country towns were the cafes run by New Australians', adding that until service stations started offering meals, 'the only way to get a meal in a country town at night was to pop down to the Greeks' (Dow & Factor 1991: 134–5; Kennedy 1976: 44; Price 1963; Tsounis 1971a).

More than 20 years after the end of World War Two, non-British migrants could not make public pronouncements against the status quo without coming under the scrutiny of the secret service, the police force or the immigration author-ities. Australia, as an essentially isolated Victorian society, perceived itself as largely homogeneous, by 1947. Conse-quently, 'uniformity was held up for emulation', a view that was further reinforced through a policy of assimilation (Encel & Bryson 1984: 176–7). Languages other than English were still viewed as underground languages and taught by clergy and untrained instructors. The Hellenes, although having es-tablished their first schools at the turn of the twentieth century—almost immediately following the establishment of their Greek Orthodox Communities in Sydney and Mel-bourne—were still, in the 1950s, forbidden by legislation passed during the Great War to offer day-school education in languages other than English. According to Tamis:

a 1957 report on Greek afternoon schools in Australia suggested that their function should be restricted to that of Sunday Schools. The rationale for this was that only religious instruction should be taught because 'the Australian commu-nity will not tolerate any language acquisition effort for tongues [that is Greek] and they will press for the elimination of any ethnic activity on their soil' (Tamis 1988: 528).

Suddenly, this homogeneity, although protected by legisla-tion for assimilation, was challenged by the emergence of mass communications systems, an unprecedented expansion in manufacturing industry, increased urbanisation and the post-World War Two mass-migration program. An increasingly suburban lifestyle and the baby boom led Australia to become a consumer-oriented society.

Paradoxically, this emphasis on homogeneity did not always stop those who were members of organised labour from challenging the order of the status quo. For example, by the early 1950s, some members of the Greek Left and the CPA were already entangled in a struggle for citizenship rights and the abolition of the Dictation Test. One prominent member of the Greek Left, Jim Anastassiou from Cyprus, a member of the Building Workers Industrial Union and later a delegate and a member of the Committee of Management of the same union, went to great lengths in his fight for the abolition of the Dictation Test. In a recent interview with Anastassiou, George Chatzevasiles reveals the successful outcome of his struggle against the Australian bureaucracy in connection to the Dictation Test:

> Dr Evatt, the great constitutional lawyer and ALP leader, had advised Jim Anastassiou that failing the spelling [Dictation] Test did not take appeal, because [it was] the Government had the constitutional right to expel him from Australia. As it is apparent, Jim was not expelled, not because of the Government's generosity as much as the support of unionised labour. About five thousand waterside workers and other unionised labourers got together in the Town Hall and voted that 'there will be no ship which will transport Jim Anastassiou from Australia!' Finally, this terrible law was eliminated, and if today we are not in danger, we owe it to people like Jim Anastassiou who gave the battles so we can enjoy equality and multiculturalism . . . (Chatzivasiles 1995).

The Left's struggle for the abolition of the Dictation Test coincided with the building of factories geared for mass production of goods, which became centres (characteristically analogous to the sheep station), where often hundreds or even thousands of people worked. During this period, many migrants arrived 'on a two year contract to undertake manual labourers' employment, as a condition of their entry' (Borrie 1949: 44). Migrants were regarded as cheap labour, designed to help Australia to achieve rapid economic development. Hellenes and the majority of southern European migrants were employed as Australia's 'factory fodder' (Collins 1975; Collins 1988). Reflecting on this period, the editors of *Paroikia* (February 1986), characterised this migration as a kind of 'conscripted' labour force, for the completion of certain projects. The majority of this labour force consisted of 'individuals who presumably had limited commitments' outside their need for work and some cash. The Hellenes, first males and then females, who were brought to Australia arrived mainly by ship. These ships, especially those carrying the 'brides', created unforgettable emotional upheaval and were described as the 'ships of tears . . . the ships of loneliness and of desperation . . .' (*Paroikia*, March 1986: 46). As Mourikis observes:

> in the beginning were the shiploads of men. Those who were to fill the factories and mobilise them. Those who would open the roads and lay down the rail lines. Those who would build the hydroelectric power stations (such as the Snowy Mountain Hydro Electricity Scheme). Then were the shiploads of women. The 'ships with the brides', as the Australian newspapers were writing with irony at the time. As for the 'labour' demand, it was unprecedented! (Mourikis 1986: 38).

By the early 1960s, the 'ships with the brides' had been supplemented by 'airplanes with the brides' as a means of their speedier arrival. Either way, this arrangement was designed to contain most immigrants' socio-economic achievement within specific occupations. These categories involved jobs which Australians themselves did not want to do (Encel & Bryson 1984: 178). At the peak of their arrival between 1964–5, Greek migrants were largely involved in unskilled occupations and mainly employed in factories which used Fordist techniques to maximise production.[1] During this period, 68.6 per cent of migrants were classified as unskilled labour, with only 3.7 per cent in the professional and semi-professional categories, compared with 61.6 per cent and 1.6 per cent respectively for Italian migrants, but 14.9 per cent and 16.4 per cent respectively for British migrants. Overall, as Price observes, only some of those Greeks who arrived in the immediate postwar period managed to succeed in establishing themselves in some kind of independent business (Price 1968: 10–11). Some 20 per cent of Greek and Italian migrants belonged to 'employed' (that is, self-employed) categories— compared with 12 per cent of British migrants; 11 per cent of German migrants; and 7 per cent of Maltese migrants (Price 1968: 11). These categories included work in agriculture, retailing and food stores—for example, milk bars or fish and

Illustration 7.6   Many Hellene migrants were obliged to work for the greater part of their working lives as assembly 'hands' in factories such as this GMH plant. (*Source*: Christos Mourikis, *Parikia-Greek Monthly Review*, Dec. 1985: 35.)

chip shops—and were all areas in which Greeks succeeded. Agriculture, however, as in inter-war years, posed many challenges and most Greeks avoided it, with only a small proportion of migrants becoming involved in agriculture in Australia.

The high proportion of Greek employees in the factories has been a subject of intense debate over many years with racism, 'even in diluted form', continuing to provide the 'justification for the super-exploitation of migrant labour by alleging directly or indirectly that migrants are inferior' (Collins 1975: 123). Some have argued (Hunt 1972, 1978: 86–116) that Greek involvement in the manufacturing industry was inevitable because they arrived in such large numbers during the postwar period and thus could not be absorbed within the Greek shopkeeper communities. According to Zangalis, however, it was not simply because Greeks arrived in large numbers that they could not be absorbed in the Greek shopkeeper communities. It was because:

Illustration 7.7 Above, at a Melbourne Commonwealth government clothing factory in 1959, workers are having a break to celebrate an imminent Christmas. Approximately 100 Hellene, and another 700 Italian, Yugoslavs, German and other Australian women worked uninterruptedly next to each other as machinists under the Fordist-type production model. Front right, Maria Andreaki is sitting opposite co-worker Eudokia. (*Source*: Dimitra Temelcos)

there was no other place to go to without capital. The little money they were getting, they were spending it to raise families and paying off the mortgages of their houses. At the same time, Australians did not want small business people, they wanted migrants to work in the factories and stay in the factories (Interview with Zangalis, 1995).

Unable to be absorbed within the shopkeeper communities, the newcomers were often viewed with contempt by the well-established Greeks. Class differences were further intensified by political conflict in the struggle for leadership within the Hellenic communities of Australia. This conflict was further intensified by the 'great split' between the Hellenic lay community organisations and the newly-founded Holy Archdiocese of the Greek Orthodox Church of Australia (established in 1959) (Tsounis 1971a). As Collins commented, 'central to this

201

struggle for dominance in the Greek community was the tension between class and ethnicity, particularly after the emergence of multiculturalism' (Collins 1988: 94).

Issues of class difference became apparent even on the factory floor, where many different national groups were destined to work side by side. According to Zangalis, Greek workers became increasingly active through their participation in the industrial unions and this involvement was strengthened by the role of the Left. In instancing the participation of Greeks in industrial unions, Zangalis stresses that out of 100 CPA members who were working at General Motors in the 1950s, about 50 were Greeks. This was indicative of the fact that 'we didn't see unionised Labour as a temporary phenomenon but as something continuous that involved the workers' class struggle'. Within this framework, Greeks could see that 'the answers to their problems were in their cooperation with other migrants, and generally with other workers . . .'. 'Once this was clear, then through the unions, they became participants in the affairs of this country and not just spectators.' Zangalis argues further this cooperation could only have been achieved in the factories, as it was throughout the 1950s and 1960s, 'because the factories enabled the interaction of many ethnic groups at the same time'. In fact, comparatively, Greeks had the highest proportion of union participation of all migrant groups: '90 per cent of Greeks in the 1950s and 1960s being union members' and many, motivated by their Hellenic predisposition for democracy, were not content to be just members. They wanted to be, and often became, representatives, delegates and organisers, thus succeeding more than any other non-British migrant population group (Collins 1988; Interview with Zangalis, 1995). Zangalis also stresses that:

> The point I wish to make here is that although the Greeks had no Trade Union or factory work experience, within 5–6 years of being in industry in Australia, they provided the largest number of delegates and other union activists among migrants after the British (Interview with Zangalis, 1995).

In spite of Greek workers' interest in unions, their representation in the higher-ranking positions, for example, union official, remained limited. Tsounis (1971a) lists only 20 Greeks

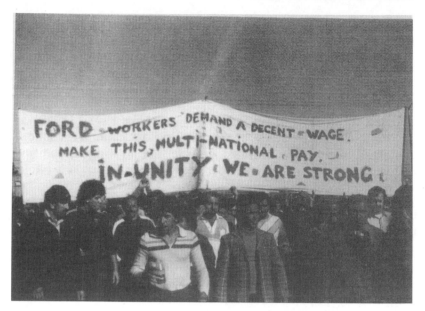

Illustration 7.8   Hellene workers joined with other migrants during the Ford Motor plant strikes of the early 1970s. (*Source*: 90th Anniversary Album of GOCM&V.)

who held union positions throughout Australia—this was minimum participation in positions of power and occurred because such positions were denied to Greeks and other migrants, although they formed the main labouring force in the manufacturing industry. None the less, according to Zangalis, within the manufacturing industry itself, 'Greeks were almost always the forerunners in establishing *cooperation* with other migrants and Australian workers' and, for this reason, they 'were promoted as delegates and organisers in order to enable the unions to function on the base level, in the job environment' (Interview with Zangalis, 1995).

The Greek officials pressed hard to achieve improved working conditions and wages, 'which often led to industrial strikes throughout the 1960s and 1970s'. According to Zangalis, Hellenic involvement in strikes included the General Motors strikes in both 1961 and 1964; the Aircraft Industry and the Dunlop Rubber strikes; the Kitchen Union Lever, Railways, Building Industry, Liquor Trades (including Beer and Restaurant), Waterside Workers, Seaman's Union strikes and others. In the 1973 Ford Broadmeadows strike, Greeks were the most militant group (Interview with Zangalis, 1995; Collins 1975; Collins 1988; Lever 1984). In an article entitled 'Greek Community Backs Strikes With Words and Money', Hawkins wrote, '. . . Greeks certainly were prominent both at the riot on Wednesday and the meeting on Friday which decided to strike indefinitely . . .' (Hawkins 1973: 18–19).

Paradoxically, despite such mobilisation, immigrant labour remained highly concentrated in the nation's manufacturing industry and, ironically, this was seen by the Australian public as a direct outcome of the abilities of Greek migrants, not as a situation created by the host society which denied migrants the better jobs. On the one hand, it was acknowledged that migrant labour should be integrated within the wider economy but, on the other hand, little was being done to help migrants and their children make that transition (Storer 1975; Collins 1988). As Hunt (1972) and Taft (1972: 87) have both pointed out, despite popular expectations, the reality was that immigrant integration could not really occur unless migrants were able to make connections with the host society. Formal contact, through education and inter-marriage, would not really occur until the second generation, therefore it was all but inevitable that many of the first generation remained in unskilled or labouring occupations.

The high proportion of southern European migrants involved in unskilled occupations, along with their residential patterns, led to the formation of predominantly migrant neighbourhoods, which many locals saw as 'ghettos' (Hunt 1972; Taft 1972; Collins 1988). It was argued that national 'ghettos' were self-perpetuating through the establishment of ethnic institutions and the use of languages other than English. However, it has now been acknowledged that such self-perpetuation—in many cases—reflected the failure of Australian institutions to provide improved social structures which would incorporate the migrants' experience. It cannot be denied that Australian institutions failed to go beyond the rationale of 'teaching sufficient fluency in English for the child to be absorbed into the economy above the level of unskilled labourer' (Taft 1972: 86).

Throughout the 1960s and much of the 1970s immigrants' upward mobility remained limited and this led to serious repercussions in periods of recession, when immigrant unemployment was almost always higher than that in the rest of the Australian labour force. As Collins put it: 'southern European immigrants function not only as a permanent addition to the secondary industry workforce, but also as a "buffer" group which absorbs disproportionately the unemployment generated in the business cycle' (Collins 1975: 117). As in the inter-war period, postwar Greek immigrants often started their struggle for upward mobility after being unemployed for long periods. For example, in the 1961 economic crisis, of the 300 unemployed individuals who marched to the Victorian Parliament protesting their unemployment situation, about 80 were Greeks, while another 5,000 out of 30,000 Greeks living in Victoria were unemployed (*Herald*, 30 May 1961: 3). Similarly, in the 1972 recession, unemployment among Greeks was 3.9 per cent, in comparison to 3.2 per cent for Italians and 2.1 per cent for all Australians (Collins 1975).

The economic status of immigrant labour was highlighted in the Henderson Report on *People in Poverty* (1969). This study showed that immigrants' earning power was limited to minimum income earnings, in comparison with other Australians. This discrimination, when combined with prohibitive housing costs and a lack of suitable housing prevented migrants from experiencing upward social mobility—with often unforeseeable implications for their future and that of their children (Henderson, Harcourt & Harper 1969, 1975; Collins 1975).[2]

The impact of immigrant experience in shaping the perceptions and attitudes of Australians has been highlighted in various studies. Public opinion surveys carried out between 1948 and 1978 raised questions of acceptability, and documented contemporary Australian attitudes towards various migrant groups and the prevalent opposition to the entry of most ethnic groups—with the exception of British migrants. It is important to note that the 'rating of favourability towards a national group was determined by its similarity to the Australian lifestyle and one's share in English history' (Callan 1986: 71). A survey taken in 1948 indicates that 32 per cent of Australians thought that Greeks should be kept out and 42 per cent considered that only a few should be let in. Only 8 per cent of Australians wanted to encourage the Greeks to come (Alomes, Dober & Hellier 1984: 13). Later surveys, often using the Oeser and Hammond (1954) research as a bench mark, reported more positive attitudes towards German, Greek and Italian immigrants, together with the widespread belief that migrants *could* assimilate (Taft 1966; Richardson & Taft 1968; FitzGerald 1988). The Perth studies (Taft 1966; Richardson & Taft 1968) indicated a widespread belief that immigrants *should* assimilate and, though prejudice still existed, it did not have a strong emotional basis. However, British-Australians still only rarely invited immigrants into their homes (Stoller 1966; Jupp 1966).

Despite a general improvement in attitudes towards the Greeks and other migrants over time (Taft 1978; Callan 1986: 71), some hostility remained intact during the postwar years. This hostility was expressed in the form of verbal attacks on migrants through a number of derogatory epithets. For example, Greeks were called 'wogs', 'fish and chips', 'greasy Greeks', 'dagoes', 'strangers', 'foreigners', 'aliens', 'migrants', 'them' as against 'us'—to name just a few means by which Australians could exclude the unwanted (Interview with Patriarcheas, 1981; Interview with Trahanas, 1991). As Janiszewski and Alexakis stress:

> Unfortunately though, as with the Anglo-Celt, stereotypes have also been imposed and feverishly maintained . . . With the Greeks, an 'urban stereotype' of the Greek fish-and-chip shop owner or cafe proprietor, or the 'folkloric stereotype' of Greek festivals and dancers in traditional costumes, predominate. Accumulatively, such attitudes effectively 'marginalise' Greek-Australians . . . as being dwellers of the outer perimeters or fringes of mainstream Australian society (Janiszewski & Alexakis 1989: 72).

Host society attitudes did not change following the industrialisation and socio-economic transformation of the postwar period, nor did this economic progress end the socio-economic inequalities experienced by various migrants and working-class Australians (Collins 1976; Encel & Bryson 1984: 176–7). On the contrary, these factors and the sudden socio-economic transformation of Australian society prevented a smooth social transition. In addition, there were other forces which continued to fuel xenophobic attitudes. Fear of the

Illustration 7.9 Hellenes and other southern Europeans were often stereotyped and called names such as 'wogs', as shown by the graffiti in Melbourne. (*Source: Parikia-Greek Monthly Review,* Dec. 1985: 37.)

'yellow peril' continued to dominate public opinion and the impact of the Cold War and anti-communist propaganda, particularly in the wake of the Chinese Revolution and the Korean and Vietnamese wars, aggravated the tensions of life in Australia. All these factors, together with the large-scale migration of the postwar period, resulted in increasing levels of discrimination against foreigners. Consequently, host society attitudes towards the Hellenic presence in Australia were shaped by many contrasting socio-economic indicators which created a confusing state of affairs. As Alomes, Dober and Hellier point out:

> The reaction against alien 'foreign immigrants' was similar to fears about communism and invasion. Images of disease, or at least dirt and smell, of race and of evil were common in

popular perceptions of migrants (Alomes, Dober & Hellier 1984: 13).

The anxiety about communism was intensified by Menzies' public speeches and the Liberal government's anti-communist campaigns, which created rising political and public hysteria (Alomes, Dober & Hellier 1984: 2, 10). Given the anti-communist hysteria of the period and the high Greek migrant membership in both the CPA and their own Greek Workers' Leagues organisations throughout Australia, governments did not take kindly to their presence. As a consequence, the activities of the Greek Left were monitored by the special branch of the police force (Tsounis 1971a; *Neos Kosmos*, 13 March 1995).

This anti-communist hysteria forced the Federal government into the 'infamous' decision to conscript Greeks and other immigrants into the Australian Armed Forces. What eventuated was the conscription of young Greek migrants, such as George Kallianis, who were not even Australian citizens and had been in the country for less than a year. Conscription outraged the Hellenic community and feelings ran even higher against the Liberal government when Greeks were forced to undergo medical examinations by Australian recruiting officers, to establish if they were 'fit' enough to serve in the Australian Armed Forces. Those found fit could be and were sent to Vietnam. In fact, a recently revealed list of 170 Hellenic names shows them as being among the 50,000 Australians and others who served in Vietnam (*Greek Times*, 29 April 1995: 1, 2). By the mid-1960s, the Hellenic ethnic press—especially the *Hellenic Herald* and *Neos Kosmos*—were on the attack against the government and ran many headlines against the war. These papers encouraged young Greeks to return home and live, if they had to, on 'olives and bread', rather than fight in an 'unjust, 'imperialist war' away from home. The Greek Left, in conjunction with the CPA and other Australian organisations (Tsounis 1971a, 1971b), became extremely vocal and, through their own Greek Workers' Leagues' organisational publications and radio programs, encouraged the community to mobilise against Hellenic and Australian participation in the war (Hearn 1971: 151).

Conscription of migrants was an extreme example of the government's policy of assimilation. Academic and public opinion of the time held that for immigrants—and especially their Australian-born children—acculturation needed to be acceptable to Australian ways (Taft 1972: 87).

According to Martin, the general Australian response to immigrants from the 1950s to the 1970s endorsed the Commonwealth government's 'forceful promotion of assimilation policy. In short, immigrants were expected to assimilate without aid or encouragement from the locals and if they did not it was their fault' (Martin 1953: 81). Martin also contrasted social reality with what some perceived as an idealised version of life in Australia, which most people wanted migrants to accept, but which few Australians could achieve themselves (Ibid.).

The expectation of immigrant assimilation often outraged Hellenes who, according to Grambas, had been 'deceived by Australia's recruiting officers in Greece. These officials had failed to inform recruited migrants about factory labouring, working conditions and assimilation. They had not informed the Hellenes that they were to live in the inner industrial "slums" and polluted environments, and that they intended to convert them as they did from rural to industrial workers within a week of their arrival'. Australian officials had said nothing about racism or the exclusion of migrants from the wider range of the host society's socio-economic practices, nor that they would have to fight to assert their 'rights' almost immediately after their arrival (Interview with Grambas, 1991). Grambas' view is shared by Trahanas, who states in addition that Australians asked Greeks, Italians and other Europeans to come to Australia but, following settlement, Australians failed to exhibit a sense of *philotimo* and *philoxenia* because they were *aphilotimoi*, and did not know what *philoxenia* was. They did not have a sense of *philotimo*, because Australian culture was nationalistic and, above all, materialistic. Trahanas insisted that materialism was all that mattered:

> It was taken for granted that Hellenes came to Australia to stay and not because of the economic destruction that was brought about in Greece due to the events of the Second World War, and the role attributed to monopoly capitalism in investing capital elsewhere and thus targeting the transfer around of innocent people (Interview with Trahanas, 1991).

209

In conclusion, this chapter has provided an account of the experiences of Hellenic migrants and the pattern of social mobility in the context of the host society's public and popular attitudes during the inter-war and postwar periods. In spite of the contribution made by migrants in general—and Greeks in particular—to Australia, Australian racial discrimination against them, although waning over time, was not eradicated during this period. Before World War Two, racism, combined with the exclusion of southern Europeans from the job market which was controlled by British-Australians, forced Greeks to remain in their shopkeepers' communities, with equally segregated labour in the nation's expanding manufacturing industry during the postwar period. This expansion was the main cause of Australia's southern European mass-migration program. Exploitation of migrant labour led to the increasing organisation of Greeks within the Left movement, which challenged the Dictation Test and the policy of assimilation. Many Greek workers joined industrial unions, thus becoming a major force in many state and national industrial strikes. How the migrants' campaigns for their rights became part of a wider social movement is discussed in Chapter 8.

Whitlam and beyond

Policy changes initiated during the Whitlam and post-Whitlam periods mark the end of one historical era and the beginning of another, in which Australian government administrations started to introduce vital and often radical changes in migration policy. By the 1970s, the migrant campaigns for social change in Australia had found many sympathisers within the Left movement and the ALP, among whom were ALP leader Gough Whitlam and his Minister for Immigration, Al Grassby, whose famous 1973 speech on the 'Family of Nations' sowed the philosophical seeds for the establishment of an Australian multiculturalism, and a redefinition of the assimilationist terms 'migrants' and 'new Australians'. By introducing the concepts 'ethnos' and 'ethnicity', Grassby's speech laid the basis for the emergence of 'multiculturalism'—as understood and defined by the Ethnic Rights Movement (ERM). His views found strong support within various academic circles and ethnic communities, although the term 'multiculturalism' itself did not appear in government reports until 1977 (Grassby in Bowen 1977; Castles et al. 1988).

The policy shift rhetorically marked in the 'Family of Nations' speech both acknowledged and heightened the increasingly vocal role of the Greek Left in asserting ethnic rights within the Australian bureaucracy. By the early 1970s, the Left's initiatives were strengthened by the involvement of the Australian Greek Welfare and other Hellenic community organisations. This period saw several Greek leaders enter mainstream debate for an Australian multiculturalism. As the Greek-Australian lawyer George Papadopoulos observes:

> In the beginning the Greek Welfare was the first overtly and aggressively ethnic agency, particularly in terms of the 1970s and working from a rights-based approach. This is not to say there were not other ethnic-specific agencies but that they operated on a quieter and at that time a more welfare (charitable?) based approach. In essence they were passive about their ethnicity . . . (Papadopoulos 1993: 1).

In contrast, Greek members of the ERM loudly demanded government recognition of Australia as a polyethnic nation rather than a monolingual, monocultural society. Papadopoulos, a prominent member of the ERM, argued that 'Greeks were among the forerunners for rights in Australia'. Unlike other immigrant communities, 'Greeks were very vocal about multiculturalism and the need for a more open and tolerant society' (Interview with Papadopoulos, 1992). A similar observation was made by Trahanas, who stated that Australia needed social change because, until then, the viewpoint of Greeks, like that of all non-British migrants, was considered at worst irrelevant and at best of secondary importance. He further stresses that:

> the voice of migrants and of Hellenes in particular was not heard. No one asked the Hellenes what their needs were or why they actually migrated to this country; at the same time, the Australian public was kept in the dark as to why Greek migrants had come to their country (Interview with Trahanas, 1991).

One method of excluding the migrant voice was the denial of their naturalisation. According to Collins (1975: 121), the authorities used this method to exclude those who were politically active, especially those of the Left. Some Greek migrants were denied Australian naturalisation, for example, a number of those who were involved in the formation of the Melbourne branch of the 'Committee for the Restoration of Democracy' in Greece following the 1967 colonels' coup.[1]

This Committee, with Dennis Sikiotis as its secretary,

Illustration 8.1 Prime Minister Gough Whitlam with self-exiled Andreas Papandreou, future Prime Minister of Greece, in Melbourne in 1974 at the invitation of a coordinated effort by the Hellene-Australians and the Melbourne Committee for the Restoration of Democracy in Greece. (*Source: Neos Kosmos.*)

lobbied politicians, unions and government administrators with its demands for Australian intervention in the cause of restoration of democracy in Greece, the end of discrimination against those who were denied citizenship rights due to the refusal of the Australian authorities to grant basic human rights, and the introduction of social change following the demographic changes that occurred because of the postwar mass immigration. On the Committee were 15 prominent members of the Greek Left and the Centre Unity forces of the political spectrum, several of whom directly or indirectly had been entangled in a struggle for citizenship rights and social change in Australia since the 1950s. Among them were George Zangalis (Railways Union), Dennis Sikiotis (an academic at the Royal Melbourne Institute of Technology) and

Christos Mourikis (a waterside worker in the 1950s and, from the 1960s, a journalist). Mourikis' case had previously reached the New South Wales Parliament chambers (Cavanagh 1965). According to Zangalis, there were about 1,000 individuals, of whom up to 100 were Hellenes who, although residents for more than 15 years, were unable to gain Australian citizenship. Successive Australian governments had denied them citizenship because they were active on the Left, extremely vocal in the anti-Vietnam campaigns and 'rights for migrants' movement and advocated the need for improvement in working conditions and remuneration for all Australian workers. Zangalis also recalls that:

> Giovanni Sgro and myself became citizens in 1973 but I repeat there were more than 1,000 people who were denied naturalisation without any excuse apart of course from being active in a non-Liberal party, in political and social organisation activities (Interview with Zangalis, 1993).[2]

Zangalis argues that the struggles of the ERM enabled ethnic communities to bring the important issues and concerns of the migrant experience to the attention of the authorities. He emphasises that, in an attempt to meet the varying needs of migrants, 'the Ethnic Communities, or the migrant workers' movement, or the Ethnic Rights Movement if you like' organised various conferences in the 1970s, including the Migrant Education Conference, the Communist Party of Australia (CPA) Conference, and the Conference on Health, which empowered migrants to elect their leaders and forced governments, for the first time, to consult with ethnic communities about ethnic issues and provisions. The Ethnic Rights Movement:

> forced society to face up to this reality, that Australia is different, and that demographically and socially there are different classes of people in the work force where migrants go . . . ethnic background is not and it should not be seen as synonymous to inferior in economic, social and political status (Interview with Zangalis, 1993).

These issues were articulated in the *Ethnic Rights Power and Participation* 'agenda', prepared by the ERM (Storer

1975). It contained a number of articles addressing the multi-cultural needs of ethnic population groups in Australian society. Contributions were solicited from Greeks and other authors—of predominantly non-British ethnic origins. The issues raised informed debate over government policy under the Whitlam administration and thereby contributed to reforms which were continued and extended under the Fraser and subsequent Labor government administrations (Interview with Papadopoulos, 1992).

According to Matheson, the debate for rights has 'never ended', with ongoing initiatives such as the Galbally Report (1978) and the Jupp Report (1986). The Galbally recommen-dations, for example, helped to establish SBS ethnic radio and television programs and to improve education provisions for the teaching of languages other than English, including 'bilingual' programs at both primary and secondary levels in various Australian states. Almost ten years after the Galbally Report, the Jupp Report (1986) reviewed what had taken place in terms of policy and migrant initiatives and made proposals for future structures, policies and programs that were designed to ensure the coordination of services delivery (Jupp 1986). For Mathe-son, the positive results of this ongoing campaign can be seen in such areas as education, where Greeks have been able to establish their own schools—at both primary and secondary levels—and incorporate Hellenic language and culture into the mainstream teaching curriculum. This was a radical departure from the days of the White Australia Policy, when migrants were not allowed to speak their own language in public. In 1994, there were about six bilingual Hellenic schools nationally, with most being in the states of Victoria and New South Wales. Although these schools were under-equipped to meet a more balanced bilingual and multicultural education of their students, in broad terms multiculturalism had enabled Hellenes to improve on the status of cultural deficit they had previously experienced through the partial incorporation of their own language and culture within the curriculum of government schools and, therefore, within the broader framework of the educational system operating in different Australian states.

> In the area of education the objectives . . . were in respect of languages and culture; the maintenance of languages, the notion of community, and the value of cultural diversity, I

think we succeeded. I don't think it's perfect, we have a long way to go . . . the respect for diversity, the richness is very much a part of Australia. In that broad objective we succeeded (Interview with Matheson, 1993).

Others have contested the 'success' of 'multiculturalism'. Zangalis pointed out that various members of the ERM preferred the compound terms 'polyethnic' and 'polyethnicity' instead of 'multiculturalism' because Australia is a 'polyethnic society' and the mosaic ethnic character of Australian society is better captured by use of this term (Interview with Zangalis, 1993). Similarly, Jayasuriya (1991, 1993) commented that the term 'multiculturalism', in its normative sense, is a 'way of thinking about issues of migrant settlement which replaced the rigid monocultural assimilation of the 1950s and 1960s. In essence, multiculturalism signified that variant cultures can flourish in harmony side by side, provided that there is an acceptance of the commonalities of society embodied in the political and legal system' (Jayasuriya 1993: 1). This conception remains an unresolved issue politically and legally, and 'signifies the paradox that what cultural pluralism needs is to reconcile commonalities, and the existence of cultural differences' with an overriding universalism (Jayasuriya 1993: 1). The author further adds that what recent reports:

and in particular the Labor Government's National Agenda (OMA 1988), have been reluctant to do is to present a coherent and defensible rationale for multiculturalism in the 1990s. This needs to take account of the inherent strains and contradictions of the old model, without losing sight of the tangible achievements of the past, as well as to address sensibly, the needs and concerns of the host society and ethnic minorities. The denial of difference and adherence to universalism, [allows only for a] symbolic form of multiculturalism which extols the value of cultural difference provided it is relegated to the private domain as manifestation of one's ethnicity and culture (Jayasuriya 1993: 6).

Even the concept 'ethnic' has been used by certain authorities wrongly or in order to show difference between the British-Australians and other migrants. Unfortunately:

216

'marginalisation' is commonly evidenced by incorrect and divisionist use of the word 'ethnic' in Australia, to refer to all cultural groups other than the Anglo-Celts (Janiszewski & Alexakis 1989a: 72).

It follows, therefore, that multiculturalism came into existence as a generalised government policy in order to achieve the opposite to ghetto-like residential and occupational enclaves, by providing access and equity for all Australian citizens irrespective of their ethnic background. With corresponding government recognition ethnic communities have gained legal rights to linguistic and cultural maintenance. In addition, the provision of legal protection through the *Racial Discrimination Act*, 1975 and the ratification of the International Convention on the Elimination of All Kinds of Racial Discrimination, was welcomed by all members of the Hellenic community and consequently encouraged significant residential and social participation in the mainstream Australian society.

In practice, however, despite multiculturalism, government decision-making often discriminated against certain migrants. The implementation of anti-discrimination laws did not stop injustice occurring against specific ethnic population groups who lived on the margins of Australian society. As Zangalis (1993) argues, post-Whitlam administrations have failed to consult with representatives of ethnic communities (one of the key objectives of the ERM) and left the decision-making in the hands of selected bureaucrats—irrespective of the background and understanding of the views and opinions of those affected. This has resulted in decisions being taken that are detrimental to ethnic community minorities. Reflecting on the immigrant experience, Bottomley observes:

> Although it is undoubtedly true that Australian institutions have still not really faced the task of providing services and opportunities for immigrants and their offspring, those who define policy and practice need a more radical reorientation to take into account the different kinds of cultural capital held by people of non-English speaking background (Bottomley 1991: 104).

What this suggests is that the fear of cultural difference has not been sufficiently eliminated in Australia. A recent

217

survey found that 55 per cent of general respondents thought that multiculturalism led to urban concentrations of minorities (Jupp, McRobbie & York 1990: 12), and the determination of certain ethnic groups to make their voices heard has often been criticised and condemned in offensive and defamatory ways by government bureaucrats and the mass media. As mentioned, Greek migrants who were vocal about the establishment of policies that celebrated cultural difference and granted migrants rights were viewed with 'envy' by their hosts (Bottomley 1993: 13; Interview with Sidiropulos, 1995). A well-known example of this envy was the so-called 'socio-medical syndrome' that became known by varying names such as the 'Greek back', 'Mediterranean back' or 'migrant back', all of which replaced the 'Irish back'. This 'migrant back syndrome' even gained political credence within the Australian bureaucracy and became formally known as the 'Greek Conspiracy Case' against the Department of Social Security. This title, as used, for several years, by a section of the mass media, aimed at stigmatising the Hellenic community through manipulated news stories and ignored the resulting emotional impact on Greek migrants. In fact, this attitude was nothing more than a blatant government attack, through overt and covert discrimination, against the Hellenic community for being vocal about migrants' rights. They were accused of malingering in order to defraud the Department of Social Security. Many injured workers (Greeks were only one minority among many) were unlawfully arrested by the police and had their pensions cut, while others were too scared to claim benefits to which they were entitled (Aitkin 1977; *Contact* (*Epaphe*) 1984: 21–6). In response to this situation, the Greek-born Labor MLA for Richmond, Theo Sidiropoulos, questioned the legality of the actions of the then Social Security Minister, Senator Guilfoyle, over the alleged fraud:

> I told the Victorian Parliament that there were criminal elements in every community and that the headlines about the alleged fraud discriminated against not only Australian Greeks, but 'ethnic Australians'. I emphasised that this discrimination marked a sharp contrast to privileges enjoyed by the Chief Secretary, Mr Dickie, during the land deals inquiry. Also that the media headline had not been seen announcing

Illustration 8.2 ALP MPs in Melbourne, 1986, with a visiting delega-
tion. Theo Sidiropoulos (far right) was the first
Greek-born member of the Victorian Parliament, and
Andrew Theophanous (3rd from left) the first Greek-
born member of the House of Representatives. (*Source*:
T. Sidiropoulos)

'White Anglo-Saxon, Australian fraud', and that there was no
mention of the Australian Housing Commission officers
involved . . . and that the outrage in some conservative
quarters about the amount of money going out of the country
in social services payments would have been better directed
at multi-national companies such as Utah which had paid
$141.2 million in dividends to its United States parent
company the previous year (Interview with Sidiropoulos,
1995).

Bottomley argues that this is a phenomenon of state
intervention that 'goes beyond the efficacy of icons of Australian democracy celebrated in works such as the FitzGerald
Report' (Bottomley 1993: 13). She further argues that state
legislation has exceeded both what multiculturalism stands for
and democratic practices by ignoring the rule of law and the

individual's right to freedom of speech. In explaining this point the author stresses that:

> powerful emotions have revealed themselves countless times in Australia, not only in the complex relations between Aboriginal people and settlers, but also in various anti-immigrant campaigns and in national scandals such as the 1978–83 social security witch-hunt where virtually all Greek-speakers were slurred into a mess of potage as cheats, liars and organised criminals, hundreds were arrested in dawn raids on their homes, untold millions of dollars of taxpayers' money was spent in legal and related expenses involving extremely shady practices by public authorities, and the whole circus resulted in dismissal of all charges, after the longest and most expensive legal proceeding in the history of British law (Bottomley 1993: 13).

It seems that the only people to benefit from the 'Greek Conspiracy Case' were the Australian media and the legal profession.

Despite the lack of evidence to prove accusations often made against selected sections of the population, through their control of the 'immense' public power of the state, bureaucrats tend to either ignore or devalue the importance of cultural identity and the dichotomy between the 'private' and 'public' spheres of life. Moreover, the burcaucrats, with their

> homogeneous identities defined within the contours of that power by definition deny the challenge of the cultural difference. The pluralist policy of multiculturalism has valorised ethnicity and played down other forms of power relations, such as those based on gender and class (Bottomley 1993: 15).

Multiculturalism, as Zangalis notes, has not improved working conditions and remuneration for Australian workers, nor has it led to a greater proportion of migrants being elected as union officials or addressed poverty in Australia. Although Greek migrants have remained highly active in industrial unions, and have had the largest number of representatives as well as members of any non-British ethnic population group since the Second World War, they are, even now, under-represented in jobs as high union officials. In summing up his reasoning for these failures Zangalis states, 'in a world of injustice it is difficult to achieve justice' (Interviews with Zangalis, 1993, 1995). That is, in spite of the adoption of multiculturalism and their many years of concerted effort Greeks, like other working-class migrants, remain on the margins of the Australian economic and occupational structures (Henderson 1975; Collins 1988). It is in this sense that multiculturalism departed from the 'rights objectives', at least as they were envisaged by the Greek Left. Papadopoulos comments that:

> in recent years Australia's discussions of Multiculturalism are . . . vitiated by reliance on ethnicity as a non-dependent variable and by omitting class, race and gender from certain key elements of discussions re policy and issues . . . (Papadopoulos 1993: 1).

Obvious class differences can be found in the occupational hierarchy which multiculturalism has not helped to alleviate, with most southern Europeans continuing to be occupationally disadvantaged. According to the 1976 ABS Census (see Appendix 5), most Greeks were still involved in the 'Tradesmen, etc.' occupations (61.23 per cent of females and 50.67 per cent of males), while their participation in the professional and administrative occupations was only 3.15 per cent and 10.67 per cent respectively. In comparison, the figures for British-Australians employed in manual occupations were significantly lower (37.61 per cent of males and 7.31 per cent of females), with a much higher participation rate in professional and administrative occupations (26.1 per cent for males and 11.75 per cent for females). Similarly, the modal category for British-Australian females was 'Clerical Workers'. Only 6.95 per cent of Greek women were employed in this category, with their modal category being 'Tradesmen, etc.'.

This lack of occupational dispersion of Greeks into the broader Australian economic market was linked to the host society's unreadiness as a receiving society. Australia failed to recognise and capitalise on migrant skills and qualifications obtained from overseas (non-British) institutions. For example, during the postwar period, with the Australian Medical

Association dominating the profession, Greek doctors were often forced to join other highly-qualified migrants in seeking employment in manual labouring occupations. This meant that when bridging courses to re-train qualified migrants according to Australian standards were introduced in the late 1970s, government policy had already stranded many thousands of individuals in unskilled occupations. Although bridging courses have been increased over the last 20 years, only a small proportion of migrants have completed them and, equally, only a small proportion have managed to obtain employment in their chosen field. According to the chairman of Ethnic Affairs of South Australia, of the 3,000 doctors, for example, who had (by 1994) completed a bridging course, only 800 managed to pass the course's stringent requirements. Although the results of those who undertake bridging courses in other disciplines may be proportional, at least the debate for the recognition of overseas qualifications is still going on (Nocella 1994).

A report prepared by the Bilingual Consultancy Network (BCN) (1994) for OMA and the National Office of Overseas Skills Recognition (NOOSR) has made a series of recommendations it considers necessary to facilitate the recognition of overseas skills and qualifications. The report found that of the 72 migrants interviewed from Asian, European and Arabic backgrounds, only one in four participants who arrived under the family migration scheme had their qualifications assessed pre-migration and they were often unemployed because their qualifications were not recognised in Australia. Similarly, many 'participants were confused about the migration assessment purposes and the formal skills/qualifications recognition required by individual associations and trades'. In remembering the postwar Hellenic migrant experience in Australia, Trahanas estimates:

> that up to about 20 per cent of Greek migrants had either completed high school or were tertiary students in Greece prior to migration, not to mention the graduates. Many stopped studies for financial or other family reasons to come to Australia. Although many had excellent academic results from our studies. When we arrived in Australia neither government authorities nor any other organisation asked us

what could be done with our qualifications, our skills and abilities . . . no one encouraged or guided us how to improve our chances to get a better job with our skills or qualifications or make use of our motivation and determination. Instead, we were all lumped together in the factory as labour force. Soon we realised that all Australians were concerned about was to increase the numbers of their European working hands. It follows that when we came here in the 1950s and 1960s Australia not only did not have the infrastructure as a receiving society nor was it willing to create the ground to help its migrants improve their lot (Interview with Trahanas, 1991).

After years of concerted effort, many Greeks managed to find better jobs and break away from the factory labour force. According to the 1981 ABS Census, the income status, occupational and educational mobility of Greeks and other ethnic groups in Australia now began to reverse the trends previously observed (see Appendix 6). It is observed that the first- and second-generation Australian- and British-born showed a high degree of similarity across the occupational and educational spectrum (Hugo 1986). In contrast, the NESB migrants, particularly the Greeks, Italians and 'Yugoslavs', exhibited the greatest occupational divergence and increasing attainment of higher educational qualifications in subsequent generations. In 1981, almost half of the Greek (47.1 per cent) and over half of both the Italian (51.3 per cent) and Yugoslavian (58.6 per cent) first-generation migrants were employed as tradesmen and unskilled workers; a quarter or less of the second generation were employed in these occupational categories (Greeks 20.7 per cent; Italians 25.5 per cent; 'Yugoslavs' 25 per cent). Thus, there had been a significant shift between the first and the second generations—from tradesmen and unskilled labourers to a whole range of practices in the 'top end' of the occupational ladder. To illustrate this change, there has also been a significant shift in the professional occupations—from 5.7 per cent to 17.4 per cent—between first- and second-generation Greeks. These same intergenerational shifts were also observed for other southern European ethnic groups: (from 5.7 per cent to 12.6 per cent for Italians and 4.9 per cent to 14.8 per cent for the 'Yugoslavs'). In contrast, the 1981 Census shows that occupational mobility of first- and second-generation British and Irish migrants and Australians has been horizontal and static (with 23.6 per cent of these groups remaining in trades and unskilled occupations and 18.4 per cent in professional categories) (Hugo 1986; Collins 1988: 189–91). Similarly, according to the 1986 Census, there has been further occupational divergence in ethnic groups, with a drastic increase in the number of Greeks in the 'Self-Employed' occupational category, (more than 28 per cent of all Greeks in New South Wales were recorded as being self-employed and employers) (Castles 1991). The figures suggest that there is a clear departure from previous occupational practices (see Appendix 7). A similar trend has been observed in the area of tertiary educational qualifications obtained between generations. By 1981 the figures had risen from 1.4 per cent to 7.2 per cent for Greeks; 2.2 per cent to 5.3 per cent for Italians; 1.6 per cent to 5.7 per cent for the 'Yugoslavs'; and 7.9 per cent to 7.8 per cent for Australians. This trend is further elaborated by an inter-generational mobility study between first- and second-generation migrants prepared by the Bureau of Immigration Research (BIR). The study, which is based on the 1991 Census, shows that while Greeks have the highest proportion of people with no tertiary qualification, at the same time they also have the highest proportion of individuals between two generations who have gained a degree from tertiary institutions (18.8 per cent of Greeks surveyed gained degrees in contrast to 13.1 per cent of Italians, 15.2 per cent of 'Yugoslavs' and 10.8 per cent of Australians) (see Appendix 8).

Other Hellenes continued to pioneer industries such as opal mining and pearl fishing. In fact, for over a century Hellenes have made a significant contribution to the establishment of the Australian pearl industry and the increasing numbers of Kalymnians brought to Australia during the postwar period meant that Hellenes became the nation's foremost pearl luggers and traders in Darwin, Broome and elsewhere (Janiszewski & Alexakis 1989a: 72). Many others sought their fortune in the opal mines of Lightning Ridge, Coober Pedy and Mintabie and, in some cases, managed to gain control of a large part of the mining and marketing of opals (Interview with Karefylakis, 1994).

Illustration 8.3   For most migrants upward social mobility within Australia has been a struggle to achieve. However, as the illustration shows, Stephen and Maria Themelios' family has been one of the success stories. All three daughters succeeded in getting their degrees from the University of Melbourne. (*Source*: Dimitra Temelcos)

On the other hand, in industries such as agriculture, Hellenic participation remained almost static between the 1970s and 1980s. This in part reflects the comparatively low number of Greeks who entered into agricultural occupations. Many of those who succeeded in purchasing farm properties in the 1960s and 1970s did so through hard work and thrift. The purchase of farm properties was often the cause of internal chain migration by many Greeks, a practice which sometimes resulted in the conversion of predominantly British-Australian areas into southern European ones. Such conversions occurred despite the efforts of local inhabitants to prevent large numbers of southern Europeans from entering British-Australian areas. As Price observes (1963), in some farm districts such as Mildura, Shepparton and Murrumbidgee, 'often deserted and derelict lands sold by British-Australians to pay off debts were bought by Greeks'. Similarly, land sales in Robinvale and the Riverland meant that many Greeks who had managed to save for a deposit and with the banks' encouragement borrowed the rest of the money, were able to purchase farms and, from this starting point, most made very significant inroads into land and building ownership. By 1988, therefore, in some towns of the Riverland (for example, Renmark, Berri, Loxton, Barmera, Paringa and Monash), Greek fruit-growers owned up to 25 per cent of the irrigated land (Renmark Irrigation Records 1988; Berri Land Irrigation Records 1988).

Discrimination continued, however, against Greek agriculturalists in the Riverland, Mildura, Shepparton and elsewhere. The local authorities, through their control of the Land and Irrigation Authorities of the Riverland, created regular problems for Greek and other migrant fruit-growers in relation to the timing and volume of irrigated water. Similarly, in contrast to British-Australian farmers, Greek growers faced severe economic problems due to exploitation from the Riverland Fruit and Wine Co-operatives, who often failed to pay for the produce they purchased, with the result that many growers lost large amounts of money (see Appendix 9). British-Australians, having full control of the administration of the fruit-growing industry, were able to use hidden agenda tactics that enabled them to extract greater benefits from that industry for themselves, thus depriving Greeks and other non-British migrants of their rights (Interview with Dedes, 1988).

Throughout the postwar era, especially in the 1970s and 1980s, Greek fruit-growers in the Riverland organised themselves and became politically mobile in an attempt to achieve their 'rights'. They did this firstly by electing a committee,[3] secondly by exerting significant political pressure on both the local then the Federal and South Australian governments. According to Dedes, towards the late 1970s, 200 cars were driven to the South Australian–Victorian border at Kealba. The purpose of this mobilisation:

> was to close the highway (number 20) that links Victoria to South Australia and New South Wales. We believed in this way we would make the Federal Government show interest for our economic devastation. When we arrived there the police intervened and told to us to stop because we were obstructing the traffic . . . ! The message finally arrived at the government in Canberra not only because of the rally

Illustration 8.4 Hellenic family of fruit-growers picking fruit in Renmark during 1965. Rear, left to right: brothers Angelos and Panayiotis Kalantzis, Anna Vlachos, Voula Kalfantis. Front, left to right: Yiannis Kalantzis, Konstantina Kalantzis, Dionysios Vlachos. (*Source*: Y. Kalantzis)

but because of our poverty here in the Riverland and, consequently, the continuation of our campaigns and efforts. The Fraser government had sent Ian Sinclair, Minister of Agriculture and leader of the National Country Party. When he came, on 19 December 1978, the word was spread quickly and about 1,000 of us got together at the Renmark football oval. When we asked him to find ways so we could sell our produce so we can get paid for it, he told us that 'there was an economic crisis and that the Government will try and look for a solution'. I told him that we suffer economically and that we have difficulties in meeting our bank loans terms, and he told me 'you should go to the unemployment office [and get the dole]' . . . In other words, these were the Government incentives believe it or not . . . Then I told him that this is a nice answer—to want to convert people who operated small businesses into bludgers. In reaction to this, he took his comb out of his pocket and started to comb his hair so he can be photographed and look beautiful in the newspaper. The Federal government had given us the PULL

227

SCHEME both before and after our mobilisation which was a failure, because it meant that we had to uproot our trees and vines and were to be compensated (as some did later) with $800–$1,000 an acre. It was obvious from the beginning that his scheme did not and could not have worked because it was not a productive solution to our crisis . . . since if you uprooted a tree or a vine as some of us did under this scheme, we had to wait for at least five years for new produce (Interview with Dedes, 1988).

While the demonstrators may not have achieved all their goals, their ability to mobilise at this level demonstrated a capacity to organise and apply political pressure on Australian governments to improve developments in agriculture and the fruit-growing industry (Interview with Dedes, 1988).

These initial changes were followed by significant changes in the level of Hellenic cultural homogeneity due to the processes of settlement and resettlement. Initially, Hellenic migration was characterised by a very high level of homogeneity, based on a common nationality, identity and religion (with, for example, 95 per cent of all Greek migrants belonging to the Greek Orthodox Church) and manifested in intensified resettlement concentration in the larger metropolitan areas of Australia. Such concentration enabled chain-migration mechanisms to operate in a way that brought relatives and friends from the same village, town, or other regions of Greece to join their compatriots in urban settlements. There, by creating social enclaves, the Greeks, Italians and other immigrant communities created residential formations that gave the impression of ghetto settlements (Burnley 1976, 1977). These settlement concentrations had a strong impact on previous neighbourhood structures, as the original British-Australian inhabitants felt compelled to move out to the newly-built suburban neighbourhoods, thus leaving the densely-populated polluted industrial environments to the newly-arrived immigrants.

Maturity of settlement, accompanied by government policy changes in favour of migrant resettlement, made Hellenic residential mobility inevitable. By 1986 (ABS Census) many Greeks had moved out to some of the newly-built, cleaner and more affluent suburbs. This mobility started with Greeks moving between inner areas within the industrial centres and

Illustration 8.5 Hellene fruit-growers meeting Minister of Agriculture Ian Sinclair during their mobilisation at Renmark SA on 19 December 1978. Here, growers Panayiotis Zervoulias and Evangelos Dedes make their point to the Minister. (*Source*: The Adelaide *Advertiser*, Dec. 20, 1978: 1 and also E. Dedes)

resettlement only gradually progressed to inner-outer and outer suburbs. The rate of this movement (between inner city to inner-outer city and outer suburbs) ranged from 4 to 50 per cent in different areas over the period from 1976 to 1991 (see Appendix 10). According to a Bell's BIR study of the period from 1981 to 1986, Greeks, like Italians, display a significant movement away from the 'ecological niches' of the inner suburbs in the major capital cities. He stresses that:

patterns of net migration of the Greek-born are distinctive, with substantial losses from the inner-city regions of Sydney (region number 01) totalling more than 4,000 persons in aggregate. There were compensating net gains of Greek-born persons in St George-Sutherland (03) and Canterbury-Bankstown (04) regions (812 and 660 persons respectively), and in the inner-eastern (27) region of Melbourne (1,371 persons). These patterns again reflect progressive outward diffusion of the Greek-born from their traditional regions of first settlement in the inner suburbs. Net gains and losses of Greek-born persons elsewhere in Australia are comparatively small, reflecting the smaller number of Greek-born persons in the remaining states and the larger geographic size of the regions in their capital cities (Bell 1992: 191, 194).

This mobility was the product of many interrelated factors, including many Greeks' failure to achieve their initial objectives (for example, to return to Greece with sufficient wealth), the lack of timely and adequate policies adopted by Hellenic governments to encourage repatriation and the granting of rights to ethnic groups in Australia through the establishment of multiculturalism. All these factors resulted in the inner suburbs becoming 'transitional zones' for subsequent migrant resettlement within the Australian social space.

As well as achieving residential mobility, Greeks succeeded in a whole range of other areas including: inter-ethnic marriage; mainstream political participation; and the adoption of Australian citizenship. Studies by the BIR have shown Greeks to be among the top six non-British ethnic population groups in Australia in terms of Australian citizenship (BIR 1990, 1994). According to the 1976 ABS Census figures (Price 1979), 65.33 per cent of those born in Greece, who had been in Australia for less than 20 years, had taken up citizenship. This number increased to 90.7 per cent in 1986 and, by 1991, had reached an average of 94.2 per cent for the whole population born in Greece and 96 per cent for those who had been in Australia for 15 years or longer (BIR 1986: 10; 1994: 16).

Similarly, the marital status of postwar Greek migrants was strongly affected by the length of residency in Australia. In the mid-1960s, during the early stage of their settlement, Greeks remained very highly endogamous, with 88 per cent marrying partners from the same country. This is in contrast to Italians, with 64 per cent of endogamous marriages, and non-British northern Europeans, with approximately 60 per cent endogamous marriages during the same period (Immigra-

Table 8.1   Marriages among Greeks in Australia

Year	1975	1980	1985	1990	1991	1992
Total Greek Marriages	1,732	1,541	1,988	2,324	2,118	1,808
Inter-Christian Marriages	256	348	535	761	663	599

Source: (Holy Archdiocese of the Greek Orthodox Church of Australia 1994)

tion Advisory Council 1969). However, as Greek settlement matured, statistics indicate that there was an increase in the number of inter-marriages (Immigration Advisory Council 1969; Price 1989). Price (1989: 35–6) has shown that, by 1988, 25 per cent of second-generation Greek women entered into mixed marriages. Similarly, according to the archives of the Holy Archdiocese of the Greek Orthodox Church of Australia (1994), by 1992 more than 33.1 per cent of all Greeks were marrying outside their own ethnic population. As illustrated in Table 8.1, between 1975 and 1992 the rate of inter-marriages celebrated within the Greek Orthodox Church was constantly increasing, from 14.8 per cent in 1975 to 33.1 per cent in 1992.

The figures indicate that during this period inter-Christian marriages entered into by Greeks increased by more than 123 per cent. In addition to the marriages celebrated within the Greek Orthodox Church, there must have been a significant number of mixed marriages outside this institution. In some parts of the country such as Western Australia, where Hellenic settlement is more mature and the group size proportionally smaller, inter-marriage is also greater, with 64.3 per cent of all Greeks now choosing non-Greek partners (Holy Archdiocese of the Greek Orthodox Church of Australia 1994). These findings suggest that the greater the maturity of Hellenic ethnic settlements, the greater the degree of inter-ethnic marriage among Hellenes which, in turn, suggests that the passage of time is a key feature in inter-ethnic interaction.

As well as the abovementioned changes in Greek migrants' status, greater social interaction between Greeks and Australian society, since the adoption of multiculturalism, has resulted in the increasing absorption of Hellenic organisations within broader society networks, together with an increasing involvement of leaders of Hellenic origin within these networks. Since the 1970s, in contrast to the earlier postwar period, Greek-Australians have shown significant levels of social involvement and political participation outside their immediate communal organisations (Petrolias 1959; Davies 1972; Tsounis 1971a, 1971b; Hearn 1971). As discussed earlier, this increased social interaction was initiated mainly through the activities of the Greek Left (Tsounis 1971a, 1971b; Interview with Zangalis, 1993; Interview with Zangalis 1995). 'In both cases the field of operation was mainly the Greek ethnic communities in Australia and the principal agencies through which the Greek Left acted were workers' clubs, that had Grecian focus' (Tsounis 1971a: 55). Similarly, Hearn (1971: 149) stressed that although 'Greek and politics are often regarded as synonymous, in Australia this relationship is fully operative within the confines of the Greek community which is eminently suited for the purpose'. In fact, as Papadopoulos points out:

> At the time of the formation of the Greek Welfare [early 1970s], only the various elements of the Greek Left, principally the Communist Party branches, did any sort of social policy discussion—consider the issues of *Epitheorisis* and the *Greek Left Review* and the *Neos Kosmos* newspaper. The Left analyses were, however, maintained within constrained frameworks, in particular by over-reliance on class as a non-independent variable . . . At the . . . time (other than the Communists), no other political party had any ethnic affairs policies or ethnic branches . . . , Greek branches of the Australian Labour Party were then forming. But they became more publicly involved and influential in policy discussion and communal issues in . . . the later 1970s (Papadopoulos 1993: 1).

As Australian political parties began to accept Greek and other southern European migrants as members, their active involvement in Australian politics became only a matter of time. Greeks were now able to divert their focus from the CPA, which had served their needs and framed their ideological perceptions during the pre- and early postwar periods, to other parties, including the ALP and the Liberal/National parties (both of which until the 1950s had refused the participation of non-British migrants) (Jupp 1966; Storer 1975). Consequently, Greeks had remained preoccupied with the politics of their own communities (Petrolias 1959; Tsounis 1971a, 1975), leading Reich to comment that 'social mobility and the drive for status, privilege and power have been taking place largely within the Greek communities' organisations in important spheres of social and cultural life giving the Greeks ample opportunities for social and political positions which have generally been denied to them by the Australian society' (Reich 1981: 171).[4]

According to Collins (1975), in order to understand the lack of migrant involvement in Australian politics it is necessary to locate the discussion of the migrant labour experience within a Marxist analysis of Australian capitalism. He stresses that immigrant labour under capitalism formed the function of an 'industrial reserve army', artificially divided from indigenous workers, who were elevated to a 'labour aristocracy' by the granting to them of special privileges. Immigrant participation in Australian politics, according to this framework, could be best realised if immigrants and the 'indigenous working class' united to break the barriers of racism and the 'labour aristocracy' created by capitalism. Only then could the capitalist political order be overcome and exploitation of the workers be brought to an end. Until that time, migrant workers, as an underclass, would be denied participation in mainstream Australian institutions—including political parties.

Aitkin (1977) maintains that in spite of 'talk of Italian and Greek ghetto formation, there were very few parliamentary constituencies until the mid-1970s'. He argues that social mobility of migrants failed to disturb the equilibrium of the party system and that massive immigration also had little effect—with migrants having to accept the only party choices offered to them, resulting in only marginal benefit to the non-Labor bloc. Bottomley (1976: 95) pointed out the resistance of Australian institutions towards migrants and the pressure on political parties to absorb them into existing party structures rather than forming ethnic branches. 'Anglo-conformism, combined with class-location, constrained and pre-defined the life chances of those from less-favoured ethnic groups, while the same groups were under-represented in the political system at all levels' (Bottomley 1979: 13). Allan (1981) emphasises that party loyalties can be affected by single government actions or mistakes as, for example, the

'Mediterranean' or 'Greek back' syndrome which led to the infamous Social Security scandal. As Allan notes, 'the so-called Greek Conspiracy Case involving the alleged use of fraud by a number of Greeks to obtain Social Security pensions . . . turned many Greek-ethnics against the Liberal Party' (Allan 1981: 22; Jupp 1988).

None the less, as Greeks became increasingly mobile socially, there was evidence of increasing Hellenic participation in all political parties. After the initial establishment of political party branches by the CPA (Jupp 1966, cited in Storer 1975), the ALP followed suit in Victoria in the 1970s, offering non-British migrants the opportunity to set up party branches by different ethnic populations. Initially, the ALP was seen to be as racist as the Liberal Party but, social change during the postwar period, combined with the realisation that with the 'migrant vote' it could win power after 23 years in opposition, convinced it to encourage the establishment of different ethnic branches.[5]

The establishment of ethnic branches, therefore, led to the emergence of Greek participation in ALP politics as a strong political force. As a result, Greeks have arguably higher participation in Australian politics than any other non-Anglo ethnic group (Jupp 1988: 145). Allan emphasises that the Victorian ALP experienced great ethnic transformation and that the initial dominance of the Irish Catholics, followed by that of the Anglo-Protestants after 1955, is now under challenge from the Greeks (Allan 1985: 133–43). Jupp emphasises that 'such control is not sinister, and should not be looked as such as it is by some members of the ALP. Greek control is not likely to prove any worse, and may even be of higher calibre than that of other groups in control of local councils' (1988: 148).

The new level of Hellenic participation in Australian life reflects the beginning of migrants' political incorporation within the structures of Australian society. One measure of this incorporation is the increasing number of Members of Parliament of Hellenic origin serving the Australian nation (Allan 1985; Jupp 1988). No longer do Greek-Australians have to campaign for leadership positions within Hellenic-Australian organisations alone—as was the case until the early 1970s (Petrolias 1959; Tsounis 1971a, 1971b, 1975; Reich 1981).

Instead, they now have the choice to participate, if they so wish, in the general society's political arena. In fact, in 1995, the secretary of Greek ethnic branches of the Victorian ALP, Michail, confirmed the existence of 11 ALP Greek ethnic branches in Melbourne alone (generally located in areas with high Greek populations) (Allan 1985: 136; Interview with Michail, 1995). Similarly, 20 years after the initial establishment of the Greek branches of the ALP, in 1994 there were still 1,200 members of these branches (Interview with Sidiropulos, 1995). In addition, many more Greek immigrants or their children were participating in English-speaking branches in Melbourne, with one estimate by the Victorian ALP (Interview with Michail, 1995) that, by 1994, approximately 200 Greek persons were participating in five Victorian English-speaking branches. Similarly, the Liberal Party acknowledges the existence of at least two bilingual Greek branches in Melbourne, with an increasing number of individuals from the Hellenic community taking up membership. From only five members in the 1950s, Greek membership of the Liberal Party of Victoria, in 1994, had increased to at least 500 out of the total membership in Victoria of 20,000 (Petrolias 1959; Interview with Karavitis, 1995).[6] The number of Greeks standing for pre-selection in both of the major Australian parties (especially in the ALP) has, similarly, shown an increase and, while the proportion of Greeks granted pre-selection in the coalition of the Liberal/National Parties remains marginal, it none the less marks a departure from the previous disinterest in migrant politics demonstrated by the Liberal Party.

In 1995, there were at least 15 Greek-Australian politicians—representing both the Liberal and the ALP parties—elected to the Federal and various state parliaments (see Appendix 6).[7] An important feature of migrant participation in Australian political life is that MPs of Hellenic ethnic origin do not have to depend solely on the resources and support of the Hellenic community, but draw from the broader base of Australian society. Conversely, although Greek voters support Greek candidates, ultimately their vote is given to candidates according to the policies and party they represent, whether it is the ALP or the Liberal/National Party.

Illustration 8.6 Bipartisan endorsement of multiculturalism. Representatives of both major political parties at the Antipodes Festival of the Greek Orthodox Community of Melbourne and Victoria. (GOCM&V) March 1992.

As with most other voters, Greek voters differentiate between parties and support candidates according to their perception of how political and economic issues affect their lives. Over the last ten years, the mass media, including the previously exclusively pro-Labor newspaper *Neos Kosmos*, have increasingly covered the activities of the Liberal Party and, in particular, the activities of Greek Liberals. There has not only been a polarisation of support between the two major parties, but also a growth in support for and commitment to new minor parties.

The 'Greenies', with their conservationist views, have made significant gains within the Hellenic community, due, in no small part, to the establishment of an independent Hellenic conservationist body in Melbourne. Although not identified as political, the 'Greek Greenies' have sought community support for conservationist issues, campaigning for the conservation and protection of the Australian environment and natural resources.

This political diversification reflects both the social and economic changes within Australia's Hellenic population out-

Illustration 8.7   Hellenes marching in the anti-nuclear campaign of
1983. During the 1980s, Hellenes featured in many
Australian demonstrations for peace and disarmament.
(*Source*: 90th Anniversary Album of the GOCM&V.)

lined previously and the increasing incorporation of Hellenes
in a wide range of influential positions. As Tsounis states:

> We observe a fairly large . . . Hellenic presence in the
> political life of the country: within labour unions . . . in a
> level of leadership positions in unions; there is participation
> in many political parties and in other political and social
> organisations; with participation in local government being
> fairly evident . . . there are three Hellenes in positions as
> mayors in three of the six capital cities—in Perth, Adelaide,
> and in Hobart—cities which have relatively less Hellenism;
> Parliamentarians in State and Federal Parliaments—and at
> least one Federal Minister and other Ministers in State
> Governments or as appointed advisers, as in Ethnic Affairs
> Commissions (Tsounis 1989a: 8).

Tsounis adds that, by being empowered to participate in

the political life of the country, Hellenism is increasingly being incorporated into the legal and political system of Australia, with all of its attendant rights and obligations. For the majority of Hellenes, the choices they make at this level are largely irrelevant to what happens within the *paroikies* (Hellenic communities abroad) and their *koinotites* (lay community organisations) and whether there is internal conflict and divisions (Tsounis 1989a: 9). Greek participation at all political levels reflects the success of multiculturalism in facilitating migrant participation in the social, economic and political life of the broader community. Despite this participation, the Hellenic migration experience remains one of a continuous struggle for rights and equality within an evolving multicultural framework. This evolution, which is distinguished by migrants' increasing social and political participation, incorporation within the wider community and upward social mobility will be demonstrated graphically in Chapter 9.

Social mobility and political behaviour of Greeks in Australia

Many Greeks migrated to Australia in search of a better life. How successful were they in achieving this goal?

This chapter is based on a random survey of 353 Greek immigrants in Melbourne, Victoria, and country areas of the Riverland, South Australia. It looks at a range of factors which are good indicators of participants' social mobility over the period of their lives in Australia including residence, occupation, income and class. It shows that Greek immigrants started in Australia as a reasonably homogenous group, but have experienced increasing socio-economic differentiation over time. Drawing on this class analysis, it also explores the political behaviour of Greeks in Australia, assessing the significant factors affecting party affiliation.

RESIDENTIAL MOBILITY

Residential mobility is a good indicator of the social mobility of a population group. As families improve their financial and social situations, they often move to wealthier suburbs, which in Australian cities is often reflected in moves from the poorer inner to the wealthier outer suburbs.

The majority of Greek immigrants in Victoria started their lives in the inner suburbs of Melbourne. The people interviewed in the survey who started in the inner suburbs mostly

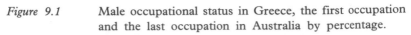

Figure 9.1   Male occupational status in Greece, the first occupation and the last occupation in Australia by percentage.

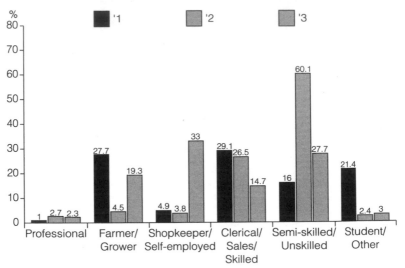

still live there, but around 20 per cent of this group have moved to the wealthier outer suburbs and about 8 per cent have moved to the country. This movement has been largely in one direction; few have moved from the outer suburbs and the country into the inner suburbs during the period of the field study.

OCCUPATIONAL MOBILITY

Changes in occupation are also good indicators of social mobility, reflecting not only changes in social class, but also in economic status.

As Figure 9.1 shows, nearly 80 per cent of the men in the survey were either farmers, clerical workers and sales people or students before they left Greece. Upon arrival in Australia, their occupations often changed dramatically. Sixty per cent were employed in semi-skilled or unskilled occupations and 26 per cent in clerical, sales or other skilled professions. In other words, many skilled male workers were obliged to take unskilled work when they first moved to Australia.

240

However, as the graph shows, many were able to move into higher status and better-paying occupations over time.

Those who classified themselves as farmers or self-employed in Greece had, in most cases, been involved in family businesses and thus the means of production was family-owned. In contrast, if they became farmers in Australia they personally owned the means of production. Equally important is the fact that many of the unskilled and semi-skilled occupations in Greece during the post-World War Two period employed people who had experienced largely multi-skilled occupations within the semi-agrarian economy. This experience was obtained within a setting where there was a minimal division of labour, with little or nothing known about the Fordist model or division of labour as known in the industrially advanced western economies. Instead, collaboration with other members of the community—especially within the extended family network—and regular informative and ana-lytical debates in the *agora*, allowed workers to pursue a more democratically collective effort, in contrast to the single-task occupations later assigned to them in the developing industrial economy of Australia. Such industrial occupations involved extensive division of labour through labour segmentation in routinised tasks.

The story for women is similar. Prior to migration, around 77.4 per cent of the adult women in the survey worked in agriculture, clerical, sales or other professional jobs or were students. This trend is similar to the male participants' occu-pational distribution in Greece (see Figure 9.1). Soon after arriving in Australia, the female occupational shift was dra-matic, to the extent that 74.7 per cent of this ethnic population were employed in semi-skilled and unskilled occupations in the manufacturing industry. The occupational shift affecting Hellene females is so significant because, in contrast, only 22.4 per cent of this population sample held the same occupational status in Greece. Figure 9.2 also shows that women were less able to move into higher status occupations than men over time.

These Australian figures do not, however, tell the whole story of occupational mobility among Hellenes. In fact, many Greek migrants may have already experienced a major change in occupation before they migrated. After World War Two,

241

Figure 9.2   Female occupational status in Greece, the first occupation in Australia and the last occupation in Australia by percentage.

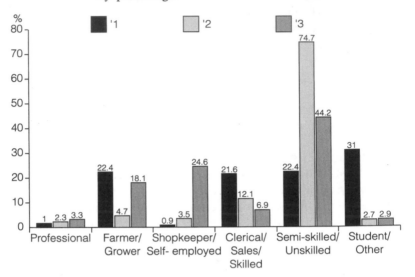

agriculture in Greece was poorly managed and many people were forced to migrate to the cities in search of employment opportunities. As a result, proportionally many more were employed in services and small industries in Greece than in Australia. Unlike their countrymen in distant Australia, movement in search of work in cities offered Hellenes the opportunity not only to retain their farm property in their village or town of origin, but also to cultivate it. This cultivation was often arranged by organising their employment commitments in the cities in such a way that enabled them either to make occasional visits during the year to their place of origin or to appoint another local farmer to cultivate their produce, thus ensuring they were provided with the foods and fruits to which they were accustomed while residing in the cities. In addition, they were able, more than the Hellenes in Australia, to enjoy their holidays in the ways to which they were accustomed: returning to the countryside to celebrate the seasons of the year in traditional ways and in their accustomed physical environments. In contrast, although Hellenes in Australia retained contact with their country of

Figure 9.3   Percentage distribution of main occupations in Greece
for both male and female participants.

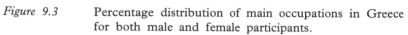

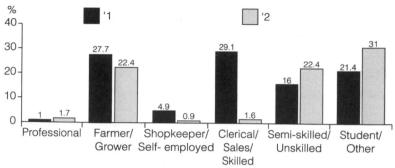

origin they found it very difficult, if not impossible, to continue
their traditional cultural practices, as in the country of their
origin, because of the distances involved and the prevailing
social and economic climate in the host society.

A significant finding of the survey is that there was
relatively little difference in occupational status between Greek
men and women before and after they first arrived in Australia.
The semi-agricultural economy of Greece was essentially based
on the structure of the extended family unit, where individual
members of given families usually collaborated in occupational
practices, regardless of gender. At the same time, the experiences obtained in the *agora* debates and the social memory
maintained over generations means that people can be supported in their endeavours by the precedents of those who
had undertaken similar tasks in the past. Social memory
provided participants in Australia with a framework of accounts
and values for the worth of their work and helped to limit
the anxiety they experienced because of migration and alienation. It enabled them, for example, to avoid to some extent
the conflicts caused by single-task occupations and the rigid
hierarchical control of the 'bosses' who ensured the maximum
exploitation of their workers—either through segmented labour
or the denial of their democratic rights as the true makers
of goods produced in Australian industry. In this sense,
social memory operated as a buffer against the stress or
emotional conflict experienced by migrant workers due to the
occupational tasks and working conditions in capitalist indus-

243

Figure 9.4   Percentage distribution of first occupations in Australia
for both male and female participants.

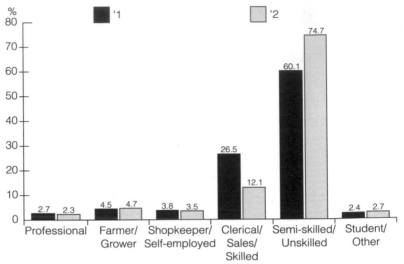

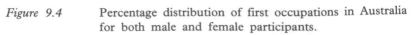

trialist structures based on the Fordist model. Most Hellene
migrants whose work experience in their place of origin
involved extensive cooperation and collaboration with the
extended family network and the community at large experienced mental and emotional stress in the host society, when
confronted by the rigidly segregated occupations and production line tasks of the occupational structure of Australia's
capitalist industrial economy.

   In contrast to Figure 9.3, Figure 9.4 shows the occupational status of males and females following settlement in
Australia. Most of the occupational categories had equivalent proportions of representation, except for the
semi-skilled/unskilled and clerical/sales/skilled categories. In the
semi-skilled category, females had a higher proportional representation than males (by 14.6 per cent). In the clerical
category, males had a higher representation of 14.5 per cent.
This minor difference agrees with the earlier conjecture that
male and female immigrants had similar occupational status
upon arrival in Australia, although the females did initially
enter a slightly lower occupational status. Although in terms
of gender females appeared to have been exploited more than

Figure 9.5   Percentage distribution of last occupations in Australia for both male and female participants.

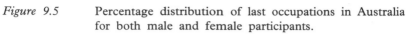
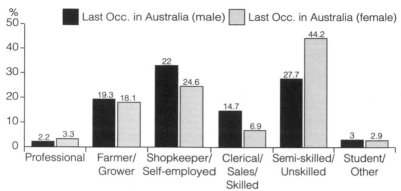

males, generally migrant labour experience and their high participation in the unskilled and semi-skilled occupations could be understood better by the Marxist analysis in terms of reserve army of labour and labour segmentation in Australia as argued by Collins (Collins 1975, 1986, 1988; Castles et al. 1988).

Figure 9.5 shows the beginnings of a difference between the occupational status of the male and female participants. This dissimilarity between genders is apparent with females having less opportunity to rise in occupational status than males, as is shown in the comparison of last occupation held by both males and females in Australia. Most importantly, there is a diversification of the occupation status of the participants that is indicative of a permanent shift away from the single, unskilled task occupational practices, initially available to Greek immigrants, towards their participation in a much wider range of occupational categories that reflect a broader section of the Australian labour market.

After World War Two, the majority of Greek immigrants, both male and female, suffered downward occupational mobility through their mass entry into the unskilled and semi-skilled jobs in the industrial economy of Australia. As discussed in Chapters 7 and 8, there were many reasons for this downward mobility, including Australia's immigration policy, host society attitudes, language difficulties, the single-task occupational practices offered and misunderstanding of the Hellenic values that formed an integral part of the Hellenic concept of *philotimo*. This connection between values and work was important, since labour exploitation was high and foreign workers were disempowered in terms of improving or developing their personal skills. The non-portability of trades also contributed to limiting occupational mobility. It could be argued that the employment status of Hellene migrants in Australia imitated the distribution of occupational status of the semi-agricultural economy of Greece, but this would be an erroneous supposition as the migrants had learned many skills that were portable in their home country. On the contrary, in Australia, it is seen that the final occupation tends to mirror the original occupation or skills that were attained in Greece. This trend could have been facilitated in an earlier time period if the single-task semi-skilled or unskilled occupations available in Australia had become more multi-skilled or multi-task occupations.

Over time, Hellenic occupational mobility in Australia is indicative of a highly significant transition to higher or diverse occupations and/or levels of employment. With the exception of the professional occupational category (as seen in Figure 9.5), there is an issue of gender bias against the female migrants, whose transition to higher occupational status appears to have been more difficult, even after they had been in Australia the same number of years as the males and had been fully employed in the Australian labour market for that time.

INCOME AND CLASS

As shown, Greek migrants have been able to achieve a degree of residential and occupational mobility over time. The survey results show that this led to changes in class position.

Participants in the survey were grouped in three class categories according to family income, number of properties and property value.

Sixty-five per cent of inner suburbs residents had a lower to lower-middle income status, while only a third of country residents were in this bracket. Twenty-seven per cent of inner

Figure 9.6   Class categories based on family income

Class	Family Income	Property Value	No. Properties
Lower-Lower Middle	<$40,000	<$160,000	0 or 1
Middle	>$40,000 and <$60,000	>$160,000 and <$250,000	2
Upper	>$60,000	> $250,000	>=3

suburbs residents were middle class, increasing to 50 per cent of country residents. Outer suburbs residents had a higher level of affluence than inner suburbs residents as is typical of the Australian population as a whole.

The number of people in the lower to lower-middle class category declined over time. Eighty per cent of participants who had been in Australia for under 15 years fell into the lowest bracket, while only a third of participants are in this bracket after 25 years in Australia. Fifty per cent had reached middle-class status after living in Australia for over 25 years.

It is possible that these figures are skewed by the fact that some individuals who were unsuccessful in Australia may have returned to Greece. While the Australian socio-economic system has historically pushed migrants into menial jobs, it has done nothing for unsuccessful migrants who become destitute. However, these unsuccessful immigrants did not make up a large proportion of the immigrant population when social class is defined in Weberian terms.

The rise to the middle and upper classes of migrants resident in Australia for a period of between 16 and 30 years stops after 31 years. The lower to lower-middle class then rises significantly, with a decrease in the middle and upper classes by 50 per cent and roughly 33 per cent, respectively. This may be due to the fact that residents of over 30 years in Australia are probably moving into old age and may be pensioners. Also, Hellenes, as a family-oriented population group, often make extensive efforts to help their children succeed financially and otherwise, by purchasing them a home or by offering financial assistance when it would otherwise have been important to save for their old age. Such sacrifices often cause financial difficulties for elderly Hellenes who, no longer able to work, suffer in poverty.

As is to be expected, the research indicates a strong

correlation between occupation and class status among men. Survey participants working in clerical, sales and semi- or unskilled jobs are more likely to belong to the lower classes in terms of income and assets. Professionals and farmers are more likely to be middle class. The pattern is similar for women, although more women working in clerical and sales areas are likely to belong to the middle class.

Only 10 per cent of the participants in the lower income group bracket anticipate moving to a different suburb or area in the next few years, while 35 per cent of those in the upper income bracket expect to move. Clearly, those with higher incomes are more residentially mobile than those with lower incomes.

In summary, the survey showed that as immigrants attained a middle-class economic standing, they were likely to move from primarily inner-suburban living to the outer suburbs and country, and from clerical and unskilled work to professional and self-employed work.

POLITICAL BEHAVIOUR AND VOTING PREFERENCES

This section analyses voting trends of Greek immigrants by tracing the history of the survey participants' voting behaviour between their country of origin and their host society, as well as by their residential, occupational and economic status. Voting preferences have been coded into 'left' and 'right' categories. The 'left' wing political parties in Australian politics are designated as the ALP, Democrats, Socialist parties and Communist parties. The 'right' wing political parties are the Liberal, the National and Country parties and also any further right-wing political party organisations.

The survey participants and their fathers had very similar voting preferences in Greece, with around 40 per cent voting for left-wing parties and 60 per cent for right-wing parties. The situation changed markedly once they moved to Australia, with around 80 per cent of participants voting for left-wing parties on average and 20 per cent for right-wing parties. This radical shift from predominantly right-wing affiliation in Greece to strong left-wing affiliation in Australia reflects the

Figure 9.7   Shows percentage of participants voting left- or right-wing (ALP and Liberal/National parties) politics respectively by the number of years in Australia.

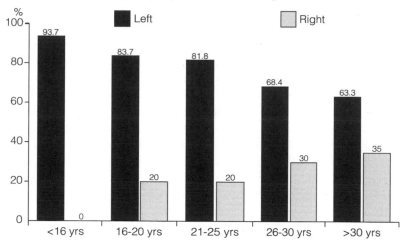

interest in migrant workers' needs shown by Labor governments since the 1970s (as discussed in Chapter 7).

However, the 80 per cent preference for left-wing parties is not consistent. Rather, nearly 95 per cent of participants who have been in Australia for less than 15 years vote for left-wing parties. The preference for left-wing parties tends to decline for those who have been resident in Australia for longer, with only 65 per cent of those who have been in Australia for over 30 years voting for left-wing parties.

The initial preference for left-wing parties, especially the ALP, and the eventual shift toward conservative politics, has a longstanding history in Hellenic political culture and the political behaviour of Greeks in Australia. The political history of Greece, especially during the years following the World War Two, involved administrations by right-wing governments and foreign powers such as the United States that undermined the political stability of the Hellenic nation. Right-wing governments not only undermined the political aspirations of the left-wing parties but also were responsible for depriving many hundreds of thousands of young Hellenes of their livelihood through their lack of agricultural and welfare policies. Following settlement in Australia, it was conservative administrations that forced Hellenes, along with many other immigrants, to work in the manufacturing industry and assimilate in their host society's culture.

In contrast, Prime Minister Whitlam, a worthy statesman in the mould of Pericles (in the eyes of many Hellene immigrants), made Promethean efforts against the intervention of foreign interest in Australia and, to a great extent, succeeded in providing Australians with a set of policies and a vision for a more equitable society for the future. His administration provided new policies but, of more importance to the Hellene migrants in Australia, it also provided hope for a voice and democracy for all Australians, irrespective of ethnicity, class or gender. For this reason, Hellenes regarded him as the 'greatest politician in Australia's history' and as an Australian with a strong sense of *philotimo* (*Greek Times*, Friday 14 April 1978: 1, 5). The subsequent shift to the right, however, signifies a change in the perceptions of immigrant life in society, which has started to come to terms with the presence of different ethnic population groups, enabling many to accept or be accepted by the new society and thus to choose the party of their own preference, according to their individual interests or perceptions, similar to those of other Australians.

Men and women working in agriculture, self-employed men and women and professional women tended to show a greater preference for right-wing parties than those working in less skilled occupations. Overall, participants from the middle and upper classes were more likely to vote for right-wing parties than those from lower socio-economic backgrounds. Around 11 per cent of lower to lower-middle-class participants vote for right-wing parties, rising to 26 per cent of middle-class and 37 per cent of upper-class participants.

Country residents were more likely to vote for right-wing parties than their metropolitan counterparts, with a preference for the National Party over the Liberal Party. Left-wing parties receive double the number of votes of right-wing parties in the country, as opposed to five times as many in metropolitan areas.

Around 20 per cent were frequently swinging voters, and those with a general preference for right-wing parties more likely to swing their vote than left-wing voters.

CONCLUSION

The immigrants who came here to become quickly affluent and return to Greece did not do so. Instead, they chose to reside in Australia and the willingness to return to Greece was either postponed or became a mere personal matter, irrespective of economic gains which may or may not have been made while working hard in Australia. Returning to Greece became a personal, not a collective ethnic interest, irrespective of economic status acquired following many years of settlement.

Change of residential area in relation to economic mobility is open to question. This change has been shown to be statistically significant, but the question 'Why?' is still unanswered. Inner-city residences can be council-owned, cheap or private single-fronted Victorian cottages that are 'worth a fortune' on today's market. Those who have attained upper-class status and are economically able, may still choose to live among their own as of old. Those who moved out from the inner industrial areas to outer suburban or country areas could well have been drawn back to the agrarian lifestyle from which they came. Occupational and accompanying economic upward mobility attests to the determination to succeed, a dominant trait in the Hellenic character. Time in Australia, however, has been shown to be significantly associated with upward social mobility, together with a change in political party affiliation. The closure of the host society to immigrants' participation in political and organisational life had a very significant impact on the voting patterns of Greeks in Australia for many years. Only now, two decades after the struggle for 'ethnic rights' and the subsequent enactment of the policy of multiculturalism, are Australia's Greeks (with their increasing naturalisation) demonstrating a change back to the political affiliations of their former country and generally reflecting that their voting patterns are in accordance with their particular socio-economic position within Australia's social stratification system.

10

Discussion and implications

This study paints a complex picture of the Hellenic community in Australia—one of the many migrant communities which has had to come to terms with a new society which, until relatively recent times, had not been either accepting or tolerant of ethnic, cultural and racial differences. The process of settlement and attainment of social mobility by the Hellenes, as this study illustrates, has been long and hard. Simplistic and superficial formulations such as the 'passage of time' cannot adequately explain this process as they ignore the complex nature of the lived reality of cultural adjustment, struggle, accommodation, deprivation and sacrifice that individuals, families and communities have to make.

My research investigated the ethnic factor in social mobility. Ethnic groups arriving in Australia *en masse*, especially in the 1950s and 1960s, found themselves consistently encapsulated in the so-called 'ethnic enclaves'—residentially, occupationally and economically—often until subsequent generations broke away from the 'social mobility traps'. Many first-generation immigrants were forced into the secondary labour market, especially in the manufacturing industry, due to a number of social factors operating against them. These included migrants' lack of language and labour market skills and the refusal by the host society to recognise the skills and qualifications of newly-settled migrants.

In this broader context, at least until the 1970s, the

experience of southern Europeans in Australia was the experience of a southern European microcosm with different national origins in the context of one single nation state, namely Australia. Their struggle for acceptance or for the creation of a southern European social space was simultaneously a real and an imaginary reflection of the social tensions, political conflict and economic antagonism found within the single nation states of their European homeland, prior to and after their migration and settlement in Australia. These tensions were transmitted—both consciously and unconsciously—to the other end of the world by individual social actors, and can be mirrored in the struggles of the South against the materially and industrially wealthier North in the contemporary history of the European Community (EC). The tensions of the debate about North and South or about 'centre' and 'periphery' in the EC with its economic and political ramifications—whether real or imaginary—has been central in Australian social sciences. It has remained a great divide in the debate among Australian academics and other sceptics throughout this century about the 'quality' difference between northern European and southern European immigrants. In other words, southern European migrants, whether Hellenes or Italians, Maltese or Yugoslavs, faced all the racial, cultural, economic and legal implications which have been evident in the history of European colonisation, together with the contemporary implications of the nation state, all of which had lasting effects on migrants and their children.

This research supports the thesis that the marginalisation of ethnic groups in Australia has traditionally been based on the migrant's country of origin, ethnic or cultural background, or racial and gender differences (Collins 1986). As Collins states, 'the two most important sources of late capitalism's reserve army have been female and migrant labour, reflecting an internationalisation of the division of labour' (Collins 1986: 57). As a consequence, the marginalisation of ethnic groups in Australia has been subject to dual labour market strategies found also in other capitalist societies such as the western European nation states (Dimitreas 1981; Collins 1986: 43; Castles, Booth & Wallace 1984).

The post-World War Two Australian labour force was highly segmented. The labour market ensured the maximum exploitation of labour through a strategy of 'divide and con-quer' of the working classes, including migrant workers. The social relations which the capitalist mode of production creates have traditionally forced migrant workers to become segmented within the labour market, not only in terms of work practices but also in accordance with their respective ethnic origins and gender (Collins 1986; Castles et al. 1988: 26). Labour seg-mentation, therefore, often blocks the upward social mobility of immigrants who, alternatively, have been encouraged or directed toward certain settlement and employment zone areas or into the small business sector. Historically, there has been a strong link between country of birth, gender and types of employment people are likely to obtain. As Castles, Cope, Kalantzis and Morrisey argue:

> Segmentation means exclusion of certain individuals or ethnic groups from entering some categories of employment in favour of some other individuals or ethnic groups for a significant amount of time length after arrival. Segmentation means that job opportunities are not based on a person's work ability, qualification and productivity, but also on non-economic ascriptive criteria, linked to ideologies of gender, race and ethnicity. Labour markets are structured to place women, migrants and racial minorities at a disadvantage, and their low-status positions are in turn taken as practical proof of innate inferiority (Castles et al. 1988: 26).

Despite the segmentation of the labour force and the marginalisation of southern European ethnic population groups this study indicates that, through concerted effort and struggle over many years, Greeks have become socially mobile within Australian society.

Specifically, by focusing on the so-called 'push' side of migration, the study stresses the existence in continuity through time apparent in the Hellenic cultural features and values which contributed to the decision to migrate away from familiar social and geographic places to remote countries of the world such as Australia. It indicated how Australia's Greek pioneers, encouraged by myths and legends to travel or migrate, became the forerunners of Greek chain migration and that, through their social achievements, they managed to set in motion the foundations for the subsequent Hellenic post-World War Two mass migration to this Antipodean country. It was argued that out-migration became necessary because of both domestic and externally imposed limitations upon the political and economic progress of the new state.

It was argued that, throughout modern Australian history, the 'pull' side of immigration remained a fairly selective process directly affected by the availability of employment opportunities which also remained highly discriminatory against southern Europeans. The Hellenic migrant experience was not exceptional compared to that of other southern European ethnic immigrant groups. Before World War Two, lack of economic opportunity and discrimination by employers forced Greeks either to live and work in closed, essentially 'shopkeeper communities', or to become itinerant seasonal workers (Gilchrist 1985; Price 1963; Tsounis 1971a). During the mass immigration program from the 1950s to the 1970s, new arrivals were attracted by and concentrated in the easily accessible unskilled labouring occupations, from which few were able to escape. They were still there at the beginning of the 1980s, according to the 1981 Census data (Storer 1985b).

By the late 1970s, a number of factors, including the adoption of a policy of multiculturalism and maturity of settlement, led to Greeks beginning to appear, albeit in small numbers, at levels of power within the structures of the host society, for example, as parliamentarians and business community leaders (ABS 1981). Since then Hellenic incorporation in Australia's broader societal network is evident economically, socially, politically and culturally. As this study indicates, while this incorporation of Hellenes into general Australian structures is recent, aspirations to upward social mobility have always been present in the Hellenic immigrant community in Australia, even when prevailing attitudes and cultural trends compelled them to be latent.

Greeks in Australia are now increasingly spread throughout the existing social stratification system, and it can be argued that Australia's 'experiment' of mass immigration of non-English-speaking background immigrants during the postwar period has proven significantly successful, in the longer term, for both the Hellenic community and the host Australian society.

This study also argues that migration, migration settlement and social mobility or immobility within receiving societies can neither be understood or defined in terms of a single theory, such as neoclassic or Marxist, nor comprehended in terms of a single discipline. Indeed, the complexity of external and internal socio-economic forces operating behind people's decisions to migrate requires both a multi-theoretical and a multi-disciplinary approach.

Although the construction of a Weberian-based model—because of the inclusion of 'status'—provides for a more complex analysis of stratification than a Marxist model, such a model was found to be more appropriate for demographically and economically stable societies than for societies which experience rapid social change due to migration. The Weberian model 'breaks down' in the study of migration because ethnicity either brings with it characteristics of its own understanding of power, status and class, or because it creates varying dimensions of power, class and status which operate both inside and outside the existing status system of the host society. In the Weberian model, society is seen to function on stable, mainly inherited rewards, in contrast to the dynamics of 'class struggle' as defined by Marx.

The study of migration and migrant mobility cannot be clearly understood nor defined if status is placed above class struggle in terms of significance. In Marxist class terms, most postwar Hellene immigrants have been proletarians and even sub-proletarians (Collins 1975, 1986; ABS 1981; Collins 1988). This lack of power in class terms has produced a long-term struggle of intensely hard work on the part of immigrants to enable them to enter the dominant class through the attainment of financial power. It is only relatively recently that the official policy of multiculturalism has rendered the Weberian model potentially relevant to providing for the allocation of status to ethnic groups. Yet the bulk of the migrant experience has been and remains in the context of class struggle. It is evident that Weber's views on migration are not clearly defined. Weber, like Marx, was concerned with the consequences of industrialisation and the rise of capitalism. He noted the importance of religion and what he called the 'Protestant ethic', which he regarded as being responsible for capital accumulation and which helped to bring about the rise of modern capitalism with its related disciplinary code imposed on the workforce. He was less impressed by this system's disintegrating effects and he saw migration, for example, as an incidental factor creating new employment opportunities for new social classes and ethnic status groups (Richmond 1988: 31).

Although neither Weber nor Marx directly addressed the question of race, there have been indications of interest in a more dynamic and accessible contribution to a Marxist analysis of racism, although the debate remains undeveloped (Solomos 1986: 84–109). Specifically, Marxist approaches to racism have focused on social relations and the role of the capitalist state in reproducing or countering racist practices. They have touched on issues such as the origins of racist ideologies and the role of the capitalist state's institutions in reproducing the political and cultural ideology of racism, and located them within the conflict of class struggle within the capitalist economic system. Coupled with questions of political and ideological reproduction, the question of ownership of the cultural 'means of production' in relation to racial and ethnic minority cultures needs to be debated and defined within an expanded and integrated Marxist theoretical framework.

The ethnic factor, however, cannot be inserted so easily into conventional sociological models such as the Weberian structuralist–functionalist model. These models fall short in tackling the historical importance of migration as a force of transition or social change, where the cause of such development is linked with the effect of real issues in host societies that ultimately lead to increasing ethnic stratification. Neither is it possible, in Marxist terms, to justify and to understand studies based on Weberian structuralist–functionalist sociological perspectives, if capitalism is the cause of labour transfer in order to exploit it. Nor is it possible to state that in the Australian situation social classes are characterised by a closure due to endogamy, because historically different ethnic groups have a tendency to inter-marry widely in society (Price 1988; BIR 1990). Past studies on migrants have utilised horizontal measurements which are not committed to a vertical analysis of migration or a radical critique of Australian society (see, for example, Birrell 1987 and Burns 1977). In contrast, this study has utilised both horizontal *and* vertical approaches in order to chart a more comprehensive and critical picture of the upward movement of migrants across a number of indices such as occupation, education and place of residence. This approach has contributed to an overall view of migrant mobility within the existing social stratification system, and has helped to ascertain if there has been any qualitative change in the status of migrants as a result of their social mobility in Australia.

Multiculturalism as an integrative mechanism has indeed occurred for postwar Greek migrants, their children and grandchildren. They now appear to have gained acceptance into, and themselves accept, the 'Australian way of life', at the same time preserving their own culture and values by membership of their ethnic clubs and associations. However, in the continuing history of Hellenic incorporation into Australia's social milieu there still remain unanswered questions—whether remaining in Australia was by choice, economic circumstances, or related to *philotimo* or *entrope* (shame)—which cannot be ascertained by this particular research. It is proposed that future research examines the extent to which acceptance of Greeks is not simply a product of government policy, such as the policy of multiculturalism, but reflects positive changes in line with the subjective perceptions and feelings of Australians towards Hellenes, that is, to establish evidence of the true level of acceptance between the two groups. To this end, investigation of the perceptions, attitudes and behaviours of other (non-Greek) society members toward Hellenes—and their perceptions of second- and third-generation Greek-Australians—could be enlightening. A replication of the study in other states that uses the same residential classifications and takes into consideration the nation's enormous social changes in the last eight years, could give a clearer picture of the success of multiculturalism for Greek-Australians.

Much of the migrant success in Australia, as in any receiving society, is associated with the type of 'social incorporation' model in operation for the accommodation of migrant workers and their families. The absence of a formal social incorporation model militates against the further development of a partnership based on equity rather than the social marginalisation of the ethnic groups in Australian society. What has been increasingly evident during the postwar years, is that if greater involvement of various ethnic population groups in Australia's social, economic and political structures is to occur, a tolerant and liberal model of social incorporation based on social justice and diversity is required. Admittedly, formal incorporation of migrants in this country is far greater than in most countries of western Europe, where during the first two decades migrants are seen as temporary 'guest workers', and only after a considerable period of time are they regarded as settlers (Castles, Booth & Wallace 1984: 4; Castles 1988). In Australia, as in Britain, in addition to the fact that new arrivals are offered immigrant status and related legal protection, there has also been an absence of major legal obstacles connected with the migrant settlement processes. As Castles, Booth and Wallace have stressed, in Australia—in contrast to other European countries such as West Germany—the expectation of permanent residency, even if not universal, causes the migrant community to become settled relatively quickly. These authors argue that a lack of socio-economic balance in regard to the improvement of migrant life in Australia has meant that there have not been readily accessible opportunities for migrants. Instead, there have been various hindrances that have obstructed people's movement across the social strata. As a result, migrants often require many years of settlement and substantial amounts of effort before they experience any discernible advancement in socio-economic terms.

Despite the absence of a fundamental model of social incorporation at both structural and cultural levels, and the failure of the policy of multiculturalism to respond to many migrants' needs, it can be argued that, even in its mildest form as a political campaign slogan or political rhetoric, multiculturalism has helped to show Australians the merits of other cultures. It has helped to reduce the prejudice of the host society, which many ethnic population groups, especially those from non-English-speaking backgrounds, saw as oppressive, both institutionally and culturally. Multiculturalism has also mitigated against ghetto formation by encouraging migrants to venture out of their ethnic communities into the social and institutional ranks of the host society.

Although Australia has not adequately managed to develop a complete multicultural model, none the less it has managed over the last two decades to develop and incorporate diverse ethnic, institutional and cultural responses. These experiences have placed Australia in an advantageous position among many nations of the international community and especially with those nations located in its own immediate geographical region, most of which are sending rather than receiving societies, either because of economic poverty or industrial underdevelopment. The continuing migrations of people crossing international borders place new demands on nation states' administrations to accommodate racial and ethnic diversity. In its ability to cope with the new challenges, the state faces a future which is difficult to predict, especially in light of the increasing demands placed on its legal and political system, the almost endless financial pressures and the need for economic reform associated with an internationally integrated economy. Increasing globalisation is leading to the blurring of the boundaries of the nation state. As a result, there are the ever more demanding questions of citizenship and the intervention of the state's law beyond its national borders in order to offer protection to its citizens and interests abroad. In addition, pressures against the state have arisen out of the increasing appearance and involvement of NGOs which deal with a variety of questions, ranging from human rights (of migrants and others) to environmental issues, all of which complicate the modern government options of an already diminishing notion of the nation state.

For many Hellenes, the movement for success now brings them, together with other Australians, before the challenges which face their adopted country in the context of regional economic integration of cultural diversity within an increasingly socio-economically incorporated world. It is within these new contexts that many Greek-Australians are already crossing the borders of the countries of the Pacific and South East Asia for business purposes or in search of better remuneration for their professional services and skills.

However, these new contexts do not mean some of the older questions on migration and mobility can now be left unexplored. Future investigations need to examine the impact of the migration experience on those who, after many years of concerted effort in industrial work structured by Fordist production techniques and segmented labour markets, suffered injuries and sickness, were retrenched and forced to join the unemployment queues following the economic restructuring of the 1980s (Social Justice Consultative Council 1992). These are ongoing issues central to our understanding and assessment of the success or failure of Hellenic migration to Australia up to the present and into the future. The challenges awaiting Australia in the future bring together other Australians with the descendants of Odysseus in a common struggle for success. The struggle for a better life has not ended in Hellenic migration and the subsequent social mobility within the adopted country. Instead, it continues (as the myths and legends have it) beyond their present and past *agoras*, beyond the horizons of the furthest mountains and the endless Australian plains, towards the other unknown and unexplored destinations of the Asia Pacific and the world, thus, inevitably applying their ultimate ancient tradition—όπου γης και πατρίς (where there is earth, there is home).

Appendices

Appendix 1
Interview Schedule

(1) When did you come to Australia?

(2) Did you come on your own or with your family?

(3) Why did you come to Australia?

(4) Which part of Greece are you from?

(5) Is this your original Greek name or have you changed it?

(6) What was your occupation in Greece?

(7) What were your parents' occupations?

(8) Where did you first arrive/settle in Australia?

(9) Did you live on your own, or with: (a) friends; or (b) relatives?

(10) What were your first impressions of Australia?

(11) What were most Greeks doing for a living in those days?

(12) Why were they involved in such occupations?

(13) Was it easy to get a job?

(14) What was/is your job history?

(15) Did you experience any racism in Australia during settlement?

(16) Did you meet with other Greeks?

(17) Did you join Greek or Australian organisations?

(18) Do you remember/recall other Greeks and their activities during the earlier years?

(19) Were any Greeks in Australian political parties?

(20) Did you join a political party and, if so, why?

(21) How many hours a week did Greeks work during the early days

(or in contrast to the postwar period)?

(22) (a) Did you join a mainstream organisation, and (b) was there any racism?

(23) Has a lack of proficiency in English caused any problems for you in Australia?

(24) Did the fact that you are of Hellenic origin pose any problems for you?

(25) Have you been a member of Hellenic community organisations?

(26) What was it like for Greeks in Australia during the inter-war years?

(27) How did the Greeks who came to Australia during the prewar years view the Greeks who came to Australia during the mass migration of the postwar years?

(28) Do you have any children?

(29) How did you feel about your children growing up in Australia (satisfied/dissatisfied)?

(30) Do your children keep in close contact with you?

(31) What do your children do for a living/occupation?

(32) Do your children celebrate the Greek holidays with you?

(33) Are your children married to (or wish to marry) Greeks or non-Greeks?

(34) Do you intend to return to Greece?

Appendix 2
Interview Questions

(1) (a) Where were you born/raised? (b) How long have you been in Australia?

(2) What is your occupation? (a) in Greece/Cyprus/Egypt/other? (b) in Australia?

(3) Which part of Greece/Cyprus/Egypt/other do you come from?

(4) What made you come to Australia?

(5) Did you have relations in Australia?

(6) Did anyone else migrate from your village/town to Australia or to other parts of the world?

(7) (a) How did you imagine Australia to be prior to your migration? (b) How did you find out about Australia?

(8) Has Australia fulfilled your expectations? (Explain.)

(9) Retrospectively, has Australia provided you with answers to what you were/have been searching for? (Did you fulfil your goals and aspirations?)

(10) Has Australia given you the opportunity to provide your children with what they need in life?

(11) Has Australian society (mainstream) and Australians at large treated you as you expected them to?

(12) Have you been able to get the kind of job and the kind of rewards you hoped for or have there been any barriers against you achieving them?

(13) What kind of forces operated in Greece (social, political,

economic) that accentuated the mentality of out-migration?

(14) (a) Was out-migration a necessity from Greece/Cyprus/other?
(b) Why did the Greek governments not take any measures to curtail migration or did they encourage out-migration?

(15) What about the Greek political parties, what were their views on mass out-migration?

(16) Other than travel agents, were there any other organisations who were interested in Hellenic out-migration? (If so, who were they and why?)

(17) How long did you intend to stay in Australia?

(18) What did you expect to achieve in Australia?

(19) Have there been any barriers which stopped you from achieving your goals?

(20) What was your occupational status prior to migration?

(21) What has your occupational history been in Australia?

(22) Has Australian society provided you (and other Greeks) with hospitality?

(23) To what extent have you or are you participating across the mainstream society's social and organisational life?

(24) (a) Which organisation(s) was/were this/these?
(b) What were its objectives?
(c) Have these objectives been achieved?
(d) Who else was in that organisation?
(e) What was your role in that organisation?
(f) Did the organisation meet its objectives?

(24) In contrast to earlier years do you think Greek-Australians are now gaining entry in sufficient numbers to mainstream organisations?

FURTHER QUESTIONS FOR SECOND-GENERATION AUSTRALIANS OF HELLENIC DESCENT

(25) If born/raised in Australia, when did your parents come to Australia?

(26) Which part of Greece/Cyprus/Egypt/other did they come from?

(27) What was your parents' occupation in Australia?

(28) What is your occupation?

(29) Have you been involved in any Australian political organisation?

(30) Have you been involved in any other mainstream organisation(s)?

(31) Have you been a member of any Hellenic community organisation?

(32) If you are involved in an Australian political organisation have you been discriminated against because of your ethnicity (Greek)?

(33) Did you have to join some radical political organisation out of social necessity?

(34) (a) Have you heard of the existence of radical/other Hellenic community organisations? (b) Have you been involved in any?

(35) Are your friends of Hellenic origin involved in political organisations? If so, which ones?

(36) Do you usually identify as an Australian or as an Australian of Hellenic origin among Greeks and British-Australians?

Appendix 3 Anglicisation of Hellenic Names

Some of the names that have been either partly or totally Anglicised include: Peter Alexander, Anthony Barber, John Black (Mavrokefalos), Nicholas Brown, Spiridon Candiottis, John Carpattes, Athanasius (John) Carpatus, Demetrius Carra, Lafar Constantine, William Constantine, Constantine Crocos, George Doicos, Samuel Donnes (Andonis?), Nicholas Emelsen, Con Fischer (Constantine Argyropoulos), Andoni Fossilo (Phasoulas), George Georges (Georgouras), Antony Ioannou, John Kapazzo, Nicholas Karkoe, Dennis Key (Dionisios Korkuchakeys), Leonidas Koledas, Constantine Lalechos, Nicholas Lambert, John Lewis, Andreas Lukas (Lekatsas), Vacillius Macryannis, John Manolato, Michael Manusu, George Marks, Nicholas Megne, Jeremiah Mitaxa, George Morphesis, Themetre Moustaka, James Nicklos, John Pannam, Nicholas Paris, John Pericles, Jeremiah Perry (Apozogy or Apergis), Peter Stevens (Panayiotis Tsirginis), Jeremiah Williams (Vasilakis), and Joachim (James) Zannis—among many others.

Appendix 4 Money Lost by Greek Fruit-growers in the Riverland

(For legal reasons the name of the co-operative and its manager have been deleted. The co-operative changed its name in the mid-1980s when it was sold to private enterprise.)

Various informants in the Riverland stressed that they had lost large sums of money because local fruit industries deceived and exploited them. Specifically, it was alleged that, due to lack of appropriate control, the management of one specified fruit co-operative and, especially, the person who was managing it over a number of years in the 1970s and 1980s, cheated the growers because he failed to honour their agreements and pay them for fruit purchased over several years, although the co-operative was making vast profits over the same period. According to Dedes:

> [there] were other private factories outside Adelaide there too people lost lots and lots of money, but the local fruit co-operative known as * * * was the Hiroshima of the Riverland. There was no 'new Australian' who was not complaining about it or who did not lose something in the range of ten to seventy thousand dollars each, money which was almost equivalent for each to buy another house or fruit block, because it involved several years of work (Interview with Dedes, 1988).

Dedes mentions the names of some of the people who lost significant sums of money as a result of their agreement with the co-operative. He states categorically that, in Renmark alone some of the people who lost money were: Soterios Polymeneas ($10,000); Yiannis Alexandropoulos ($12,000); Demetrios Arnaoutis ($60,000); Stefanos Grevezas ($65–70,000); Tzanavaras ($10–12,000); Peter Markeas ($10–15,000); Stavros Markes and Antonis Sourtzis ($29,000); Christos Polymeneas ($20,000); and Yiorgos Atsaves ($25,000). The huge trouble that occurred in the Riverland affected the fruit-growers of Loxton, Berri, Barmera and Monash, many of whom were Hellenes (Interview with Dedes, 1988). Many growers also lost the money that they had invested in the same co-operative, before it was privatised.

Appendix 5 Comparison of Greek-born in Melbourne LGAs (1976, 1981 & 1986 Census)

LGA	1976 Numbers % Change	1981 Numbers % Change	1986 Numbers % Change	1991 Numbers
(3000–5000)				
Doncaster/ Templestowe	1364+4.03	2241+45.07	3251+16.36	3783
Moorabbin	2723+9.36	2978+2.72	3059+6.86	3269
Northcote	6291–17.07	5217–13.57	4509–27.50	3911
Oakleigh	4290+4.90	4500–5.33	4260–2.86	4138
Preston	3677+4.03	3825–4.47	3654–5.83	3441
Whitlesea	3471+23.97	4303+5.25	4529+1.70	4606
(1200–2999)				
Broadmeadows	1703+5.58	1798+0.28	1803+3.88	1873
Brunswick	4401–17.72	3621–21.29	2850–15.23	2416
Camberwell	1452+11.36	1617–4.70	1541+4.35	1608
Caulfield	1949–10.21	1750–8.00	1610–2.05	1577
Coburg	2459–3.42	2375–0.34	2367–5.79	2230
Footscray	2918–14.50	2495–20.48	1984–16.83	1650
Keilor	1389+22.61	1703+20.43	2051+16.14	2382
Malvern	1573–14.43	1346–8.99	1225–1.06	1212
Nunawading	1090+49.17	1626+4.43	1698+4.06	1767
Richmond	3835–35.15	2487–29.07	1764–24.26	1336
Prahran	3707–24.68	2792–26.58	2050–17.41	1693
Sunshine	1926+9.09	2101–3.33	2031–5.91	1911
Springvale	1405+12.88	1586–4.22	1519+9.28	1660
Waverley	1626+46.76	2386+18.44	2826+12.84	3189

Sources of Appendix 5:
ABS Censuses 1976, 1981, 1986, 1991,
Victorian Ethnic Affairs Commission, *The Population of Victoria According to Birthplace and Language 1986.*

Australian Bureau of Statistics, *Census on Population and Housing 1991.* Although settlement within some of the inner suburbs (for example, Brunswick, Coburg, Richmond, Prahran, Footscray, Northcote) remains fairly high, there is no doubt that there has been a very significant movement away from the inner/industrial suburbs towards the better, cleaner or socio-economically more affluent suburbs such as Doncaster/Templestowe (Northeastern), Waverly (Eastern) and also Keilor (Northwestern).

Appendix 6 Australian MPs of Hellenic or part-Hellenic Origin: 1995

	State or Federal	Party	Electoral area	First elected
Victoria				
Theophanous, A.	Federal	ALP	Calwell	1980
Andrianopoulos, A.	State	ALP	St Albans	1985
Dollis, D.*	State	ALP	Richmond	1988
Theophanous, T.	State	ALP	Jiga-Jiga	1988
Pandazopoulos, J.	State	ALP	Dandenong	1992
Georgiou, P.	Federal	Liberal	Kooyong	1994
Katsambanis, P.	State	Liberal	Monash	1995
New South Wales				
Morris, P.	Federal	ALP	Shortland	1972
Morris, A.	Federal	ALP	Newcastle	1983
Kaldis, J.	State	ALP	(Upper House)	1978
Samios, J.	State	Liberal	(Upper House)	1984
Photios, M.	State	Liberal	Ryde/Ermington	1988
Souris, G.	State	National	Upper Hunter	1988
South Australia				
Bolkus, N.	Federal	ALP	(Senate)	1980
Dondas, G.S.	State	Liberal	(Legislative)	1993
Queensland				
Fouras, G.	State	ALP	Ashgrove	1992

Source: *Neos Kosmos,* 17 October 1994, Melbourne.

Note: Dollis replaced former MP, T. Sidiropoulos in Richmond. In Queensland, the first Australian of Hellenic origin was elected, George Georges, who represented the people of Queensland in the senate (ALP) of the Federal Parliament from 1968 until the 1980s. Representing the people of the Northern Territory in the State Parliament was Nicholas Manuel Dontas who was elected in Casuarina in 1974 and served in a number of positions, including Speaker of the House until 1993.

Notes

CHAPTER 1

1. Throughout this book, the author has used 'Greek' or 'Hellene' and 'Hellenic' interchangeably. While 'Greek' is more readily understood by non-Hellenic Australians, Hellene-Australians prefer 'Hellene(s)' as a name which they use among themselves. While the singular for Greek is Hellene, the plural is Hellenes.
2. According to Byrne (1977: 248), the term 'migrant' in Australia is used to distinguish those who are born in Australia from those who are not, while the expression 'migrant family', refers to those families where one or more persons are not born in Australia.
3. There are various theoretical assumptions as to the definition of 'postmodern society'. However, here it is meant as a society which assumes greater openness of institutional structures and greater democratisation of work and working tasks. It is assumed that such openness has coincided with greater mobility of labour between and within nation states and also with increasing technological innovations in the areas of computer or microchip technology, satellite communications and transportation as well as with an increasing social, cultural and economic interdependency or such integration in a national and international context.
4. The term NESB, or NESBIANS as it is often jokingly referred to, has derogatory implications and is often regarded as a deficit term because it implies ethnic population minorities do not

273

form part of the mainstream population group. The author is aware that the term has a variety of connotations and limitations and has used it to show something of the views and perceptions of people who migrated to Australia. The author is also aware that the term does not adequately capture the existence and identity of individuals and the different ethnic communities. Instead, the term 'ethnic community' is gaining strong currency (Jayasuriya 1993) nationally and is also a more acceptable term to use internationally. The term 'ethnic community' has a long and well-established history and is robustly defined in international law.

5. Hellenic community, or Ελληνική Παροικία (*Paroiki[es]* = plural) as the Greeks name their respective Australian Hellenic communities established in different Australian states, is here understood as a collectivity of individuals who are totally or partially of Hellenic ethnic origin, who share the Hellenic ethnic culture and who live and work in Australia.

6. 'Diaspora' or Hellenic dispersement refers to the awareness in Greece (found both in Hellenic history and folk traditions), that there have always been Hellene travellers, adventurers, explorers and migrants who go abroad and establish Hellenic communities. Hellenic diaspora has been a product of many factors, including the island nature of the country but also a product of Hellenism itself that often had to survive long periods of time abroad by establishing Hellenic *Paroikies*.

CHAPTER 2

1. Initial outlays for transportation expense and lost earnings while migrants look for work will be renumerated by anticipated higher earnings in the place of destination.

2. The Organisation for Economic Cooperation and Development (OECD) has also used the neoclassic economic model to explain and justify the causes for human migratory currents. This is shown in OECD publication listings of migrant categories required by host societies. As Descloitres (1967: 35) comments, OECD publications make this apparent by stating explicitly that the main cause for migrant employment is the lack of labourers needed to fill in job vacancies in different places or sections of industry necessary for the economic development of receiving countries.

3. Generally, according to Marx (1983), the 'reserve army' is an inexhaustible reservoir of disposable labour power, and

this is not limited to national boundaries. Instead, it embraces every country and, by doing so extends along with it the class struggle under capitalism. Marx distinguishes three types of 'reserve army' or labour surplus: (a) the surplus-population existing in the floating form; (b) the relative surplus-population existing in a latent form; and (c) the relative surplus-population existing in stagnant form. Each of these types have distinctive features of labour surplus (Marx 1983: 600–2).

4. Remittances are said to create or reinforce in some way the so-called 'migration mentality' or a kind of popular thinking across different nation states of the world.

CHAPTER 3

1. *Philotimo* means one of many things or several things at the same time including: self-esteem, honour, pride, and altruism, democracy, fairness, egalitarianism, generosity, the definition of work, diligence, cooperation, collaboration, individualism, egoism.

2. This saying forms part of the tradition which is mentioned often among Hellenes. I am indebted to my mother Stavroula Spyrea-Dimitrea for reminding me of it as a central value so often throughout my life.

3. In the form of contemporary Cretan folklore or demotic verse known as *mantinatha*, a relative statement is used to make a point in reference to a person's intellectual, ethical or physical ability. An example often quoted in everyday discussion by people of Cretan origin—in Australia and in Greece—reads as follows: Σαν είναι ο τράγος δυνατός δεν τον κρατάει μάντρα ('If the billy goat is strong, he will not be contained/restricted by the walls').

4. The Seven Wise Men of Antiquity were: Solon the Athenian, Thales of Militus, Cleovoulos from Lindos, Chilon the Lacedaemonian, Pittakos from Lesbos, Dias the Prineus, Periandros the Corinthian.

5. *Philotimo* requires that the socio-economic structures of a social system be open and democratic, enabling all citizens to pursue their socio-economic goals in a fair way. As an ancient Greek compound noun, *philotimo* means *philos* and *timi* (friend & honour), but at the same time it produces a whole series of related meanings and has many more antecedents and consequents. It is often linked to words and notions like democracy, altruism, individualism, group or

family pride and integrity, progress, being a good worker, truthfulness, achievement, freedom, and in certain circumstances self-sufficiency or self-reliance, in the sense of being related to diligence (*procomenos*) and work (*douleiá as the verb 'to work' but not douleía* as 'slavery'). It is interesting in this context to note that when in countries of settlement like Australia, Hellenes expect to have access to these social and economic opportunities and thus not to have to resort to socially unacceptable means to succeed.

6. The Italians in the United States or Australia similarly refer to *il bosso*, as distinct from *il padrone*, and two styles of employment.

CHAPTER 4

1. Such views are often shared by people from all socio-economic backgrounds, that is, by individuals who often participate in popular culture discussions within Hellenic cafes and Hellenic community forums in Australia.
2. Although it is mentioned (Gilchrist 1985) that Ghikas was taken captive along with his crew (numbering about 32 individuals), no other information is recorded about his crew.
3. Michael and Sarah had twelve children most of whom followed different but in some cases successful careers across the socio-economic structure of the Australian society (Messaris, May 1988).
4. The discovery of the 'actual' number of early Greek arrivals in Australia has not been an easy enterprise for those researchers who have attempted to search the official records of the different colonies, because many of these Greek pioneers' names seem to have been Anglicised. See Appendix 4 for a list of names that have been partly or totally Anglicised.

CHAPTER 5

1. Food shortages during World War Two, especially in the cities, had also encouraged rural migrants to retain ownership of their small land blocks, hoping sooner or later to return to their beloved and historic localities.
2. This treaty established the borders between Greece and

Turkey and divided the populations between the two countries.

CHAPTER 6

1. Until the 1967 referendum, the Population Census did not include Aborigines. It was estimated that their number had fallen to 95,000 by 1901 (Borrie 1954).
2. There were two known exceptions to this. These were the 335 northern Italians (in 1881), and the wives and children of the Maltese plantation workers already settled in Australia, who replaced the Kanakas as coloured labour (Price 1963: 98; Borrie 1954: 9).

CHAPTER 7

1. Fordist is an industrial technique which involves work in routinised occupations, based on single tasks with extensive division of labour, in which most postwar Hellene immigrants to Australia were involved for many years following settlement.
2. Henderson's report on *People in Poverty* (1969) found that many southern Europeans were experiencing high levels of poverty. Henderson showed that when income earned and housing costs are combined in the calculation, then 29.3 per cent of Italians and 22.9 of Greeks were living in poverty. These findings were reinforced by a later study on Poverty (1975), known as *Interim Report of the Australian Government Commission of Inquiry into Poverty*.

CHAPTER 8

1. The individuals involved in this organisation represented the wider section of the *Paroikia* and were an important historical force which influenced future developments in Australian and Greek politics. By its foundation, on 18 June 1967, this committee (that had replaced the previous Committee for the Support of Democracy in Greece), was partly the continuation of the Lambrakis Committee, founded by the Left in Melbourne in 1964 in the name of a left-wing MP Grigoris

Lambrakis, (who was in addition a marathon runner and a champion of peace and disarmament), following his assassination in Greece in 1963. Subsequently, the greater forces of the Left (known as PAM), were joined by the Centre Unity forces (known as PAK) of the community that supported the veteran politician George Papandreou's struggles for democracy in Greece. A number of community leaders served on the committee that was formed in 1967 and ran until 1974, when democracy was restored in Greece. Among them were: Victor Nollis (President), Dennis Sikiotis (Secretary), Theodoros (Theo) Sidiropoulos (Treasurer—who later became the first Australian parliamentarian born in Greece to serve in the state of Victoria), Christos Mourikis, Kyriakidou Lefkothea, Leo Doukakaros, Stelios Stathis, Nikos Linolakis, Takis Gogos, Yiannis (John) Tsitas, Georgia Liakou, A. Demoyiannis, N. Gotsis, Plutarch Deliyiannis, M. Papapanayiotou, George Zangalis, Panayiotis Stoicos, Vassilis Keramas, Yiannis (John) Zigouras, George Papadopoulos, Stathis Stathopoulos and Christos Fifis. At the same time, most of these people (who were also members of the Greek Orthodox community of Melbourne and Victoria) were directly or indirectly behind the Hellenic community's efforts to promote social change in Australia, much of which came at the same time from within the greater Ethnic Rights Movement (Interview with Sidiropoulos, 17 April 1995).

2. The establishment of the committee was of a temporary nature, and involved, among others: Tom Oikonomou (the coordinator), with Peter Zervoulias, Peter Markeas, Sotiris Polymemeas, and Vangelis Dedes as members (Interview with Dedes, 26 April 1995).

3. In quoting Tsounis, Reich (1981) claims that the number of positions increased with the segmentation of communities and the growth of various organisations until there about 600 such formal organisations nationally—with about 10,000 important positions—the most important of which was that of president. The majority of these organisations were in Melbourne and Sydney (Tsounis 1975; Reich 1981: 174).

4. According to Jupp (1988: 144), as early as '1958 ALP Leader H.V. Evatt recognised the existence of great potential support for the ALP from Greek-ethnics'. This view appears in his 'policy speech for the 1958 Federal elections, where Evatt sought to win Greek-ethnic support by promising to support justice for Cyprus while Greece was in diplomatic dispute

with Britain over the future of the then British-occupied island'.

5. The Liberal Party does not keep separate figures for each ethnic community group. But according to Con Karavitis (Interview, 7 January 1995) who was pre-selected to represent the Liberal Party in the area of Pascoevale in the last elections for the state of Victoria and who was very active in organising Hellenic community support for his pre-selection, there were no less than 500 members of the Hellenic community in the Liberal Party in Victoria. Similarly, according to Frank Hingan (Interview, 24 April 1995) from the head office of the Liberal Party in Victoria, an increasing number of Greeks are now members of the Liberal Party. He stated that the Liberal Party has 100,000 members nationally, of which 20,000 were in Victoria, and that there are more than 500 Greek members. Hingan also estimated that the proportion of Greek participation in the Liberal Party in other parts of the country, such as Queensland and Western Australia, would be even higher.

6. Thirteen out of at least 15 MPs of Hellenic origin were elected, predominantly in the inner suburbs of Sydney and Melbourne (where most Hellenes in Australia had settled). Seven were elected in Melbourne and another six in Sydney.

Bibliography

ABS, Australian Bureau of Statistics 1976, Census.
——1981, Census.
——1986, Census.
——1991, Census.
——1991b, Census. Community Profiles, Greece-Born, Bureau of Immigration Research (BIR) 1994, AGPS, Canberra.
ACOSS 1976, 'Immigrants and mental health: A discussion paper', Standing Committee on Migration Issues, ACOSS, Sydney.
Adams, W. 1968, 'The brain drain' in T. Nichols (ed.), *Capital and Labour: Studies in the Capitalist Labour Process*, Athlone Press, London.
Afendras, A.E. 1987, 'Greek Australians, ethnolinguistic vitality and multicultural policy', Department of Education, University of the Aegean, Rhodes. Paper prepared for Greek Australian Conference, Melbourne.
Aitkin, D. 1977, *Stability and Change in Australian Politics*, Australian National University Press, Canberra.
Alexakis, E. and Janiszewski, L. 1988, 'A brief history of the Greek presence in New South Wales', in the Ninetieth Anniversary Album, Lefkoma, Greek Orthodox Community of Sydney and New South Wales, Sydney.
——1989a, 'A fragment of Australia's emerging new social history and self-image: white gold, deep blue: Greeks in the Australian pearling industry 1880's–1980's' in *O Kosmos*, Second Annual Edition, (Special Edition—Historical Feature December 1989), Dulwich Hill, Sydney, pp. 72–5.

——1989b, 'Greek Australians in their own image', National project and touring exhibition, Petersham, Sydney.

——1991, 'E Istoria ton proton ellinon tes australias' (The History of the First Hellenes), in *Skepsis*, 26 May, Hellenic Connection, Coburg, Victoria.

Alexander, Peter 1987, Interview, 29 January, Coburg, Victoria.

Allan, L. 1981, 'The ethnic factor and Australian politics', *Journal of Higher School Certificate Politics*, Vol. 9, No. 1, Melbourne.

——1985, 'Ethnic politics in ALP', in P.R. Hay, J. Halligan, J. Warhurst and B. Coster (eds), *Essays on Victorian Politics*, Warrnambool Institute Press, pp. 133–43.

Alomes, S., Dober, M. and Hellier, D. 1984, 'The social context of postwar conservatism', in A. Curthoys, and J. Merritt (eds), *Australia's First Cold War: Society, Communism and Culture*, Vol. 1, Allen & Unwin, Sydney.

Amin, S. 1977, *Imperialism and Unequal Development*, Harvester Press, Hassocks.

Andrewes, A. 1984, *Greek Society*, Linotype Juliana, Singapore.

Appleyard, R.T. 1971, *Immigration: Policy and Progress*, Australian Institute of Political Science, Sydney.

Appleyard, R.T. and Amera, A. 1978, *Greek Migrant Education in Australia: A Parent View*, Department of Economics, University of Western Australia, Report 1/78.

Armstrong, F. and Wearing, J.A. 1980, *Socio-Economic Indicators for Victoria, Stage Two*, Public Policy Studies Monograph. No. 2, The University of Melbourne, Parkville.

Arrowsmith, J. and Zangalis, G. 1965, *The Story of General Motors in Australia . . . The Golden Holden*, International Bookshop, Melbourne.

Australia, National Population Inquiry 1975, *Population and Australia: A Demographic Analysis and Projection*, First Report, Chairman W.D. Borrie, AGPS, Canberra.

Australia, National Population Inquiry 1978, *Population and Australia: Recent Demographic Trends and their Implications*, Supplementary Report, AGPS, Canberra.

Australia, Review of Post Arrival Programs and Services to *Migrants 1978, Migrant Services and Programs, Report and Appendices*, Vols 1 and 2, AGPS, Canberra.

Australian Encyclopaedia 1983, *Volume 13*, Bay Books Pty. Ltd., Kensington, New South Wales.

Australian Ethnic Affairs Council 1977, *Australia as a Multicultural Society*, J. Zybrzycki (Chairman), submission to the Australian Population and Immigration Council, AGPS, Canberra.

Australian Immigration 1971, *Consolidated Statistics*, AGPS, Canberra.

Australian Immigration and Population Council 1976, *Immigration Policies and Australia's Population*, Green Paper.

——1983, *Consolidated Statistics No. 13, 1982*, AGPS, Canberra.

Australian Population and Immigration Council 1976, *A Decade of Migrant Settlement: Report on the 1973 Immigration Survey*, Social Studies Committee, J.I. Martin (Chairman), AGPS, Canberra.

Australian-Greek Welfare Society 1985, 'Social relationships of young people', *Greek Action Bulletin*, Vol. 9(2), 17–23.

Babbie, E. 1992, *The Practice of Social Research*, 6th edn, Wadsworth Publishing Co., California.

Baxter, J., Emmison, M. and Western, J. 1991, *Class Analysis and Contemporary Australia*, Macmillan, South Melbourne.

Bell, M. 1992, *Internal Migration in Australia 1981–1986*, Applied Population Research Unit, The University of Queensland, produced for the Joint Commonwealth/State/Territory Population and Immigration Research Program, Bureau of Immigration Research, AGPS, Canberra.

Bella, J.I. and Moraitis, S. 1970, 'Knights in armour—a follow-up study of injuries after legal settlement', *Medical Journal of Australia*, 22 August, pp. 355–61.

Berger, P., Berger, B. and Kellner, H. 1973, *The Homeless Mind*, Random House, New York.

Berri Land Irrigation Records 1988, Berri, Riverland, South Australia.

Bianco, J. 1989, *Languages Action Plan*, Ministry of Education, Victoria.

Bilingual Consultancy Network 1994, *Consultation on the Process for Recognition of Overseas Skills*, Office of Multicultural Affairs (OMA), Department of The Prime Minister and Cabinet, Canberra.

Birrell, R. 1987, 'The educational achievement of non-English speaking background students and the politics of the community language movement', in *Economics of Immigration*, Proceedings of a Conference, (Joint conference of ANU and DIEA: The Economics of Immigration) 22–3 April, Australian National University, Canberra.

Birrell, R. and Hay, C. (eds) 1978, *The Immigration Issue in Australia*, Department of Sociology, La Trobe University, Melbourne.

Birrell, R., and Khoo, S.E. 1995, *The Second Generation*, Bureau of Immigration, Multicultural and Population Research, South Carlton, Victoria.

Birrell, R. and Birrell, T. 1981, *Australian Studies. An Issue of People: Population and Australian Society*, Longman Cheshire, Melbourne.

Bombas, L. 1989, *O Ellinismos tou Kanada (Canada's Hellenism: A Bibliographic Guide)*, General Secretariat for Greeks Abroad (Hellenic Ministry of Culture), Athens.

Borrie W.D. 1949, *Immigration: Australia's Problems and Prospects*, Angus & Robertson, Sydney.

——1954, *Italians and Germans in Australia: A Study of Assimilation*, F.W. Cheshire, Melbourne.

Botsas, N. E. 1982, 'The American Hellenes: phases of Greek migration', in S. Rovcek and B. Eisenberg (eds), *American Ethnic Politics*, Greenwood Press, Connecticut.

Bottomley, G. 1973, *Community and Continuity Among Greeks in Sydney*, Macquarie University, Sydney.

——1976, 'Migration and ethnicity', Committee on Community Relations Final Report, AGPS, Canberra.

——1979, *After the Odyssey: A Study of Greek Australians*, University of Queensland Press, St Lucia, Queensland.

——1991, 'Representing the "second generation": subjects, objects and ways of knowing', in G. Bottomley, M., de Lepervanche, and J.A. Martin (eds), *Intersections: Gender, Culture, Ethnicity*, Allen & Unwin, Sydney.

——1993, 'Post-multiculturalism? The theory and practice of heterogeneity' (paper presented to a conference on Post-Colonial Formations: Nations, Culture, Policy, at Griffith University, Queensland, 7–11 June, 1993).

Bottomley, G. and de Lepervanche, M. 1984, *Ethnicity, Class and Gender in Australia*, Allen & Unwin, Sydney.

Bottomley, G., de Lepervanche, M. and Martin, J.A. (eds) 1991, *Intersections: Gender, Culture, Ethnicity*, Allen & Unwin, Sydney.

Bottomley, J. 1973, *The Greek Orthodox Community in Melbourne*, Fitzroy Ecumenical Centre. Melbourne.

Bowen, M. 1977, *Australia 2000: The Ethnic Impact*, proceedings of the first national conference on Cultural Pluralism and Ethnic Groups in Australia, University of New England, Armidale, New South Wales.

Boyd, M. 1989, 'Family and personal networks in international migration: recent developments and new agendas', *International Migration Review*, Vol. 23, pp. 638–70.

Broom, L., Selznick, P., and Broom, D.H. 1981, *Sociology: A*

Text with Adapted Readings, 7th edn, Harper & Row, New York.

Bryman, Alan 1992, *Quantity and Quality in Social Research*, Routledge, London.

Buckland, D. 1971, 'The assimilation of Greek migrants', in F.S. Steven (ed.), *Racism, the Australian Experience: A Study in Race Prejudice in Australia*, Vol. 1, ANZ Book Co., Sydney, pp. 124–34.

——1972, *The Greek Family in Australia and the Process of Migration*, ANZAAS 44th Congress, Sydney.

Bulmer, M. 1982, *Social Research Ethics*, Macmillan, London.

Burbridge, A., Caputo, J. and Rosenblatt, L. 1982, *They Said We'd Get Jobs: Employment, Unemployment and Training of Migrant Workers*, Centre for Urban Research and Action, Fitzroy, Victoria.

Bureau of Immigration Research (BIR) 1990, *Community Profiles: Greece-born Statistics Section*, AGPS, Canberra.

——1994, *Community Profiles: Greece-born Statistics Section*, AGPS, Canberra.

Burn, A.R. 1930, *Minoans, Philistines, and Greeks, 1400–900BC*, K. Paul Trench, Trubner, London.

Burnley, I.H. and Walker, S.R. 1977, 'Social adjustment of ethnic groups at the neighbourhood level: a research proposal', in M. Bowen (ed.), *Australia 2000: The Ethnic Impact*, University of New England, Armidale, New South Wales, pp. 188–91.

Burnley, I.H. 1973, 'Greek immigrants in Melbourne', *Social Survey*, No. 22, Kew, Victoria, pp. 145–52.

——1974, *Urbanization in Australia: The Postwar Experience*, Cambridge University Press, Cambridge.

——1976, 'Greek settlement in Sydney', *Australian Geographer*, Vol. 13, No. 3, pp. 200–14.

——1977, 'Resettlement of immigrant communities in urban Australia', in M. Bowen (ed.), *Australia 2000: The Ethnic Impact*, University of New England, Armidale, New South Wales, pp. 142–73.

Burnley, I.H., Pryor, R.J. and Rowland, D. (eds), 1980, *Mobility and Community Change in Australia*, University of Queensland Press, St Lucia, Queensland.

Burns, A. 1977, 'Entering a job: some comparisons between Greek migrant employees in Sydney factories with Greek migrant employees in three Newcastle factories', in M. Bowen (ed.), *Australia 2000: The Ethnic Impact*, University of New England, Armidale, New South Wales, pp. 223–45.

Byrne, E. 1977, 'The migrant family—transitions', in M. Bowen (ed.), *Australia 2000: The Ethnic Impact*, University of New England, Armidale, New South Wales, pp. 247–55.

Cahill, D. 1990, *Intermarriages in International Context: A Study of Filipina Women Married to Australian, Japanese and Swiss Men*, Scalabrini Migration Centre, Philippines.

Callan, J.V. 1986, *Australian Minority Groups*, Harcourt Brace Jovanovich, New South Wales.

Calwell, A.A. 1972, *Immigration, Policy and Progress*, Cecil J. Morley, Melbourne.

Castles, F.G. 1967, *Pressure Groups and Political Culture*, Routledge & Kegan Paul, London.

Castles, S. 1988, 'Temporary migrant workers, economic and social aspects', in the *Report* of the Committee to Advise on Australia's Immigration Policies, Section 1.10, AGPS, Canberra.

——1991, 'From migrant worker to ethnic entrepreneur', in D. Goodman, D.J. O'Hearn and C. Wallace-Crabbe (eds), *Multicultural Australia: The Challenges of Change*, Scribe, Newham, Victoria, pp. 178–91.

Castles, S. and Kosack, G. 1980, 'The function of labour immigration in western European capitalism', in T. Nichols (ed.), *Capital and Labour*, Athlone Press, London.

Castles, S. and Miller, J.M. 1993, *The Age of Migration: International Population Movements in the Modern World*, Macmillan, London.

Castles, S., Booth, H. and Wallace, T. 1984, *Here for Good: Western Europe's New Ethnic Minorities*, Pluto Press, London.

Castles, S., Colleen, M., Morrisey, M., and Alcorso, C. 1989, *The Recognition of Overseas Trade Qualifications*, Bureau of Immigration Research, AGPS, Canberra.

Castles, S., Cope, B., Kalantzis, M. and Morrissey, M. 1988, *Mistaken Identity: Multiculturalism and the Demise of Nationalism in Australia*, Pluto Press, Sydney.

Cavanagh, J.L. 1965, 'On adjournment-immigration', Commonwealth of Australia, Speech, (from the 'Parliamentary Debates,' 11 May, 1965).

Chatzivasiles, George 1995, 'O Demetris Anastassiou Milaei yia ten Australia Horis Polupolitismo: Mas Eithelan deuteras Kategorias Polites' ('Demetris Anastassiou Speaks About Australia Without Multiculturalism: They Wanted us as Second Class Citizens . . . , The Migrant Battles for the Recognition of their Identity', in *Neos Kosmos*, 6 March 1995, Melbourne.

Chirkas, Christos 1988, Interview, 7 November (Committee Member of Greek Orthodox Community of Melbourne and Victoria), Melbourne, Victoria.

Cicourel, A.V. 1964, *Method and Measurement in Sociology*, Free Press, New York

Cigler, B. and Cigler, M. 1985, *Australia: A Land of Immigrants*, Jacaranda Press, Queensland.

Cigler, J.M. 1988, 'Greeks in Australia', in the *Australian Encyclopaedia*, Vol. 4, pp. 1459–60. Australian Geographic, 5th edn, New South Wales.

Clogg, R. 1985, *Greece in the 1980s*, Macmillan, London.

Collins, J. 1975, 'The politcal economy of post-war immigration', in E.L. Wheelright and K. Buckley (eds), *Essays in the Political Economy of Australian Capitalism*, Vol. 1, Australian and New Zealand Book Company, Sydney.

Collins, J. H. 1976, 'Migrants: The political void', in H. Mayer and H. Nelson (eds), *Australian Politics: A Fourth Reader*, Cheshire, Melbourne.

——1986, 'From race to ethnicity', *Australia and New Zealand Journal of Sociology*, Vol. 16, No. 1, Glen Waverley, Victoria.

Collins, J. 1988, *Migrant Hands In A Distant Land*, Pluto Press, Australia.

Cominos, G.E. 1916, *E Zoi En Afstralia (Life in Australia)*, Australia Printing and Publishing Co. Ltd., Melbourne.

Commission of Inquiry into Poverty 1975, Second Main Report, October, *Law and Poverty in Australia*, Commissioner Ronald Sackville, AGPS, Canberra.

Commission of Inquiry into Poverty 1976a, Third Main Report, March 1976, *Social Medical Aspects of Poverty in Australia*, Commissioner R.T. Fitzgerald, AGPS, Canberra.

Commission of Inquiry into Poverty 1976b, Fifth Main Report, December 1976, *Poverty and Education in Australia*, Commissioner R.T. Fitzgerald, AGPS, Canberra.

Committee on Community Relations 1975, *Final Report*, Chairman W.M. Lippman, AGPS, Canberra.

Committee Members for Kalamata Earthquake Fundraising Appeal, Interview, 26 January 1988, Melbourne.

Commonwealth Bureau of Census and Statistics 1933, Census, Australia.

——1947, Census, Australia.

Commonwealth of Australia 1940, *Certificate of Registration of Aliens*, Melbourne, Australia.

Contact (Epaphe) 1984, A Modern Greek Students' Association Publication, Melbourne.

Copeland, E. 1992, 'Global refugee policy: an agenda for the 1990s', *International Migration Review*, Vol. xxvi, No. 3, Fall, New York.

Cox, D. 1972, 'Medico-social problems in the Greek population of Melbourne: Part 1. Social and cultural background', *Medical Journal of Australia*, October, pp. 879–81.

——1974, *Towards an Understanding of the Greek Migrant*, Ecumenical Migration Centre, Richmond.

Cox, D.R. 1975, 'The adaptation of Greek boys in Melbourne', PhD thesis, School of Sociology, La Trobe University, Melbourne.

Cross, R. D. 1973, 'How historians have looked at immigrants to the United States', *International Migration Review*, Vol. viii, Nos. 1–4, Spring–Winter, New York.

Daily Standard 29/6/1925, Brisbane, Queensland.

Daniel, A. 1971, 'The measurement of class', in K. Danziger (ed.), *Socialisation*, Penguin, Harmondsworth, pp. 248–9.

——1983, *Power, Privilege and Prestige*, Longman Cheshire, Melbourne.

Davies, A. 1966, 'Migrants in politics', *Dissent*, No. 17, Winter, pp. 6–12.

——1972, *Essays in Political Sociology*, Cheshire, Melbourne.

Dawkins, P.J., Foster, W., Lowell, L. and Papademetriou, D.G. 1992, 'The microeconomic analysis of immigration in Australia and the United States', in P.G. Freeman and J. Jupp (eds), *Nations of Immigrants: Australia, the United States and International Migration*, Oxford University Press, Melbourne.

Dedes, Evangelos 1988, Interview, 23 December, Riverland, South Australia.

Dedizer, S. 1980, 'Early migration', in T. Nichols (ed.) *Capital and Labour: Studies in the Capitalist Labour Process*, Athlone Press, London.

Deliyiannis, P. 1989, 'I Parousia ton Ellenon stin Australia kai o rolos tis Koinotitas stin Ellenomatheia ton Paideion mas' ('The Hellenic presence in Australia and the role of the *Koinotita* in Hellenic education'), (paper presented in the Greek Orthodox Community of Melbourne and Victoria (GOCM&V), October).

Demos, V. 1988, 'Rapid urbanization, internal migration and rural underdevelopment in Greece: a case study', *Journal of the Hellenic Diaspora*, Vol. xv, Nos. 3 and 4.

Denzin, N.K. 1978, *The Research Act*, 2nd edn, McGraw-Hill, New York.

287

Department of Prime Minister and Cabinet 1988, *Agenda for a Multicultural Australia*, AGPS, Canberra.

Descloitres, R. 1967, *Le Travailleur étranger (The Foreign Worker)*, OCDE, Paris.

Dimitreas, Y. 1981, 'Subjective culture: the implicative ideology of Hellenes found in the concept *Philotimo*', unpublished thesis, Department of Political Science, University of Melbourne, Parkville.

——1989, 'The implication of *Philotimo* and Hellenic identity in the process of social change', *Mosaic: Journal of National Union of Greek Australian Students* (NUGAS), Melbourne.

——1992, 'Enas laos kato apo dio diaforetica systemata' ('One nation of people under two different institutional systems'), *Mosaic: Journal of the National Union of Greek Australian Students* (NUGAS), Melbourne.

Dimitreas, Y. E. 1994, 'Implications of subjective culture and Hellenic identity in the process of social transition', in H. Borland (ed.), *Communication and Identity: Local, Regional and Global, Selected Papers from the 1993 National Conference of Australian Communication Associations*, Australian and New Zealand Communication Association, ACT.

Donkin, N. 1983, *Stranger and Friend: The Greek-Australian Experience*, Dove, Melbourne.

Doukas, A. 1963, *Kato Apo Xenous Ouranous (Under Foreign Skies)*, Australian-Greek Publications Pty. Ltd., Melbourne.

Dow, G.M. and Factor, J. 1991, *Australian Childhood: An Anthology*, McPhee Gribble, Melbourne.

Edgar, D. (ed.) 1974, *Social Change in Australia: Readings in Sociology*, Cheshire, Melbourne.

——1980, *Introduction to Australian Society: A Sociological Perspective*, Prentice-Hall, Sydney.

Eisner, E. 1981, 'On the differences between scientific and artistic approaches to qualitative research', *Educational Researcher*, 10 (4): 5–9.

Ekstasis, (Journal of the Centre for Urban Research and Action (now the Fitzroy Ecumenical Centre)), all issues.

Ekdotiké Athenon 1982, *The Olympic Games in Ancient Greece*, Ekdotiké Athenon S.A., Athens.

Encel, S. 1981, *The Ethnic Dimension: Papers on Ethnicity and Pluralism by Jean Martin*, George Allen & Unwin, Sydney.

Encel, S. and Bryson, L. 1984, *Australian Society*, 4th edn, Longman Cheshire, Melbourne.

Engels, F. 1962, 'The condition of the working class in England', in *Marx and Engels on Britain*, Moscow.

Fairchild, H.P. 1911, *Greek Immigrants to the United States*, Yale University Press, New Haven.

——1925, *Immigration: A World Movement and its American Significance*, revised edn, Macmillan, New York.

Faulkner, A. (ed.) [undated c. 1972], 'Ethnic rights: recommendations for a multicultural Australia', draft paper of a Platform on Ethnic Rights, Fitzroy Ecumenical Centre, Melbourne.

Ferry, (Commissioner) 1925, 'Commissioner Ferry's Report' in Cresciani 1988, *Migrants or Mates: Italian Life in Australia*, Knockmore Enterprises, Sydney.

Filias, V. 1967, *Apopseis yia ten Diatirisi and to Metavolismo tou Koinonikou Systematos (Views About Maintenance and Change of the Social System)*. Vol. B., Nea Synora, Athens.

Firestone, W. 1987, 'Meaning in method: the rhetoric of quantitative and qualitative research', *Educational Researcher*, 16 (7): 16–21.

FitzGerald, S. (Chairman) 1988, *Immigration: A Commitment to Australia*, the *Report* of the Committee to Advise on Australia's Immigration Policies, AGPS, Canberra.

Forster, E.S. 1958, *A Short History of Modern Greece 1821–1956*, Methuen, London.

Foster, W. and Withers, G. 1992, 'Macroeconomic consequences of international migration', in P.G. Freeman, and J. Jupp (eds), *Nations of Immigrants: Australia, the United States, and International Migration*, Oxford University Press, Melbourne.

Frangioudakis, R. 1988, Interview, 12 December, Victoria, Australia.

Fraser, M. 1981, *Multiculturalism: Australia's Unique Achievement*, AGPS, Canberra.

Freeman, P. G. and Jupp, J. 1992, *Nations of Immigrants: Australia, the United States, and International Migration*, Oxford University Press, Melbourne.

Fried, M. 1964, 'Effects of social change on mental health', *American Orthopsychiatry*, Vol. 34, American Orthopsychiatric Association, New York.

——1970, 'Deprivation and migration', in E.B. Brody (ed.), *Behaviour in New Environments: Adaptation of Migrant Populations*, Sage, Beverly Hills, California.

Galbally, F. (Chairman) 1978, *Report* of the Review of Post-Arrival Progams and Services for Migrants, AGPS, Canberra.

General Secretariat for Greeks Abroad 1985, *Gnorimia me ten Ellada (Acquaintance with Hellas)*, Athens.

Georgas, J. 1991, 'Intra-family acculturation of values in Greece', *Journal of Cross-Cultural Psychology*, Vol. 22, No. 4, December, Sage, Beverley Hills, California.

George, R. 1970, 'Types of migration of the population according to professional and social composition of migrants', in C.J. Jansen (ed.), *Readings in the Sociology of Migration*, 1st edn, Pergamon Press, New York.

Georges, George 1987, Interview, 20 April, Brisbane.

Giddens, A. 1993, *Sociology*, 2nd edn, Polity Press, London.

Gilchrist, H. 1985, 'The Greek connection with early Australia: 1700–1900', unpublished paper, Melbourne.

——1992, *Australians and Greeks, The Early Years*, Vol. 1, Halstead Press, Rushcutters Bay, New South Wales.

——1995, 'Metanasteutiko reuma' ('Migration current'), *Paroikia*, *Neos Kosmos*, Supplement, 29 March, Ethnic Publications, Carlton, Victoria, pp. 34–58.

Glazer, N. and Moynihan, D.P. 1970, *Beyond the Melting Pot*, 2nd edn, MIT Press, Cambridge, Massachusetts.

Glesne, C. and Peshkin A. 1992, *Becoming Qualitative Researchers: An Introduction*, Longman, New York.

Goldlust, J. and Richmond, A.H. 1974, 'A multivariant model of immigrant adaptation', *International Migration Review*, Vol. 8, pp. 193–225.

Goldlust, J. and Richmond, A.H. 1977, 'Cognitive and linguistic acculturation of immigrants in Toronto: a multivariant analysis', *Ethnic Studies: An International Journal*, Vol. 1, No. 1, Australia International Press and Publications, Pty. Ltd. Melbourne.

Gordon, M. 1964, *Assimilation in American Life*, Oxford University Press, New York.

Gould, J. and Kolb, W.L. 1965, *A Dictionary of the Social Sciences*. Free Press of Glencoe, 3rd impression, New York.

Grambas, Yiannis 1991, Interviews, 12 March and 11 September, Melbourne, Victoria.

Grassby, A.J. (Hon) 1973, *A Multi-cultural Society for the Future*, Department of Immigration, AGPS, Canberra.

——1977, 'Community relations means us all', in M. Bowen (ed.), *Australia 2000: The Ethnic Impact*, University of New England, Armidale, New South Wales, pp. 6–15.

——[undated, *c.* 1993], 'Regional Dimensions of Australia's multicultural policy', in G. McCall and J. Connell (eds), *A World Perspective on Pacific Islander Migration*, Centre for South Pacific Studies, University of New South Wales, *Pacific Studies Monograph No. 6*, pp. 87–91.

Greek Action Bulletin 1986, 'The Greek community today', Vol. 11, June, the University of Melbourne.

Greek Orthodox Archdiocese of Australia 1992, *Hemerologion (Diary)* Redfern, New South Wales.

Greek Orthodox Community ' of Melborne and Victoria (GOCM&V) 1977, 80th Anniversary Album, Lefkoma, Melbourne.

——1987, 90th Anniversary Album, Lefkoma, Melbourne.

Greek Orthodox Community of Sydney and NSW (GOC) 1988, 90th Anniversary Album, Lefkoma, Sydney.

Greek Times (Nea Ellada) 1978, 'O Gof Ouitlam Piye Hthes yia Teleftea Fora stin Voule! ANTIO GOF MEGALE!' ('Gough Whitlam went to Parliament yesterday for the last time: good-bye great Gough!'), Friday 14 April, Melbourne.

——1988, 'Kapos etsi xekinesame' ('This is how we started'); 'E zoe kai to ergo tou Sir George Bowen kai tes Diamantinas Roma' ('The life and the accomplishments of Sir George Bowen and Diamantina Roma'), 24 December, Melbourne.

——1995, 'I 170 symparikoi pou uphretisan sto Vietnam' ('The 170 compatriots who served in Vietnam), 29 April, Melbourne.

Gregory J. 1928, *Human Migration and Future*, F.R.S.D.Sc. Publishers, London.

Gregory, T. 1989, 'Australian immigration policy and politics', *The Gatekeepers: Comparative Immigration Policy*, No. 23.

Halsey, A.A. 1972, 'Educational priority', in K. Marjoribanks (ed.) (1980), *Ethnic Families and Children's Achievements*, Allen & Unwin, Sydney.

Hamermesh, D.S. and Rees, A. 1988, *The Economics of Work and Pay*, 4th edn, Harper & Row, New York.

Hawkins, T. 1973, 'Greek community backs strikes with words—and money', *National Times*, 18–23 June, pp. 18–19.

Hearn, J.M. 1971, 'Migrant political attitudes', MA thesis, Department of Political Sciences, University of Melbourne.

Hearst, S. 1985, 'Greek families', in D. Storer (ed.), *Ethnic Family Values in Australia*, Prentice-Hall, Melbourne, pp. 121–44.

Hellenic Herald 1926, Tuesday, 16 November, p. 1.

Hellenic Ministry of Culture 1989, 'The mind and the body: athletics and motion in contemporary Greek art', *Zappeion Megaron*, 15 May.

Henderson (Report) 1975, 'Greeks in Australia', interim *Report* of the Australian Government Commission of Inquiry Into Poverty, AGPS, Canberra.

Henderson, R.F., Harcourt, A. and Harper, R.J.A. 1969, *People in Poverty: A Melbourne Study*, Cheshire, Melbourne.

Herodotus 1972, *Histories*, Penguin Books, Harmondsworth.

Hill, J.H. 1978, 'Language contact systems and human adaptations', *Journal of Anthropological Research*, Vol. 1 (April), p. 34 (Microfiche).

Hingan, F. 1995, Interview, 24 Aprril, Victoria.

Hitchcock, N.H. 1990, *Migration to Australia: An Authoritative Guide to Seeking Migrant and other Visas for Australia*, N.H. Hitchcock & Associates, New South Wales.

Holding, C. 1987, 'Victorian government, Greek government', unpublished paper, Community Tripartite Conference, 13 March, Melbourne.

Holy Archdiocese of the Greek Orthodox Community of Australia 1994, 'Statistical chapter of the Holy Archdiocese', *Registry of Statistics on Performed Marriages 1975–1992*, Sydney.

Howe, K. 1988, 'Against the quantitative–qualitative incompatible thesis, or dogmas die hard', *Educational Researcher*, 17 (8), pp. 10–16.

Hugo, G. 1986, *Australia's Changing Population: Trends and Implications*, Melbourne, Oxford University Press, Melbourne.

Hugo, G. and Menzies, B. 1980, 'Greek immigrants in the South Australian Upper Murray', in I.A. Burnley et al. (eds), *Mobility and Community Change in Australia*, University of Queensland Press, Brisbane, pp. 235–72.

Hume, S. 1991, 'Proclaiming migrant rights: the new international convention on the protection of the rights of all migrant workers and members of their families', World Council of Churches/CICARWS, *Briefing Paper No. 3*, Imprimerie Mark Picaret, Geneva, May.

Hunt, F.J. 1972, *Socialisation in Australia*, Angus & Robertson, Melbourne.

——1978, *Socialisation in Australia*, Australian International Press & Publications Pty. Ltd., Melbourne.

Iatrides, J. 1981, *Greece in the 1940s: A Nation in Crisis*, University Press of New England, Hanover.

Immigration Advisory Council Report 1969, *Immigration and the Balance of the Sexes in Australia*, a *Report* to the Minister of the State for Immigration, September.

Immigration Department 1975, *The Australian Government Commission of Inquiry Into Poverty, 1975*, Australian Immigration Consolidated Statistics.

Isaacs, E. 1976, *Greek Children in Sydney*, ANU Press, Canberra.

——1979, 'Social control and ethnicity: the socialization and repression of a Greek child at school', in de Lacey and Poole (eds), *Mosaic or Melting Pot: Cultural Evolution in Australia*, Harcourt Brace Jovanovich, New South Wales.

Isokrates 1938, *Isocrates*, trans. G. Norlin, Heinemann, London.

Ithaki, 1/5/1928, 'fortnightly Greek Language Newspaper', *Organon Ton Apantahou Ithakision (International Organ of Ithacans)*, Arsenis Bookshop, Athens.

Jakubowicz, A. 1980, *The Nature of Multiculturalism: Liberation or Co-option?*, CHOMI Reprint No. R401, Richmond.

Jansen, C.J. (ed.) 1970, *Readings in the Sociology of Migration*, Pergamon Press, New York.

Jayasuriya, D.L. 1991, 'Challenges presented to multiculturalism', *Asian Australian Focus*, Mulgrave Publishing, Melbourne.

——1993, 'Australian multiculturalism and citizenship', paper presented at the Conference of FECCA (Federation of Ethnic Communities Council of Australia), December, Fremantle, Western Australia.

Johnston, R. 1972, *Future Australians: Immigrant Children in Perth, Western Australia*, ANU Press, Canberra.

Jones, A.M. 1960, *American Immigration*, University of Chicago Press, Chicago.

Jupp. J. 1966, *Arrivals and Departures*, Cheshire, Melbourne.

——1986, *Don't Settle for Less: Report of Committee for Stage I of the Review of Migrant and Multicultural Programs and Services*, DIEA, Ethnic Affairs Branch, Canberra.

——1988, *Ethnic Politics in Australia*, Allen & Unwin, Sydney.

——1991, *Immigration*, Sydney University Press, Sydney.

Jupp, J. (ed.) 1988, *The Australian People: Encyclopaedia of the Nation, its People and their Origins*, Angus & Robertson, North Ryde, New South Wales.

Jupp J., McRobbie A. and York, B. 1990, *Metropolitan Ghettos and Ethnic Concentrations*, Office of Multicultural Affairs (OMA), University of Wollongong, Australia.

Kakakios, M. and Van der Velden 1982, 'Migrant communities and class politics: the Greek community in Australia', paper presented at the Ethnic Politics Conference, ANU, December 9–10.

Kalamaras, V. 1986, *The Bread Trap*, Elikia Books, Australia.

Kalantzis, M. and Cope, B. 1987, *Why We Need Multicultural Education: A Review of the 'Ethnic Disadvantage' Debate*, Social Literacy, Stanmore, New South Wales.

Kalantzis, Peter 1988, Interview, 23 December, Riverland, South Australia.

Kalianis, George 11/9/1967, Commonwealth of Australia: Department of Labour and National Service, National Service Registration Office, Commonwealth Centre, Spring Street., Melbourne.

Kalomoiris, Demetrios 1988, Interview, 10–15 October, Sydney.

Kamenka, E. 1986, 'Marx, communism and anarchism', in D. Muschamp (ed.), *Political Thinkers*, Macmillan, South Melbourne.

Kanarakis, G. 1977, 'Modern Greek and English consonants in contrast: an investigation of interference on the phonological and graphemic levels of English', *Ethnic Studies*, Vol. 1, No. 1, pp. 52–73.

——1978, 'Phonetic processes of modern Greek in normal conversational tempo', *Journal of the Linguistic Society of Australia*, Vol. 5, pp. 1–12.

——1979, 'A comparative study of modern Greek and English vocalic systems: findings and problems', *Mnimi*, George I. Kourmoulis, Athens, pp. 1–25.

Kapardis, A. and Tamis, A. 1988, *Australiotes Hellenes (Greeks in Australia)* River Seine Press, North Melbourne.

Karavitis, C. 1995, Interview, 7 January, Melbourne.

Karefylakis, Pavlos, 1994, Interview, 9 April, Coober Pedy, South Australia.

Kasimati, K. 1980, *Taseis kinetikotitas ergasias sten Hellenike Viomechania (Tendencies of Labour Mobility in Hellenic Industries)*, National Centre of Social Research (NCSR), Athens.

Kazantzides, S. 1988, 'Kazantzides, O Travoudouros ton Xenitemenon Hellenon', *Nostos*, Vol. 2, July, pp. 46–8. *Periodiko yia ton Apodimo Ellinismo (Greek Government Magazine for Greeks Abroad)*, Athens.

Kenna, M. 1977, 'Greek urban migrants and their rural patron saint', *Ethnic Studies*, Vol. 1(3), pp. 14–23.

Kennedy, T. 1976, Bulletin Supplement 'The Greeks: the Australian family part 3', 17 July, Australian Consolidated Press, Sydney.

Kern, K.K.L. 1966, 'Immigration and the integration process', in A. Stoller, (ed.), *New Faces: Immigration and Family Life in Australia*, Cheshire, Melbourne.

Kindleberger, C.P. 1958 'Commodity and factory prices under trade factor, price equalization', *International Economics*, revised edn, D. Irwin Homewood Inc., Illinois.

——1965, 'Emigration and economic growth', in Banca Nazionale Del Lavoro, *Quarterly Review*, September, pp. 235–64.

——1967, *Europe's Post-War Growth: The Role of Labour Supply*, Harvard University Press, Cambridge, Massachusetts.

Kindleberger, C. P. and Herrick, B. 1983, *Economic Development*, McGraw Hill, New York.

King, R. 1976, 'The dialectics of culture: Greeks in Australia', *Meanjin*, Vol. 35(2), pp. 227–40.

Kotakis, I. 1908, *E 'Ellines an Ameriki (The Hellenes in America)*, New York.

Kourvetaris, G. 1971, *First- and Second-Generation Greeks in Chicago: An Inquiry into their Stratification and Mobility Patterns*, National Centre of Social Research (NCSR), Athens.

Koutsidis, E. 1979, 'Present day Greek culture', in S. Keightley and A. Putnins (eds), *Greek Immigrants: Health, Welfare and Education*, Department of Community Welfare, Adelaide.

Koutsounadis, V. 1979, 'Cross cultural conflict between Greek children and their parents', *Greek Action Bulletin*, Vol. 4(4), pp. 12–18.

Kritz, M.M. 1987, 'International migration theories: conceptual and definitional issues', in IUSSP seminar proceedings, *Emerging Issues in International Migration*, IUSSP Seminar, Bellagio.

Kuper, A. and Kuper, J. 1985, *The Social Science Encyclopedia*, Routledge & Kegan Paul, London.

Lee, D. 1953, 'Greece', in H. Mead (ed.), *Cultural Patterns and Technical Change*, Unesco, Paris.

Legg, K. 1977, *The Nature of the Modern Greek State in Greece in Transition*, Koumoulides, J.T.A., Zeno.

Leininger, M. 1990, 'Ethnomethod: philosophic and epistemic axis to explicate transcultural knowledge', *Journal of Transcultural Nursing* 1 (2), pp. 40–51.

Lenin, V.I. 1977, *Selected Works*, Progress Publishers, Moscow.

——1978, *Imperialism: The Highest Stage of Capitalism*, Progress Publishers, Moscow.

Lever, T.C. 1984, 'A new Australian working-class politics: the case of Ford Broadmeadows', in G. Bottomley and M. de Lepervanche (eds), *Ethnicity, Class and Gender in Australia*, Allen & Unwin, Sydney.

Lewins, P. 1980, 'Putting politics into ethnic relations', paper presented at AANZAS Conference, Hobart.

Liffman, M. 1983, 'Marking Georgiou's report', *Australian Society*, David Scott, Melbourne.

Lincoln, Y.S. and Guba, E.G. 1985, *Naturalistic Inquiry*, Sage Publishing, Beverly Hills, California.

Lowenstein, W. and Loh, M. 1977, *The Immigrants*, Hyland House, Melbourne.

Luthke, M.P. and Cropley, A.J. 1990, 'Decision-making and adjustment difficulties: a counselling strategy for working with migrants', *Australian Psychologist*, Vol. 25, No. 2. July, University of Queensland Press, St Lucia, Queensland, pp. 147–64.

Lyng, J. 1927, *Non-Britishers in Australia*, Melbourne University Press, Melbourne.

Mackie, F. 1967, 'A sociological study of the influence of the Greek Church split on the assimilation of Greeks in an inner-city suburb of Melbourne', MA thesis, Department of Anthropology and Sociology, Monash University, Melbourne.

——1986, 'No future! Or cross-cultural equality', *Arena*, No. 7A, Melbourne.

Malliaris 1982, 'Metanasteusi' ('Migration'), in *Hellada Historia kai Politismos (Hellas, History and Civilization)*, Malliaris Paideia (Malliaris Education), Athens.

Manne, R. 1985, 'The Blainey affair: all for Australia', *Quadrant*, No. 209, March. Sydney.

Markus, A. and Ricklefs, M.C. (eds) 1985, *Surrender Australia?*, Allen & Unwin, Sydney.

Martin, J.I. 1972, 'Migrants—equality and ideology', Meredith Memorial Lecture, La Trobe University, Bundoora.

——1975, 'Family and bureaucracy', in C. Price (ed.), *Greeks in Australia*, ANU Press, Canberra.

Martin J. and Meade, P. 1979, *The Educational Experience of Sydney High School Students*, Report No. 1. AGPS, Canberra.

Martin, P. 1992, 'Migration and development', *International Migration Review*, Vol. xxvi, No 3, Fall, New York.

Marx, K. 1983, *Capital, a Critique of Political Economy*, Vol. 1., Lawrence & Wishart, London.

Matheson, Allan 1993, Interview, 8 November, ACTU, Melbourne, Australia.

Mavrantonis, Stratos 1988, Interview, 15–17 October, Greek Orthodox Community of Sydney and NSW, Sydney.

Mavrokefalos (Black) John 1987, Interview, 5 May, Active Hellenic Community Leader.

Mazaraki, M. 1983, 'Family law enters the twentieth century', *Greek Action Bulletin*, Vol. 8(1), pp. 3–7.

McAllister, I. and Rhonda M. 1991, 'The development of ethnic prejudice: an analysis of Australian immigrants', *Ethnic and Racial Studies*, Vol. 14, 2 April.

McKay J. and Lewins, F. 1978, 'Ethnicity and the ethnic group—a conceptual analysis and reformulation', *Ethnic and Racial Studies*, Vol. 1, No. 4, October.

Medical Journal of Australia 1972, 'Medico-social problems in the Greek community', Editorial, 14 October, pp. 855–6.

——1975, 'Migration, stress and disease', Editorial, 21 June, pp. 765–7.

——1976, 'The plight of the migrant: communication in emergency', Editorial, 18 September, pp. 433–4.

Menzies, B.J. 1980, *Agricultural Extension Among Greek Horticulturalists in the South Australian Riverland*, Research Monograph No 1, Department of Agriculture, South Australia.

Messaris, J. 1988, 'Michael Manusu: an early Greek immigrant' *Paroikia—Greek Australian Monthly Review*, May, pp. 43–4.

Messaris, P. and Kerr, D. 1983, 'Mothers' comments about TV: relation to family communication patterns', *Communication Research*, Vol. 10(2), pp. 175–94.

Messaris, J. and Koulochris, T. 1986, 'A well-kept secret . . . Trevor's "Hermes" in *To Neo*', *Greek Australian Monthly Magazine*, October, Melbourne.

Messinis S. 1992, 'Bonegilla Lives in Greece', *Kosmos*, Wednesday 14 October, Melbourne, p. 10.

Michail, Michael 1995, Interview, 26 April, Melbourne.

Milne, F. and Shergoold, P. (eds) 1984, *The Great Immigration Debate*, Federation of Ethnic Communities Council of Australia (FECCA), Sydney, Australia.

Minichiello, V., Aroni, R., Timewell, E. and Alexander, L. 1990, *In-Depth Interviewing: Researching People*, Longman Cheshire, Melbourne.

Mitsopoulos, Jim 1986, Interview, 12 September, Cairns, Queensland.

Monos, D.I. 1976, 'Upward mobility, assimilation, and the achievements of Greeks in the United States, with special emphasis on Boston and Philadelphia', PhD thesis, University of Pennsylvania, United States.

Moore, M.L. and Moschis, G.P. 1981, 'The role of family communication in family learning', *Journal of Communication*, Vol. 31(4), pp. 42–51.

Moraitis, S. 1977a, 'Greek ethnic attitudes in Australia', paper presented to the *Ethnic Injured Seminar*, Australian and New

Zealand Society of Occupational Medicine and Australian Greek Welfare Society, March 5, Melbourne.

Moraitis, S. 1977b, 'Medico-social problems in the Greek population in Melbourne. Part 2. Paediatric problems as seen by the medical practitioner', *Medical Journal of Australia*, 14 October, pp. 881–3.

Moraitis, S. and Zigouras, J.N. 1971, 'Impressions on Greek immigrants', *Medical Journal of Australia*, 13 March, pp. 598–600.

Mourikis, C. 1964a, 'O Hellenismos tes Australias' ('Australia's Hellenism'), *Dromoi* May, Year 7, No. 77, Athens, pp. 38–41.

——1985, 'I Epochi tis Bonegilla: I Diki mas epochi' ('The epoch of Bonegilla: our epoch'), *Paroikia*, December, Arion, Melbourne, pp. 20–7.

——1986, 'Ta ploia me tes nifes' ('The ships with the brides'), *Paroikia*, February, Arion, Melbourne, pp. 38–43.

——1989, Interview, 6 June, Melbourne.

Mouzelis, N. 1986, *Politics in the Semi-periphery*, Macmillan, London.

Myrdal, G. 1957, *Economic Theory and Under-developed Regions*, Duckworth, London.

Nalpantides, J.K. 1979, 'A demographic comparison of the Anglo-Australian and Greek populations of Australia', (1976) Australian Bureau of Statistics Figures, December at Clearing House on Migration Issues, Richmond, Victoria.

Najman, J.M., and Western, J.S. 1988, *A Sociology of Australian Society: Introductory Readings*, University of Queensland, St Lucia, Queensland.

National Union of Greek-Australian Students (NUGAS) 1988, *Album*, Victoria.

Neos Kosmos 1988–1994, Melbourne.

Nichols, T. 1980, *Capital and Labour: Studies in the Capitalist Labour Press*, Athlone Press, London.

Nicolaou, L. 1991, *Australian Workers and Immigrant Workers*, Allen & Unwin, Sydney.

Nocella, P. 1994, 'Riverland multicultural forum: what is the Riverland multicultural forum?', unpublished speech presented at the launch of the Riverland multicultural forum, 5 December, Berri, South Australia.

Oeser, O.A. and Hammond, S.B. 1954, *Social Structures and Personality in the City*, Routledge & Kegan Paul, London.

Office of Multicultural Affairs (OMA): Department of the Prime Minister and Cabinet 1988, *National Agenda for Multicultural Australia*, AGPS, Canberra.

Ohlin, B. 1952, *Interregional and International Trade*, Harvard University Press, Cambridge.

Omogeneia, 1988, Abbotsford, Victoria, July.

Organisation for Economic Co-operation and Development (OECD) 1976, *Migrations, croissonce et development*, Paris, pp. 55–6.

Organisation for Economic Co-operation and Development (OECD) 1988, seminar on *Returning Migrants and their Reinsertion*, prepared by N. Petropoulos, National Centre for Social Research, Athens, 10–12 May.

Papadopoulos, A. 1973, *A Comparative Study of Attitudes of Alienation Among Greek-American Children Attending Bilingual and Monolingual Programs*, University Microfilms International.

Papadopoulos, G. 1973, 'Notes on the politics of Greeks in Australia, and the effects of events in Greece upon them', *Ekstasis*, Centre for Urban Research and Action, Fitzroy, June.

——1975, 'Social organization and ethnic power: a Greek perspective', in D. Storer, (ed.), *Ethnic Rights and Participation*, Clearing House on Migration Issues and Centre for Urban Research and Action, Melbourne (CURA), pp. 39–45.

——1976, 'A perithematic strategy for social change', *Ekstasis*, CURA, Fitzroy, July.

——1988, 1991 and 1992, Interviews, 18 May 1988, 15 November 1991 and 30 March 1992, Melbourne.

——1993, 'Australian Greek welfare society, twenty years: a ruminative reflection with no apology for redundancy, the tautology, whatever . . .', Australian-Greek Welfare Society, Melbourne.

Papageorgopoulos, A. 1981, *The Greeks in Australia: A Home Away From Home*, Alpha Books, Sydney.

Parliamentary Papers, New South Wales, V. 1930–31, Lists of Names of Certain 'Communists', pp. 465–7, 23 December.

Paroikia (1995), in *Neos Kosmos*, 29 March, Ethnic Publications, Carlton, Victoria, pp. 34–58.

Pascoe, R. 1988, 'Italians in Australia: historical and social perspectives', in G. Rando and M. Aringhi (eds) (1993), *Proceedings of a Conference on The Italians in Australia: The First 200 Years*, (held at the University of Wollongong and Macquarie University, 27–9 August 1988), Department of Modern Languages, University of Wollongong, New South Wales, 1993.

Pascoe, R. 1992, 'Place and community: the construction of an

Italo-Australian space', in S. Castles, C. Alcorso, G. Rando and E. Vasta (eds), *Australia's Italians: Culture and Community in a Changing Society*, Allen & Unwin, Sydney.

Pascoe, R. and Bertola, P. 1985, 'Italian miners and the second-generation "Britishers" at Kalgoorlie, Australia', *Social History*, Vol 10, No 1.

Paton, M.Q. 1990, *Qualitative Evaluation and Research Methods*, 2nd edn, Sage Publications Inc., California.

Patriarcheas, G. 1981, Interview, 16 April, Melbourne.

Petersen, W. 1958, 'A general typology of migration', *American Sociological Review*, Vol. 23, pp. 256–66.

Petersen, W. and Thomas, B. 1968, in D.L. Sills (ed.) *International Encyclopaedia of the Social Sciences*, Vol. 10, Macmillan and Free Press.

Petrolias, J. 1959, 'Postwar Greek-Italian migrants in Melbourne', PhD thesis, Department of Political Science, University of Melbourne.

Petropoulos, N. 1986, Research program on the emigration–return migration of the Greek population: results from a microcensus 1985–86', unpublished monograph, General Secretariat for Greeks Abroad, Athens.

Polyzos, N. 1947, *Enquête sur les rétours des travailleurs migrants. Consequences des rétours en Grèce des émigrants*, OCDE, Direction de la Main d'Oeuvre et des Affaires Sociales, MS/M/4O4/365, 1970, Paris.

Polyzos N. 1986, 'Harakteristika tes demographikes krises sten Hellada' ('Characteristics of demographic crisis in Greece'), *Ellenike demographikon meleton* (EDHM), Athens.

Portes, A. 1985, 'One field, many views: competing theories of international migration', in J. Fawcett and B. Carino (eds), *Pacific Bridges: The New Immigration from Asia and the Pacific Islands*, Centre for Migration Studies, New York.

Price, C. 1963, *Southern Europeans in Australia*, ANU, Press, Canberra.

——1966, 'Post-war migration, demographic background', in A. Staller (ed.), *New Faces: Immigration and Family Life in Australia*, Cheshire, Sydney.

——1968, 'Migrant occupations', Duke of Edinburgh Commonwealth Conference, Migrants in Australian Society, background paper No. 6.

——1971, *Australian Immigration: A Bibliography and Digest*, No. 2, 1970, Department of Demography, Australian National University, Canberra.

—— (ed.) 1975a, 'Greeks in Australia', *Immigrants in Australia No. 5*, ANU Press, Canberra.

—— (ed.) 1975b, *Australian Immigration: A Review of the Demographic Effects of Post-war Immigration on the Australian Population*, Research Report No. 2 for the National Population Inquiry, AGPS, Canberra.

——1979, *Australian Immigration: A Bibliography and Digest, No. 4*, Institute of Advanced Studies, Canberra.

——1988, in J. Jupp (ed.), *The Encyclopaedia of the Australian People*, Angus & Robertson, North Ryde, New South Wales.

——1989, Statistics table with updated version of the Greek-settler loss statistics to 30/6/89, Table prepared on request, Deakin, ACT.

——[1988/89], 'The "melting pot" is working: ethnic intermarriages in Australia', *IPA Review*, Vol. 42, 3 December 1988/February 1989, pp. 34–5.

——1990, *Ethnic Groups in Australia*, Australian UMM Research Centre, Canberra.

——1993, Statistics regarding Greeks in Australia (16/3/1993). Table prepared on request. Deakin, ACT.

Psomiades, H.J. and Scourby, A. 1982, *The Greek-American Community in Transition*, Pella Publishing Company Inc., New York, pp. 137–70.

Psyroukis, N. (N.D.) *Ellinikes Paroikies (Hellenic Communities)*, Athens.

Raftopoulos, S. 1979, *E Balanda tou Ksenitemenou (The Ballad of the Immigrant)*, Melbourne.

——1988, Interview, 10 Marcy, Balwyn, Victoria.

Ravenstein, G.E. 1885, 'The laws of migration', *Journal of the Royal Statistical Society*, Vol. 48, part II, pp. 198–9.

——1889, 'The laws of migration', *Journal of the Royal Statistical Society*, Vol. 52, June, pp. 241–301.

Reich, C. 1981, 'Ethnic identity and political participation: the Greek and Jewish communities in Melbourne', PhD thesis, Monash University, Melbourne.

Reichardt, C.S. and Cook, T.D. 1979, *Beyond Qualitative Research Versus Quantitative Methods in Evaluation Research, 7–32*, Sage Publications, Beverly Hills.

Renmark Irrigation Records 1988, Renmark, Riverland, South Australia.

Report of Committee of Inquiry 1983, *The Recognition of Overseas Qualifications in Australia, Volumes 1 & 2*, AGPS, Canberra.

Rex, J. and Mason, D. 1986, *Theories of Race and Ethnic Relations*, Cambridge University Press, Cambridge.

Richardson, A. and Taft, R. 1968, 'Australian attitudes towards immigrants, a review of social survey findings', *International Migration Review*, 2, pp. 46–55.

Richmond, H.A. 1988, *Immigration and Ethnic Conflict*, Macmillan, London.

Rodakis, P. 1976, *Taxeis kai Stromata ste Neoellenike Koinonia (Classes and Stratification in Modern Hellenic Society)*, Mykenai, Athens.

Rodopoulos, L. 1975, 'Greeks helping Greeks: exploring the issues', *Antipodes*, No. 9, October.

——1978, 'Understanding the Greek family in Australia', *Australian Child and Family Welfare Quarterly*, Vol. 2(1), pp. 24–35.

——1981, 'Implementing multicultural strategies in welfare: a Greek experience', proceedings of Second National Conference of Australian Greek Welfare Workers, Melbourne, August.

Rosenthal, D. and Bornholt, L. 1988, *Expectations About Development and Anglo-Australian Facilities*, the University of Melbourne, Parkville.

Roxborough, I. 1979, *Theories of Underdevelopment*, Humanities Press, New Jersey.

Rush, M. and Althoff, P. 1971, *An Introduction to Political Sociology*, Nelson, London.

Saloutos, T. 1964, *The Greeks in the United States*, Harvard University Press, Cambridge.

Salt, J. 1989, 'A comparative overview of international trends and types, 1950–80', *International Migrant Review*, Vol. 23, pp. 431–56.

Salter, S. 1986, *Recognition of Overseas Qualifications*, Ethnic Affairs Commission, New South Wales.

Sandelowski, M. 1986, 'The problem of rigour in qualitative research', *Advances in Nursing Science*, 8 (3), pp. 27–37.

Schermenhorn, R.A. 1978 (1970), *Comparative Ethnic Relations: A Framework for Theory and Research*, Phoenix, United States.

Schwandt, T. 1989, 'Solutions to the paradigm conflict: coping with uncertainty', *Journal of Contemporary Ethnography* 17, pp. 379–407.

Scourby, A. 1984, *The Greek Americans*, Twayne Publishers, Boston.

Secret Census on Greeks 1916, Series A 385/1, Australian National Archives, Canberra.

Secretariat to the Committee to Advise on Australia's Immigration Policies 1987, *Understanding Immigration*, AGPS, Canberra.

Seitz, V. 1977, *Social Class and Ethnic Group Differences in Learning to Read*, International Reading Association, Delaware.

Sherington, G. 1980, *Australia's Immigrants 1788–1978*, George Allen & Unwin, Sydney.

Sidiropoulos, T. 1995, Interview, 17 April, Victoria.

Sills, D.L. 1959, 'Voluntary associations: instruments and objects of change', *Human Organization*, Vol. 18, No. 1, July.

Sinclair, D.A. 1980, 'The resettlement of Greek immigrants in Sydney: a kinship study', in J.H. Burnley, R.I. Pryor and D.T. Rowland (eds), *Mobility and Community Change in Australia*, Queensland University Press, Brisbane.

Skelton, R. 1974, 'Underground schools teach Greeks to live in the Past', *The Age*, 7 May, Melbourne, p. 21.

Smith, A. 1954, *The Wealth of Nations*, Vol 2, Everyman's Library, London.

Smolicz, J.J. 1975, *Ethnic Cultures in Australian Society: A Question of Cultural Interaction*, Department of Education, University of Adelaide.

——1979, *Culture and Education in a Plural Society*, Curriculum Development Centre, Canberra.

——1981a, *The Australian School Through Children's Eyes: A Polish Australian View*, Melbourne University Press, Melbourne.

——1981b, 'The three types of multilingualism', in M. Garner (ed.), *Community Languages: Their Role in Education*, River Seine Press, Melbourne, pp. 1–13.

Smolicz, J.J. and Harris, R.McD. 1976, 'Ethnic languages and immigrant youth', in M.G. Clyne (ed.), *Australia Talks: Essays on the Sociology of Australian Immigrant and Aboriginal Languages*, ANU, Canberra, pp. 131–75.

Smolicz, J.J. and Secombe, M.J. 1977, 'A study of attitudes to the introduction of ethnic language and cultures in Australian schools', *Australian Journal of Education*, 21(1), pp. 1–24.

Smyrnios, K.X. and Tonge, B. 1981, 'Immigrant Greek mothers: the anxiety of change', *Australian Social Work*, Vol. 34 (2), pp. 19–24.

Social Justice Consultative Council 1992, *Economic Restructuring & Job Loss*, Department of the Premier and Cabinet, Treasury Place, Melbourne.

Sodersten, B. 1988, *International Economics*, 2nd edn, Macmillan Education Ltd., London.

Solomon, B. 1956, *Ancestors and Immigrants*, University of Chicago Press, Chicago.

Solomos, J. 1986, 'Varieties of Marxist conceptions of "race", "class" and "state": a critical analysis', in J. Rex (ed.), *Theories of Race and Ethnic Relations*, Cambridge University Press, Cambridge.

Spinelli, G.D., Vassiliou, V. and Vassiliou, G. 1974, *Milieu Development and Male-Female Roles in Contemporary Greece*, The Athenian Institute of Anthropology, Athens.

Stahl, S., Ball, R., Inglis, C. and Gutman, P. 1993, *Global Population Movements and their Implications for Australia: An Overview of Trends and Issues*, (BIR), South Carlton, Victoria.

Stathopoulos, P. 1971, *The Greek Community of Montreal*, National Centre of Social Research, Athens.

Stefanou, Vassilis 1986, Interview, 13 October, Carlton, Victoria.

Stevens, F.S. 1974, *Racism: A Study of Race Prejudice in Australia, Vol.1, Prejudice and Xenophobia*, ANZ Book Co., Brookvale, New South Wales.

Stevens, Peter 1987, Interview, 23 January, (Political Activist of CPA and Greek Workers Leagues in Australia).

Stocker, M. and Langtry, B. 1986, 'Aristotle and polity' in D. Muschamp, (ed.), *Political Thinkers*, Macmillan, South Melbourne.

Stoller, A. 1966, *New Faces: Immigration and Family Life in Australia*, F.W. Cheshire, Melbourne.

Storer, D. 1975, *Ethnic Rights, Power and Participation: Towards a Multi-Cultural Australia*, Monograph No. 2, Clearing House on Migration Issues, Ecumenical Migration Centre and CURA, Melbourne.

——1978, 'Immigration issues in the seventies: the next steps', Notes for CURA meeting, 16 February.

——1985a, *Ethnic Family Values in Australia*, Prentice-Hall, Sydney.

——1985b, *Working Paper 5*, Victorian Ethnic Affairs Commission, Melbourne.

Svoronos, N. G. 1972, *Episkopise tes 'Ellenikes Istorias (A Review of Modern Greek History)*, 7th edn, Themelio, Athens.

Taft, R. 1966, *From Stranger to Stranger*, University of Western Australia, Perth.

——1978, 'Australian attitudes to immigrants', Meredith Memorial Lecture, Australian Multicultural Society, La Trobe University, Bundoora.

Tamis, A. 1985, 'Cultural, historical and socio-economic factors affecting the language loyalty of Greek immigrants in Victoria', *Journal of Intercultural Studies*, Vol. 6 (2), pp. 22–58.

——1988, 'Greeks', in J. Jupp (ed.), *The Australian People: An Encyclopedia of the Nation and their Origins*, Angus & Robertson, Australia.

——1991, *Early Greek Macedonian Settlement in Australia*, La Trobe University, Bundoora.

Tamis, A. 1988, Interview, 10 November, La Trobe University, Bundoora.

The Advertiser, 20/12/1978, Adelaide.

The Herald, 30/5/1961, Melbourne.

Theophanous, A. 1988, Interview, 3 September, Burke, Victoria.

Theophanous, T. 1988, 'The changing nature of Greek involvement in Australian politics', in A. Kapardis and A. Tamis (eds), *Afstraliotes Hellenes: Greeks in Australia*, River Seine Press, North Melbourne.

Theotokas, G. 1961, *Pneumatiki Poreia (Intellectual Direction)*, Vivliopoleion tes Estias I.D. Kollaroy and Sia A.E., Athens.

Thistlethwaite, F. 1960, *Migration from Europe Overseas in the Nineteenth and Twentieth Centuries*, Cambridge University Press, Cambridge.

Thomas, B. 1954, *Migration and Economic Growth: A Study of Great Britain and the Atlantic Economy*, National Institute of Economic and Social Research, Economic and Social Studies, No 12, Cambridge University Press, Cambridge.

Thucydides 1985, *History of the Peloponnesian War*, Penguin, Hammondsworth.

Tonnies, F. 1957, *Community and Society (Gemeinschaft und Gesellschaft)*, trans. and ed. C.P. Loomis, Harper Torchbooks, New York.

Trahanas, H. 1986, *Paroikia*, December, Arion Publications, Melbourne.

Trahanas, H. and Grambas, Y. 1991, Interview, 14 May, Melbourne.

Trahanas, H. 1991, Interview, 11 September, Melbourne.

Tribune, 14/6/1980, Sydney.

Tsaousis, D. 1986, 'Hellinismos-Hellenikoteta: ideologikoi kai viomatikoi axones', ('Hellenism-Hellenic: ideological and social forces'), Koinonike Demographia, Athens.

Tsotras, A. 1982, 'A study of the problems encountered by Greek Orthodox spouses, unpublished dissertation, Ballarat.

Tsoukalas, K. 1977, *Dependency and Reproduction: The Social Role of the Educational Mechanisms in Greece (1830–1922)*, Themelio, Athens.

Tsounis, M. 1971a, 'Greek communities in Australia', PhD thesis, Adelaide University, South Australia.

——1971b, 'The Greek Left In Australia', *Australian Left Review*, March.

——1974, *Greek Ethnic Schools in Australia*, Australian Immigration Monograph 1, Department of Demography, ANU, Canberra.

——1975, 'Greek communities in Australia', in C. Price (ed.), 1975a, *Immigrants in Australia No. 5*, ANU, Canberra.

——1987, *Chronico*, 6–7, M. & T. Printers, Collingwood, Victoria.

——1988a, 'How many are we really', *Paroikia*, December 1987– January 1988, Melbourne.

——1988b, 'The story of Greek-Australians: the convicts, the explorers and the first pioneers', *Paroikia*, Vol. 3, No. 26, May, pp. 42–4.

——1988c, 'Opseis kai provlemata tes istorias tou Afstralezikou 'Ellenismou' ('Views and problems of the history of Australia's Hellenism') in the 90th Anniversary Album (Lefkoma) of the Greek Orthodox Community of Sydney & New South Wales, pp. 37–65.

——1989, Interview, Brighton, South Australia,

——1989b, 'Tes genias mas ta gnorismata' ('The characteristics of our generation'), paper presented to the Greek Orthodox Community of Melbourne & Victoria (GOCM&V).

——1989c, 'The Pre-War Greek Community of Melbourne', unpublished paper, Department of Intercultural Studies, RMIT, Coburg Campus, Melbourne.

Unger, K. 1985, Regional Characteristics and Return Migration— The Case of Greece, Faculty of Sociology, University of Bielefeld.

Vakalopoulos, A.E. 1983, *O Characteras ton 'Ellenon: anichnevontas ten ethnike mas taftoteta (The Character of Hellenes: Tracing our National Identity)*, Thessalonike.

Vasilikakos, G. 1980, 1982, *E Taftoteta (The Identity)*, *Vivlio Hronias (Year Book)*, Athens.

Veglery, A. 1988, 'Differential social integration among first-generation Greeks in New York', *International Migration Review*, Vol. 22.

Velikonja, J. 1989, '25 years of international migration digest and the international migration review', *International Migration Review*, Vol. 23, Fall, Center for Migration Studies, New York, pp. 709–25.

Vgenopoulos, C. 1985, *Growth and Unemployment: The Case of*

Greek Postwar International Migration, Exantas Publications, Athens.

Victorian Ethnic Affairs Commission 1988, Immigrant Workers' Information and Human Rights, Conference Papers, Victorian Ethnic Affairs Commission, Melbourne.

Vlachos, E.C. 1964, *The Assimilation of Greeks in the United States: With Special Reference to the Greek Community of Anderson, Indiana, USA*.

Vlachos, E.C. 1968, *The Assimilation of Greeks in the United States*, The National Centre of Social Research, Athens.

Vondra, J. 1979, *Hellas Australia*, Wide Scope Publishers, Melbourne.

Voulgaris, A. and Castania, R. 1987, 'Young people and racism: the views of young people of non-English speaking background', Report prepared for workers with ethnic young people, Abbotsford, Victoria.

Wagstaff, J.M. 1985, 'The Geographical Setting', in R. Clogg, (ed.), *Greece in the 1980s*, Macmillan Press Ltd, London.

Ware, T. 1964, *The Orthodox Church*, Penguin, Middlesex.

Waters, M. 1990, *Class and Stratification: Arrangements for Socioeconomic Inequality Under Capitalism*, Longman Cheshire, Melbourne.

Weber, Max 1948, *Essays in Sociology*, trans. and ed. H.H. Gerth and C.W. Mills, Routledge & Kegan Paul, London.

——1968, *Economy and Society: An Outline of Interpretive Sociology*, trans. and ed. E. Fiscoff et al., Bedminster, New York.

Wheelwright, L.E. and Stillwell, B.J.F. 1979, *Readings in Political Economy, Vol. 2*, Australia and New Zealand Book Company, Sydney.

White, N.R. 1978, 'Ethnicity, culture and cultural pluralism', *Ethnic and Racial Studies*, Vol. 1, No. 2, April.

Wild, R.A. 1978, 'Social stratification in Australia', in C. Bell, (ed.), *Studies in Society, No. 3*, Allen & Unwin, Sydney.

Wilking, L. 1989, Interview, 10 August, Ashburton, Victoria.

Wilson, P.R. 1973, *Immigrants and Politics*, ANU Press, Canberra.

Withers, G. 1990, 'Economics, migration and interdependence', an invited keynote address to the Sesquicentenary Meetings of the New Zealand Association of Economists, University of Auckland, 22 August.

Wooden, M., Holton, R., Hugo, G. and Sloan, J. 1990, *Australian Immigration, A Survey of the Issues*, Bureau of Immigration Research (BIR), Canberra.

World Council of Churches/CICARWS 1991, 'Proclaiming migrant rights: the new international convention on the protection of the rights of all migrant workers and members of their families', *Briefing Paper No. 3*, Imprimerie Mark Picaret, Geneva.

Yin, K.R. 1989, *Case Study Research, Design and Methods*, Sage Publications, California.

Yonge, O. and Stewin, L. 1988, 'Reliability and validity: misnomers for qualitative research', *Canadian Journal of Nursing Research*, 20 (2), p. 61.

Zangalis, G. 1993, 1995, Interviews, 4 September 1993 and 11 April 1995, Melbourne.

Zubrzycki, J. 1964, *Settlers of the La Trobe Valley*, ANU Press, Canberra.

——1973, 'Immigration to ethnic conversation. Inquiry into the departures of settlers from Australia', *Parliamentary Paper No. 226*, Vol. 6. Immigration Advisory Council.

Index

Index compiled by Russell Brooks